Reading First
and Beyond

For information:

Corwin Press
A Sage Publications Company
2455 Teller Road
Thousand Oaks, California 91320
www.corwinpress.com

Sage Publications Ltd.
1 Oliver's Yard
55 City Road
London EC1Y 1SP
United Kingdom

Sage Publications India Pvt. Ltd.
B-42, Panchsheel Enclave
Post Box 4109
New Delhi 110 017 India

Printed in the United States of America

Library of Congress Cataloging-in-Publication Data

Block, Cathy Collins.
Reading First and beyond: The complete guide for teachers and literacy coaches / Cathy Collins Block, Susan E. Israel.
        p. cm.
Includes bibliographical references and index.
ISBN 1-4129-1496-5 (cloth)—ISBN 1-4129-1497-3 (pbk.)
1. Reading (Primary)—United States. 2. Reading comprehension—Study and teaching (Primary)—United States. 3. Action research in education—United States. I. Israel, Susan E. II. Title.
LB1525.B54 2005
372.4—dc'22

                                                    2004029334

This book is printed on acid-free paper.

05   06   07   08   09   10   9   8   7   6   5   4   3   2

Acquisitions Editor:	Jean Ward
Production Editor:	Melanie Birdsall
Copy Editor:	Cate Huisman
Typesetter:	C&M Digitals (P) Ltd.
Proofreader:	Mary Meagher
Indexer:	Sheila Bodell
Cover Designer:	Anthony Paular

Contents

Preface

*R*eading First and Beyond is written to assist teachers, teacher educators, administrators, literacy coaches, reading researchers, and parents to understand and implement Reading First legislation. It also demonstrates how educators and parents can extend the learning process beyond these basics in literacy instruction. This book can also be used as a textbook in undergraduate and graduate programs, and as a text with school-based learning teams and preservice or inservice study groups.

This book summarizes the key areas of Reading First and newly emerging research-based evidence concerning additional curriculum components that have been demonstrated to significantly advance students' literacy development. The key elements discussed in the book are

- Oral language
- Prekindergarten and kindergarten literacy: Phonemes and phonemic awareness
- Phonics
- Vocabulary
- Fluency
- Comprehension
- Independent reading
- Writing
- Metacognition
- Parent support

The book can assist reading programs in K–8 classrooms in many ways and serves several purposes. First, it can assist teachers who would like to know more about how to implement research-based practices that address the components of Reading First legislation in a more complete manner.

Second, it is written for teachers who have already implemented new methods but would like to enhance their repertoire of instructional strategies.

Third, it has been written as a professional development tool and resource for literacy coaches, principals, teachers, and parents who want to independently learn about Reading First components and understand how they can be, and have been, implemented in classrooms across America.

Fourth, districts that want to train teachers in methods that meet the guidelines of Reading First can use this book with confidence to develop inservice training sessions.

Fifth, this book can be used for building-level book study groups so that an entire building can be using the same literacy terms and instructional research approaches.

Sixth, this book can be used by principals to structure professional development discussions and content for monthly faculty meetings and on-site professional development programs.

Last, this book can be used for the training of literacy coaches so they can present to teachers instructional literacy strategies that are research-based.

This book is intended to contribute to the field of literacy and education by providing a guide for educators and parents to understand Reading First legislation in as comprehensive a fashion as possible. It provides explicit models as to how research-based instructional practices can be included in school programs on a daily basis. It also provides lesson plans to meet the needs of learners who struggle, learners who are learning English, and learners who excel. This book also provides methods by which teacher-directed instruction, paired instruction, independent reading, and small group instruction can be structured to include the components of Reading First.

Each chapter includes an initial *vignette of a child's thoughts* that illustrates a child successfully using the reading domains to be discussed in that chapter. This is followed by several special features to help the readers increase their knowledge in each of the key domains of literacy instruction cited above. These features are as follows:

- *What Teachers Need to Know* makes explicit a working definition of the element discussed in the chapter, provides important background knowledge of the Reading First component the chapter covers, and aids in increasing the level of understanding of that domain of literacy instruction before current research findings are introduced.
- *Research That Teachers Can Use* explains research relevant to that chapter's reading domain in terms that are easy to read and apply.
- *New Classroom-Proven, Research-Based Practices* provides three to four key lessons that address the domain described in that chapter and can be used by teachers to help all children reach higher levels of success in that content domain.
- *Tests to Assess Learning* describes concrete methods that educators can use to evaluate what students have learned.
- *Addressing Learners With Special Needs* contains concrete methods that educators can use to help learners who struggle, learners who are learning English, and learners who excel.

In summary, this book is being written to respond to the need to help guide teachers, administrators, preservice educators, and parents through the Reading First legislation and to provide a practical resource to aid instruction. Helping educators, administrators, and parents bridge the gap between key research-based evidence and reading instruction in daily classroom practices is the primary goal of this book.

Acknowledgments

We would like to acknowledge Jennifer Medved, a graduate student at the University of Dayton, for sharing some of her wonderful experiences with us, especially the idea of including parents as true partners. We would also like to acknowledge Jean Ward, our editor. She is truly an amazing editor who encouraged us to write with a unique blend of warmth and rigor with a dose of kindness and compassion.

PUBLISHER'S ACKNOWLEDGMENTS

Corwin Press would like to thank the following reviewers for their contributions:

Missy Allen
Literacy Coach and Former Reading Recovery Teacher
Bedford, TX

Joan Irwin
Vice President for Professional Development
Peoples Publishing Group, Inc.

Leslie Morris
Literacy Coach
Philadelphia Public Schools
Philadelphia, PA

Nancy McDonough
Second-Grade Teacher
Stillman School
Tenafly, NJ

About the Authors

Cathy Collins Block is a professor of education at Texas Christian University. She has taught every grade level from preschool to graduate school and was elected to serve on the Board of Directors of the International Reading Association from 2002 to 2005. She has served or is presently serving on the IBM Educational Board of Directors and on the Boards of Directors of the National Reading Conference, the Nobel Learning Communities, and the National Center for Learning Disabilities. She presently serves on the Editorial Boards for the *Journal of Educational Psychology, Reading Research Quarterly, The Reading Teacher, National Reading Conference Yearbook,* and *America Tomorrow.* She has written more than 30 books and 80 research-based articles relative to literacy instruction and teacher education. She has also served or is serving on several elementary and middle school authorial writing teams for public and private school textbooks and literacy curriculum materials. She has written for Walt Disney Corporation, PBS television stations, and other national media companies. She has received numerous honors as a teacher, including listings in *Who's Who Among America's Teachers* and *Who's Who in the World.*

Susan E. Israel is the graduate reading coordinator and assistant professor at the University of Dayton. In addition, she has served on the Alliance for Catholic Education at the University of Notre Dame. She continues to promote reading through her work with the International Reading Association and other national literacy organizations. Her most recent publication is a comprehensive volume titled *Metacognition and Literacy Learning* (2005). She researches in the areas of developmental aspects of reading comprehension, development of a child's mind, metacognition, how the brain enables reading comprehension, and neuroscience as it relates to reading processes. Her most recent article appeared in *The Reading Teacher, 58(2)* and was entitled "The ABCs of Effective Think-Alouds."

Introduction to No Child Left Behind (NCLB) and Reading First (RF)

With the Practitioner's Voice of Kimberly J. Kolba

Mr. Adams is a third-grade teacher who enjoys reading to students. Susan and Jane are two students who enjoy sharing time together reading a book during paired-reading time. During paired-reading time, Mr. Adams makes sure all students are working with a partner, so no one child feels alone. Robert came to Mr. Adams and thanked him for being his teacher. Here is what Robert said during that conversation:

Robert:	*Mr. Adams, I would like to thank you for making sure I have a partner during paired-reading time. When I was in second grade, I felt alone. It seemed that other children who were better at reading were happier because they could read. Now that I'm here I'm getting better at reading, and you make it easier for me.*
Mr. Adams:	*Robert, thank you for telling me this. You are a very good student, and I can see all the good things you do during reading. I will continue to help you find new information in books that will help you become a better reader.*

Mr. Adams thought to himself, "I am so glad that I implemented the components of No Child Left Behind and Reading First described in Reading First and Beyond. *It's working."*

The purpose of this chapter is twofold. First, we want to provide information about the important areas of No Child Left Behind and Reading First legislation and the curriculum components described in these laws that have been demonstrated to significantly increase students' literary abilities. Second, we will describe the purpose of special features that appear in every chapter of this book. These features were designed to help you expand your knowledge about critical literacy instructional domains. We want to assist you in implementing and moving beyond Reading First legislation so you can enrich all children's literacy.

Within the last decades, literacy has become the focal point for educational legislation. There are two major reasons for policy makers and government officials to have built and supported NCLB and Reading First. First, reading proficiency is the most fundamental skill critical to most, if not all, academic learning and success in school. No doubt, mathematics, social studies, science, and other content domains are essential for academic and intellectual development, but to learn information in these disciplines in school, students must know how to read. Moreover, in the United States, the ability to read proficiently is significantly related to how much a person can achieve in his or her personal and professional life (Lyon, 2002; Shaywitz, 1999). Second, the number of children in the United States who cannot read proficiently is unacceptable. For example, the National Center for Education Statistics recently published the 2003 *Reading Report Card* as part of the *Nation's Report Card* (NCES, 2003). This snapshot was a summary of reading abilities of fourth-, eighth-, and twelfth-grade students as documented by the *National Assessment of Educational Progress.* It reported a persistent trend. In the fourth grade, 37 percent of students read below the basic level nationally, which essentially renders them illiterate. Only 31 percent of fourth graders can read proficiently at this grade level or above it. These percentages must change given the evidence that most children can learn to read when provided with sufficient instruction from excellent teachers (Block, 2004; Block, Oakar, & Hirt, 2002). NCLB and Reading First legislation were written to guide us to help all children become highly literate. How this national law does so, as well as how it can be actualized in all kindergarten to Grade 3 classrooms, will be described next.

PART I: WHAT TEACHERS NEED TO KNOW ABOUT THE LEGISLATION

In the following paragraphs, we will define NCLB and Reading First and provide background information about how Reading First legislation began and is continuing to shape literacy instruction in America.

No Child Left Behind is the historic, bipartisan education reform effort that President Bush proposed his first week in office and that was passed into law on January 8, 2002. The No Child Left Behind Act of 2001 (NCLB) reauthorized the Elementary and Secondary Education Act (ESEA)—the main federal law affecting education from kindergarten through high school. NCLB is built on four principles: accountability for results, more choices for parents, greater local control and flexibility, and an emphasis on doing what works based on scientific research, as described in more detail at www.ed.gov/print/programs/ readingfirst/index.html. The No Child Left Behind Act also established Reading First as a new, high-quality evidence-based literacy policy and national program to provide excellent literacy instruction to all primary-aged students in America.

The Reading First initiative builds on the findings of many years of scientific research, which, at the request of Congress, were compiled by the National Reading Panel (NRP) in a report presented to this body in the fall of 2000 (NICHD, 2000a) and into a research synthesis commissioned by the National Academy of Sciences (Snow, Burns, & Griffin, 1998).

These projects were the most rigorous and comprehensive review of reading research relevant to teaching reading ever undertaken, and they provided clear and unequivocal evidence that the majority of children could learn to read if teachers were provided the necessary training to implement scientifically validated effective instruction. NRP analyzed research in the categories of: alphabetics (phonemic awareness and phonics), fluency, comprehension, teacher education, technology, and methodology (NICHD, 2000b). Results of this research are presented in this book.

Copies of the full NRP report have been sent to every school district in America, and the distribution continues through the National Institute for Literacy, the U.S. Department of Education, and the NICHD. The significance of this report cannot be overemphasized. The results of both the National Academy of Sciences report and the National Reading Panel report made it clear that a comprehensive, scientifically based approach to reading instruction is necessary if all children are to learn to read efficiently and effectively. Based on these findings, the essential components of all reading programs must include systematic and direct instruction in phonemic awareness, phonics, reading fluency, vocabulary development, and comprehension strategies.

In the next few paragraphs, we will address the instructional, assessment, and teacher professional development requirements of NCLB, early literacy instruction (Early Reading First initiative for preschool-aged children), and Reading First (kindergarten through Grade 3 students). The No Child Left Behind Act of 2001 requires that:

- All states must assess students' literacy and mathematic abilities in Grades 3–8, and once during Grades 10–12, by 2006, and they are to use state-designed tests.
- All teachers of core academic subjects must be judged as highly qualified and certified to teach the subject areas to which they have been assigned according to state-established certifications, which must be in place by 2006.
- All students must be assessed in science once during Grades 3–5, 6–9, and 10–12, by 2008, using state-designed tests.
- Public school choice and supplemental educational services must be provided to students in schools that have been unable to meet Adequate Yearly Progress (AYP) for two consecutive years.
- 100 percent student literacy and mathematical proficiency must be attained by all students by June of 2014.

Nothing is more important to a child's education at school than having a well-prepared teacher. That's why NCLB requires that states make sure there is a highly qualified teacher in every public school classroom by the end of the 2005–2006 school year. To be highly qualified under NCLB, a teacher must

- Have a bachelor's degree
- Be fully certified as defined by the state department of education
- Be able to demonstrate subject area competence in any core subject taught

Resources You Can Use to Implement NCLB

No Child Left Behind: A Toolkit for Teachers is a booklet that " . . . was written with teachers in mind. This booklet contains important information focusing on the teacher quality provisions and how the law supports teachers" (www.ed.gov/ teachers, 2004). At this location you can also find descriptions of educators who have significantly raised student achievement and have successfully closed the achievement gap. The U.S. Department of Education is focusing attention on exemplary classroom teachers who are successful in raising student academic achievement for all of their students—often through the use of innovative classroom strategies. These teachers will be recognized as American Stars of Teaching and will be highlighted as representatives of the thousands of teachers who, regardless of the challenges they face, are making a difference in the lives of their students.

American Stars of Teaching have been identified in each state and the District of Columbia, and they represent all grade levels and disciplines. Officials from the U.S. Department of Education will be visiting the classes of all American Stars of Teaching to congratulate them on their success as a part of the Teacher-to-Teacher Initiative. This initiative, also described on this Web site, includes teacher and principal roundtables, summer and fall teacher workshops, a Research-to-Practice Teacher Summit that was held in July 2004, toolkits for teachers, resource materials, the weekly e-mail update "Teacher E-Bytes," and a free-of-charge online professional development program.

The workshop presentations and materials from the U.S. Department of Education Teacher-to-Teacher Workshops were developed by various individuals and are being provided as illustrative examples of what might be useful to teachers. The Department is not requiring or encouraging the use of any particular methods or materials in the classroom, and the use of the methods and materials in these sessions does not constitute an endorsement by the U.S. Department of Education.

Where can you obtain additional lesson plans, teacher resources, and information on NCLB when you complete this book? The Department of Education sponsors a Web site, www.NCLB.gov. You can download exemplary, research-based lesson plans. There are many other publications as well as free materials for parents.

Research That Teachers Can Use to Implement Reading First Legislation

The development and implementation of the Reading First (RF) initiative was built on the continued recognition that many of our nation's children, particularly those from disadvantaged environments, struggle to read and read below their grade-level placements. RF is also founded on the continuing convergence of scientific evidence as to how reading develops, reading difficulties arise, and effective instruction occurs. It recognizes the need to increase reading instructional programs and professional development courses that are based on scientific research, and it requires all states to set high standards of achievement as well as to create a system of accountability to measure results. RF provides flexibility to states and local districts in meeting their specific students' needs.

In order to achieve these goals, the Reading First initiative significantly increased the federal investment in scientifically based reading research (SBRR) instruction in the early grades. Approximately one billion dollars per year for a six-year period was provided to states for school districts to implement instructional programs based on SBRR. This substantial funding increase was also predicated on data indicating that investment in high-quality reading instruction at the preschool (Early Reading First) and kindergarten through Grade 3 levels (Reading First) would help to reduce the number of children who would need special education services later because of reading failure. But it was clear that any increase in funding for reading programs would result in increased student achievement if, and only if, the U.S. Department of Education developed and put in place programmatic policies and procedures to ensure successful implementation. The probability of children benefiting from the Reading First (and Early Reading First) programs is significantly increased by the following policies:

- *Strong Statute.* The Reading First grant program states clearly that all program activities must be based on scientifically based reading research. It also requires the submission of detailed state plans and annual performance reports and explicitly allows for the discontinuance of state funding when significant progress in reducing the number of students reading below grade level is not made.
- *Significant National Activities Funds.* Reading First is allotted up to $25 million each year to allow the Department of Education to provide unprecedented funds for technical assistance and monitoring activities to support the implementation of Reading First. A specific, focused multimillion-dollar contract will provide onsite monitoring in *each* state *each* year.
- *Rigorous Application Process.* The rigorous Reading First process requires each state to create a detailed blueprint of its Reading First plan. States have not been allowed to provide vague overviews of any facet of their plans. As a result, monitors can assess how states are implementing their plans.
- *Performance Reporting.* States submit annual performance reports documenting their progress in reducing the number of students reading below grade level. States describe how they will make funding decisions, including discontinuation.
- *External Review.* External independent reviewers will determine the degree to which states and local school districts are increasing the number of students who read proficiently. The external reviewers also evaluate whether all components of Reading First are being taught consistently with appropriate fidelity.

- *Improving on REA.* For all of these reasons, the implementation of Reading First will be stronger and more focused than preceding programs such as the Reading Education for All Act (REA), the former reading law that was passed under President William Clinton's administration. Unlike previous programs, Reading First enables all students and teachers in all classrooms to participate. All states have resources to use research-based methods of instruction, as described in this book, to improve student achievement. A major difference between RF and REA is that all states and local districts are held accountable for ensuring that federal funds are explicitly tied to student reading achievement and not spent in ways that do not directly touch children's literacy needs.

Assessing Learning in Reading First Legislation

NCLB and RF require statewide assessments, a statewide and district-level system of accountability, and support for individual school-level literacy improvement plans based on these evaluations. The U.S. Department of Education and NCLB require the following evaluative actions:

State Assessments (condensed from www.ed.gov)

- By 2005–2006, states must have developed and implemented annual assessments in reading and mathematics in Grades 3–8, and at least once in Grades 10–12. By 2007–2008, states must administer annual science assessments at least once in Grades 3–5, Grades 6–9, and Grades 10–12.
- State assessments must be aligned with challenging academic content standards and challenging academic achievement standards. State standards must have the same expectations for all children and have at least three age-specific, achievement-level standards.
- State assessments must involve all students, including students with disabilities or limited English proficiency. State assessments must provide adequate accommodations for students with disabilities or limited English proficiency.
- States must ensure that districts administer tests of English proficiency—that measure oral language, reading, and writing skills in English—to all limited English-proficient students.
- State assessments must produce results disaggregated by gender, as well as by (1) major racial and ethnic groups within the student population, (2) English proficiency, (3) migrant status, (4) disability rankings, and (5) economic status of students. The assessment system must produce an interpretive, descriptive, and diagnostic report for each population subgroup, such as all data relative to a single ethnic group must be reported for that ethnic group separately from other ethnic group reports. States must report itemized score analyses to districts and schools.
- States must make results of state assessments administered in one school year available to school districts by the beginning of the next school year in a clear and understandable format.

- States must participate in biennial National Assessment of Educational Progress (NAEP) assessments in reading and mathematics for fourth and eighth graders, which began in 2002–2003, and data is examined by policy makers.
- NCLB requires states to produce annual report cards that address how *all* students are progressing in addition to information disaggregated by race, ethnicity, gender, English proficiency, migrant status, disability status, and low-income status. (Additional information concerning assessment can be found at www.nclb.gov or www.ed.gov/admins, as these Web sites are continuously updated by the Department of Education to reflect the latest adaptations and conditions affecting NCLB.)
- According to www.ed.gov, the report cards must show two-year trend data for each subject and grade tested, with a comparison between annual objectives and actual performance for each student group. The report cards must show the percentage of each group of students not tested, graduation rates for secondary school students, and information on student achievement for the district and each school. Also, these report cards must identify schools in need of improvement
- NCLB asks educators to keep parents involved in their student's progress. Districts are required to notify parents of school choice and supplemental educational service options.
- NCLB allows parents the right to request information about their children's teachers' professional qualifications.

Addressing Learners With Special Needs

In the following paragraphs, we explain how NCLB affects students with special needs.

Learners Who Struggle

Both NCLB and IDEA (Individuals with Disabilities Education Act) require students with disabilities to be assessed by the state accountability system described previously. According to the U.S. Department of Education, IDEA requires that the local educational agency develop an Individualized Education Program (IEP) for each child with a disability. This document includes information concerning how the child will be assessed and what kind of educational, developmental, and behavioral support the child will receive. Applicable accommodations to the regular assessment such as extra time, larger print, a quiet room, Braille, repeated instructions, or additional breaks may be made for students with disabilities. In Chapters 2–11, we will present methods by which students with learning disabilities can have their special learning needs met through research-based instructional practices.

Learners Who Are Learning English

NCLB and RF require students who have limited English proficiency (LEP) to be assessed and tested in reading, language arts, and math. NCLB and RF allow these students to be tested in their native language for up to three years, after which time they should be tested in English. In addition, the U.S. Department of

Education also recently clarified that newly arrived LEP students, during their first year in the United States, will be allowed to take either the English proficiency assessments or the state literacy test. States are allowed to include limited English proficient students in a school's LEP subgroup for adequate yearly progress (AYP) purposes for up to two years after these students attain English proficiency.

States are held accountable for teaching LEP students English under NCLB and RF, and they are required to develop annual measurable achievement objectives to monitor the progress of LEP students' abilities to read English. Grant recipients failing to meet their annual measurable achievement objectives for two years are required to inform the parents of LEP students of the program's inability to meet such objectives. The state requires modification of such schools' particular curriculum, program, or method of instruction if achievement objectives are not met after four years. The state will also determine if the insufficient program will still receive funding and will require educational program personnel to be replaced.

In reference to bilingual education, the previous competitive grant program required that not less than 75 percent of funds be used for programs that use a child's native language in instruction. This requirement was repealed by NCLB. States can choose the most preferred method for teaching LEP students, including bilingual education.

Parents of LEP students do have options under NCLB. It requires local education agencies (LEAs) to provide parental notification explaining why a child may need placement in a language instruction educational program. Parents also have the right to choose which instructional program they prefer for their child. LEAs are encouraged to keep parents involved and informed of their child's participation in that personally selected program.

Learners Who Excel

In this section, we will describe the special needs of gifted learners. Although RF is not designed for gifted learners (because it only requires minimum competency), this section will describe how educators can use RF research-based practices to assist gifted learners to attain highest levels of competence.

Gifted preschool and elementary school children have limited federal legislative acts designed to meet their learning needs. Only 37 states have some type of state-level mandate to provide special services to gifted readers. Only 26 states have laws that provide one or more of the following mandates on behalf of gifted readers: requirement to identify gifted readers, programmatic guidelines to build special advanced reading programs, and certifications for teachers to direct these gifted students' literacy curriculum. Many states employ regional coordinators for education of gifted children. A list of these coordinators, as well as the addresses for state-based educational advocacy and professional organizations that support gifted readers, can be found at http://ericec.org (click on Fact Sheets, then on State Resources for Gifted Education). The International Reading Association (IRA) has a special-interest group for gifted and talented readers, in which most recent research-based literacy practices are provided to members through newsletters. If you wish to join this group, the charge is minimal. Contact the president of this group at c.block@tcu.edu.

PART II: HOW TO USE THIS BOOK

In the chapters of this book, you will learn how you can use research-based instructional practices to improve all students' oral language (Chapter 2), phonological awareness (Chapter 3), understanding of phonics (Chapter 4), vocabulary (Chapter 5), fluency (Chapter 6), comprehension (Chapter 7), independent reading abilities (Chapter 8), writing (Chapter 9), and metacognition (Chapter 10), and you will learn to include parents as serious partners in helping their children learn to read (Chapter 11). You will read about scientifically validated lessons, assessment instruments, and special strategies for special literacy needs.

While the book is organized around the elements of Reading First and other research-supported instructional components for student success, we include in Table 1.1 a grid that also shows the connection between the book's content and specific IRA standards.

If you are a kindergarten or Grade 1 teacher reading this book, we recommend that you start from the beginning of the book and read each chapter in order so that you can use the information from the first few chapters at the beginning of the year and the chapters near the end of the book at the end of the year. If you are a teacher teaching in Grade 2 or 3, we recommend that you start with the chapter that most matches the curriculum objectives that you have for the beginning school year; then as you move to new curriculum objectives you may add the innovative ideas and research-based practices from the other chapters that match your exact instructional objective.

If you are a literacy coach, we recommend that you use this book either as a book study for teachers who you are coaching or as a source for demonstration lessons in individual classrooms. As a literacy coach, you may also enjoy holding faculty meetings in which you pass out one reproducible form and do a think-aloud about how all teachers at that meeting could use that particular think-aloud, form, and/or lesson to meet a specific need that they face. A think-aloud is a strategy that provides students with an opportunity to verbalize their thoughts aloud.

In every chapter you will find the following:

- *Vignette of a Child's Thoughts.* At the beginning of each chapter, this feature provides an illustration of how a component of RF legislation was applied successfully in a learning situation.
- *What Teachers Need to Know.* Throughout the book, this section is designed to present a working definition of the key literacy element described in that chapter. In every chapter, this section will provide background knowledge about a component of Reading First legislation or another scientifically validated practice in exemplary preschool-to-Grade-3 literacy programs (such as oral language, metacognition, and writing instruction).

Table 1.1   A Summary of IRA's *Standards for Reading Professionals—Revised 2003* and a Correlation of Where Those Standards Are Discussed In This Book

IRA Standard 1: Functional Knowledge	Chapters
Element 1.1. Knowledge of psychological and linguistic foundations of reading and writing processes and instruction	2, 3, 4
Element 1.2. Knowledge of reading research and histories of reading	2, 3, 4, 5, 6, 7, 8, 9, 10
Element 1.3. Knowledge of language development and reading acquisition and the variations related to cultural and linguistic diversity	2, 3, 4, 5, 6, 7, 8, 9, 10

IRA Standard 2: Instructional Strategies and Curriculum Materials	Chapters
Element 2.1. Use instructional grouping options as appropriate for accomplishing given purposes	3, 4, 5, 6, 7, 8, 9
Element 2.2. Use a wide range of instructional practices, approaches, and methods, including technology-based practices for learners at differing stages of development and from differing cultural and linguistic backgrounds	2, 3, 4, 5, 6, 7, 8, 9, 10
Element 2.3. Use a wide range of curriculum materials in effective reading instruction for learners at different stages of reading and writing development and from different cultural and linguistic backgrounds	2, 3, 4, 5, 6, 7, 8, 9, 10

IRA Standard 3: Assessment, Diagnosis, and Evaluation	Chapters
Element 3.1. Use a wide range of assessment tools and practices that range from individual and group standardized tests to individual and group informal classroom assessment strategies, including technology-based assessment tools	2, 3, 4, 5, 6, 7, 8, 9, 10
Element 3.2. Place students along a developmental continuum and identify students' proficiencies and difficulties	2, 3, 4
Element 3.3. Use assessment information to plan, evaluate, and revise effective instruction that meets the needs of all students including those at different developmental stages and those from different cultural and linguistic backgrounds	2, 3, 4, 5, 6, 7, 8, 9, 10

IRA Standard 4: Creating a Literate Environment	Chapters
Element 4.1. Use students' interests, reading abilities, and backgrounds as foundations for the reading and writing program	6, 9, 11
Element 4.2. Use a large supply of books, technology-based information, and nonprint materials representing multiple levels, broad interests, cultures, and linguistic backgrounds	2, 3, 4, 8, 9, 10
Element 4.3. Model reading and writing enthusiastically as valued lifelong readers	2, 3, 4, 5, 6, 7, 8, 9, 10

IRA Standard 5: Professional Development	Chapters
Element 5.1. Display dispositions related to reading and the teaching of reading	1, 2, 3, 4, 5, 6, 7, 8, 9, 10, 11
Element 5.2. Continue to pursue the development of professional knowledge and dispositions	1, 11
Element 5.3. Work with colleagues to observe, evaluate, and provide feedback on each other's practice	2, 3, 4, 5, 6, 7, 8, 9, 10
Element 5.4. Participate in, initiate, implement, and evaluate professional development programs	1, 11

- *Research That Teachers Can Use.* This section provides important research-based evidence that you and other educators can rely upon as you implement Reading First.
- *New Classroom-Proven, Research-Based Practices.* In this section, we present several scientifically validated instructional practices that will address the goal of the literacy domain discussed in a chapter. You can use these strategies to help children achieve success in that content domain. These practices will include a teachers' aid in many cases, such as a new graphic that has proven to be highly effective for early literacy success.
- *Tests to Assess Learning.* In this section, we will provide concrete methods that you can use to evaluate your students' progress.
- *Addressing Learners With Special Needs.* In this section, we will describe how to adapt learning and assessment techniques to meet the special students' learning needs. The needs addressed will be learning difficulties, language learning needs, and advanced literacy abilities.

SUMMARY

During these past three decades, the failure of our nation's children to read proficiently has continued to be a consistent and persistent finding. The research supported and conducted by the NICHD and other federal agencies has led to the identification of instructional and assessment strategies that can assist children to overcome reading failure. By continuously diagnosing and assessing their progress, in ways described throughout this book, high levels of literacy success can be attained. Scientific evidence has taught us that reading must be taught—directly and systematically—and that children most at risk require the most instruction with the best-prepared teachers. The guidelines within NCLB and RF were described in this chapter.

Through the activities described in the remainder of this book, reaching literacy proficiency for all is an achievable and realistic goal. By using instruction that is based on scientific research, we can view successful reading instruction with optimism for today's and tomorrow's students. At the same time, teachers can reflect on how they can individualize their instruction to match the needs of each child. This book was written to enable you and all your colleagues to walk with confidence upon the stones of scientifically validated practices that lie herein, while your work is guided by your highest aspirations for all your students as, together, you help them reach their star-filled potentials.

Research-Based Practices for Oral Language Development

With the Practitioners' Voices of Kari-Ann M. Ediger,
Jennifer R. Willcutt, and Catherine M. Bohn

On the first day of school, Ms. Ediger asked us all to say what we did over the summer. As we talked, she wrote what we said but I didn't know what she wrote! When I finished telling my story, Ms. Ediger showed me her work on the paper. She read the words that I had just told her right back to me, just the way I had said them. "How did you remember all that, Ms. Ediger?" I asked. Ms. Ediger said that the words I spoke were the same words that she had written on the paper! It's the day before winter vacation now, and I'm learning how to make the sounds of the words on paper!! I can look at what I said lots of days earlier and I can remember just what I said way back then! I'm learning to read!! That's the best!!!

—Leo, Grade 1

WHY TEACH ORAL LANGUAGE?

With so much research being focused on learning to read, you may ask "Why is there an oral language chapter in a Reading First book?" Language is one of the basic tools necessary for learning how to read. Oral language ability allows us to decode and comprehend text. Young children who receive high scores on language tests are also early readers who come from home environments rich in language (Dickinson & Tabors, 2000). Not only does language affect early reading, but it also allows children to create meaning. While oral language appears to be mastered in the preschool years, knowledge of the complexities within spoken and written language requires direct instruction before most students can understand it.

For all of these reasons and more, it is important that oral language receive an appropriate amount of attention in your literacy program. With this goal in mind, we have devoted this chapter to highlighting research-based theories of oral language development and to describing how you might implement these theories with a variety of scientifically validated lessons. We also explain how oral language abilities relate to reading achievement.

WHAT TEACHERS NEED TO KNOW

Oral language is the ability to express yourself verbally, which can include reading aloud, speaking, reciting, and conversing. Several factors influence oral language, such as cultural norms, nonstandard dialects of a single language, bilingual and second language speakers, and academic and colloquial usages within languages. Because classrooms are becoming increasingly diverse, in relation to the oral languages that students have learned prior to attending school, there is an ever-increasing need for teachers to know how to teach reading in the context of a highly diverse set of oral languages. The following scientifically based principles can assist you to ease the challenges associated with using these languages to build reading abilities.

Oral Language Ability Varies from Person to Person

Individuals vary in their ability to express themselves through oral language. Factors that can influence this ability include age, developmental growth, exposure to oral language at home, the nature of the language spoken, and the cultural climate surrounding oral language. Different arrangements of these variables can produce individual differences in oral language ability (Halliday, 1975). In addition to these factors, environmental differences, such as what cognitive and affective intensity individuals bring to the task of learning oral language, and, to some degree, the heredity and abilities of parents and grandparents, differentiate between captivating and laborious orators.

Dialect Diversity in Oral Language

Norms within cultures can affect the amount and style of oral language that is acceptable among groups of people who share a common background. In certain cultures, it is impolite for children to speak publicly among adults, which can conflict with norms in the classroom when children are expected to express themselves orally. Equally important, within certain cultural heritages, the types of discussion topics are subject to cultural norms. These cultural differences can often be difficult, especially when teachers use students' verbal feedback to assess his or her educational progress (Corson, 2001).

For instance, dialect can influence the style of oral language. African-American Vernacular English (AAVE), or *Ebonics*, and its effects on students' abilities to learn to read Standard English has been hotly debated among educators. A recent report verified that various nonstandard varieties of English are heard in the classroom, and if students' pronunciation is very different from the teacher's pronunciation, it may be difficult for students and teachers to reconcile the differences between the spoken word and the printed word (Lapp et al., 2004). This can result in confusion for the student, frequent miscommunications, and subsequent frustration with language learning. Moreover, dialect and regional differences in pronunciation occur everywhere, even among residents of the same community (Corson, 2001). For all of these reasons, a sound reading program must be grounded in instruction that builds a highly effective oral communication system for every child.

RESEARCH THAT TEACHERS CAN USE

Theories of Language Acquisition

Many theories have attempted to explain how human language developed. Behaviorists hypothesize that interactions with the environment drive language development; and that positive reinforcement encourages accurate language acquisition (Moerk, 1992; Skinner, 1957). Other scientists believe that language is acquired through social interaction (i.e., when early attempts at language are rewarded, language is slowly shaped through experimentation, reinforcement, and encouragement) (Bohannan, 1993; Cazden, 1992). Equally compelling, nativist theorists posit that language develops innately through a language acquisition device (LAD) and innate, internalized grammar rules (Chomsky, 1965; Pinker, 1994). Last, many scientists posit that language develops through the principles of constructivism (defined as "a philosophical perspective derived from the work of Immanuel Kant which views reality as existing mainly in the mind, constructed or interpreted in terms of one's own perceptions). In this perspective, an individual's prior experiences, mental structures and beliefs bear upon how experiences are interpreted" (Harris & Hodges, 1995, p. 43). Following this theory, Piaget theorized that children's oral language develops through their activities, with their first words being nouns and verbs, centered on actions, objects, and direct experiences that the child has (Piaget & Inhelder, 1969). Only at much later times do adjectives, adverbs, and subtleties of meaning develop. In like manner, Vygotsky posited that language matures through interactions with experienced adults who encourage, motivate, and offer support to young language learners (Sulzby, 1986; Vygotsky, 1978). In general, constructivists believe that children create their language based on an innate set of rules, through an active, interactive social process and that making errors is a necessary part of learning (Bohannan, 1993; Jaggar, 1985).

Based on constructivist theory, Halliday (1975, 1987) proposed the first set of principles for oral language instruction. His educational design is based on scientific studies and has become one of the leading curricular frameworks for instruction in oral language development in our country. His research found that children slowly learn how to make meaning of their experiences, which turns into oral language creation, under a master teacher's lead. This learning process continues throughout a student's life at school, when in the company of the best teachers in our profession. Under their care, students come to learn the function of even the most difficult of terms and the relevance that these words hold to a specific oral or written situation. Seven functions of oral language exist and must be instructed before many students can attain mastery of all of them: instrumental (using language to satisfy a need), regulatory (to control behavior of self and others), interactional (to get along with others), personal (to tell about oneself), heuristic (to discover and learn), imaginative (to create new ideas), and informative (to communicate information) (Halliday, 1975, 1987).

Stages of Development

Based on studies of the theories above, we know that language ability increases throughout students' development. In addition, the pace of development through the stages of language differs for each individual. During the first year of life, infants experiment with sounds they create (e.g., crying, babbling, cooing), and parents, guardians, and caregivers learn to distinguish between the noises. Babies use oral language to seek attention, can discriminate between speech sounds, and communicate nonverbally. Parental speech and body language provide affectionate, social stimulation for both children and parents. Moreover, infants are born with the ability to hear many different sound categories, including those in different languages (Sachs, 2001), but become less sensitive to sounds that are not used at home by the time they are at the age of 10–12 months (Menn & Stoel-Gammon, 2001). This developmental fact, along with evidence that a second language is difficult to acquire after adolescence, has lead educators to conclude that the primary-grade years are the most critical period in oral language acquisition (Johnson & Newport, 1989). For instance, when oral language instruction and optimal support is present at six months of age, infants can begin to combine consonant and vowel sounds into babbling. When parents or preschool teachers reinforce this babbling and attach meaning to this child's utterance, the infant begins to learn the functions of oral language described above. As a result, at about 8–12 months, children's comprehension ability increases, and the first words they utter are usually functional and meaningful (Au, Depretto, & Song, 1994). These developmental findings provide strong evidence that even during the first year of life, oral language development is an ongoing, growth-oriented experience that can prepare children to read well.

Around one to two months of age, children begin to babble in phrases that sound very sentence-like, although incoherent to adults. After 12 months, children can use telegraphic speech, including content but not function words (e.g., "want cookie," or "Mom gone"). By 18 months, children can pronounce 80% of the phonemes in English and can use 20–50 words (Bloom, 1990). During their first three years at school this aspect of oral language accelerates under the care of an exemplary teacher. In addition to the seven functions of language, by second grade, children need to have developed an understanding of the basic systems that prescribe how oral language works: phonology, morphology, semantics, syntax, and pragmatics (the social rules for language use) (Gleason, 2001).

Another dramatic stage in language development occurs between two and three years of age. Vocabulary grows from 300 to 1000 words, and most three-year olds can comprehend up to 3000 spoken words. In addition, children begin to use function words when speaking and to play with language (e.g., rhyme, repetitions). Similarly, most children use plurals and regular verbs by four years of age, and often overgeneralize irregular verbs. Children in preschool through Grade 1 talk to themselves while playing, often articulating actions (Bloom, 1990; Jewell & Zintz, 1986). For all of these reasons, when oral language incorporates these basic dimensions of English communication, the ability to call upon these basic principles when children approach written language is greatly enhanced. Oral and written language principles can be learned together in many ways and can significantly increase many students' abilities to associate sounds with letters and to associate spoken ideas to their written counterparts (Block, Rodgers, & Johnson, 2004). The more you demonstrate the complexities of the English language in its oral and, immediately after utterances, in its corresponding written form, the more rapidly students from various home languages can become successful readers.

Without such rich intermingling of teachers' oral and written demonstrations, some students, beyond five years of age, still struggle with specific sounds of individual letters and words. These children may increasingly speak more like adults and continue to assimilate vocabulary, but their knowledge of the complexities in the seven functions and five English language systems will fall farther and farther behind without your daily oral language instruction. By age five, most students will understand that words may have multiple meanings, but they will also feel increased frustration when misunderstandings occur, and subtleties communicated in complex syntactical or semantic structures will elude them. Your instruction is vital for preschoolers and kindergarteners to learn how to use humor, creative language expressions, and oral words to function in groups. With your support, their depth of noun and verb knowledge can increase, their thoughts can become more concrete, and they begin to engage in less pretend play.

By second grade, under the tutelage of a master teacher and using the lessons in this book, children continue to refine their use of complex grammatical structures in talk and in their reading comprehension. These two abilities are so intertwined that the later will be greatly restricted if correct oral language structures are not internalized. By third grade, under the care of master teachers, most students' oral grammar will become well developed, and they will become good conversationalists. Such language development and teacher knowledge-transmitting responsibilities continue throughout a child's school years (Morrow, 2001).

Development of Empathy

As you may have noticed, though individually driven, oral language begins and continues within the framework of a socially supportive environment. Just as oral language grows throughout the developmental years, so too does the social ability of children. It is important, therefore, to address the important role that social processes play in oral language and reading development. Empathy, or the ability to understand another person's perspective, is developmentally driven and enhanced through master teachers' instruction (Wigfield & Eccles, l996). From birth, and as a person's background knowledge and experiences accumulate, empathy can continually be refined through use of the research-based lessons in this chapter (Piaget & Inhelder, 1969).

This empathetic ability to understand a perspective outside a person's own internal awareness is what gives children a further context for restructuring or validating what they currently know or discover as they read. This best occurs when new information, opinions, and experiences are presented from a speaker's or literary character's perspective. In the context of listening or reading well, empathy contributes to a child's abilities to better understand and attend to the emotionally expressive cues inherent in oral and written language. In the context of reading and discourse, empathy also allows the reader to take on the perspective of a story character. Further, this emerging ability to comprehend a perspective other than their own allows readers to learn from the emotional struggles that a story character might face and the underlying reasons a character makes certain defining choices in the course of a story. When such language-complexity driven competencies are present, reading becomes pleasurable and intellectually nurturing. Neither of these benefits could occur unless these student capacities were developed; first in most cases through their teacher's well-planned, research-based oral language program. Moreover, these abilities become even more crucial when we consider the research concerning prosody. Understanding the prosody, or emotional expressions of language production, is essential if students are to attain the ability to read fluently by Grade 2. Fluent reading includes the ability to read quickly and accurately; however, the components of reading with good expression as well as comprehension are equally important (Samuels, 2002).

There are many wonderful classroom ideas for facilitating these understandings throughout this book. For instance, young learners' teachers could provide concrete examples and opportunities for students to identify emotions based on the way in which they and their peers say something or present information. For example, you could say the phrase "Hi. How are you?" in a variety of ways, using different pause points, vocal pitch inflections, and tones. The manner in which this one sentence is stated, though the words are the same, could communicate a variety of different meanings (i.e., could communicate disinterest, dislike for a person, sincere interest in the person and their answer, or possibly, a simple pleasantry or social formality). By providing the instructional opportunities throughout this book for beginning learners to identify the emotional state of the speaker and the subtleties of meanings behind the spoken words, teachers can help students not only to hear, recognize, and gain meaning from the emotions of others in an oral language context but also to lay the foundations for reading orally with good oral expression.

Emerging Perspectives of the Learner

Oral language has many uses and functions within the context of literacy learning. The following are three emerging perspectives of all of the feats that an individual must be taught to perform with regard to oral language ability.

The Speaker

First, there is language production, or expressive language. In order to communicate effectively, emerging speakers must learn to choose what to say, how they will say it, and when it is appropriate to say it so that communication is meaningful to the listener. Opportunities for using language in multiple settings and for a variety of purposes can serve to increase both the social competence and intellectual development of a child. For example, the way in which a child uses language can affect peer relationships and acceptance into social groups (Choi & Kim, 2003). Furthermore, with regard to social value, positive peer relationships offer children additional means with which to practice and enhance their language abilities (Pelligrini, Galda, Bartini & Charak, 1998). With regard to intellectual development, an effective speaker must learn how to monitor both speech output and internal dialogue (Levelt, 1999). This self-evaluation, or social metacognition, of how others react to what was said helps the child to further assimilate and accommodate educational concepts as well as social mores. The same comprehension and metacognitive system that people use to monitor their own dialogue is also used when listening to a conversational partner (Levelt, 1999; Cutler & Clifton, 1999).

The Listener

Second, when listening, students must learn how to attend to the verbal cues in a dialogue or oral discourse. They must be taught how to retain and process incoming information and integrate relevant background knowledge. Placing children in an environment that is language-rich will improve these features of receptive language development. For instance, asking children what *they* think about classroom conversation topics gives them the opportunity to understand that when participating in a discussion they need to formulate their own thoughts and responses while others are talking—yet wait for their turn to speak (Beals, 2001). Including children in discussions also helps them to become more adept at active listening, informs them of the necessity of "listening" in order for successful communication to occur, and teaches patience and respectful turn-taking. Additionally, children's explicit inclusion in such oral language experiences enhances their awareness of subtle social cues inherent in any discussion: things such as how to show someone you're listening by using good eye contact, nodding, turning toward the speaker, and nonverbal gestures that communicate interest and attention.

Oral Reading and the Reader

Lastly, there is the perspective of oral reading, which includes aspects of both expressive and receptive language. While reading orally does not necessitate the initial production of language, in terms of what one speaker will generate to say to another, it does require a speaker to interpret what is written on a page and to perform processes associated with conveying that information to others. An important distinction with regard to reading orally is that while the words on a page are represented as physically separate units of information, a listener hears speech as a continuous stream of sound (Cutler & Clifton, 1999). This means that—while a comprehension system is at work within all three perspectives—with regard to reading orally, additional cognitive systems are necessary. For example, a person with reading disabilities would likely have difficulty with word recognition and decoding; this difficulty would consequently interfere with the ability to communicate text to others although that same person's speaking ability could be quite highly functional. For a person with automatic word recognition and decoding skills, more of their cognitive resources can be directed toward speaking, along with comprehension and inference generating abilities (Samuels, 2002; Perfetti, 1999).

NEW CLASSROOM-PROVEN, RESEARCH-BASED PRACTICES

Age-Appropriate Strategies

The following research-based lessons have been proven to significantly increase students' oral language proficiencies and have enabled them to learn to read with greater ease, speed, and pleasure.

Oral Language Development Lesson 1: Increase the Amount of Daily Production of Their Own Language

It is critical to immerse young children in language-rich environments that contain a variety of contexts in which language use occurs. This could mean talking and discussing ideas as students gather for circle time, reading a book together and talking about it, generating important conversations with peers, or playing word games such as rhyming and "I Spy." Whatever the method or means, the important classroom goal is to provide an environment where language is valued and word knowledge and vocabulary increase.

Oral Language Development Lesson 2: Storytelling

Many children are natural storytellers; they simply love to talk about anything that relates to themselves and what they are interested in. As children's vocabularies begin to increase, asking them to retell a story they like, in their own words, further communicates the importance, value, and joy of learning to read. Asking children to talk, in general, about whatever they might want to talk about allows them the freedom to express what they find important and interesting as well as to practice the functions and systems of English. Guiding children through the process of telling a story can also lay the groundwork for later reading comprehension abilities. For example, if a child were to tell a story about "one time when I went to the beach," an adult could ask leading questions, such as: "What did it look like there? What did you do when you were there? Were there a lot of people at the beach? Was it fun? What did you like most or least about it? Why do you think a beach is called 'a beach'?" These sorts of questions encourage children to use their imaginations, elaborate on what they know, and begin to put words to their experiences.

Though there is simply no way to predict what the answers to such questions might be, asking these types of questions communicates interest and caring and shows that the child's perspective is valued (St. Amour, 2003). Often it is the case that feigning ignorance and asking a variety of questions can be an effective tool in discovering what children know and where the gaps in their knowledge might be. Furthermore, as a two-foot wave at the beach might likely become a twenty-foot wave in the mind of a child, asking about a memorable event can provide an opportunity to help children begin to distinguish between reality and make-believe, while at the same time supporting and encouraging their often vivid and entertaining imaginations. With regard to comprehension, asking children leading questions when they are telling a story points toward the important components of a story; and therefore, prepares them for later reading and comprehension strategies. For example, narrative stories typically have a main character, the main character takes some sort of action, and the action might happen over time. Helping children discover why a character might choose a certain path of action helps children make connections between what is explicitly stated in the text and what can be inferred from it. Asking children questions that help illuminate inferential connections in an oral story or a text aids in fostering the basic skills of comprehension.

Oral Language Lessons 3: Dialogic Reading

Similar to having children tell their own stories is dialogic reading. This process makes use of picture books as a means by which children can describe, elaborate, and "tell" the story. Where typically an adult would read a story to a child, this strategy allows children to have control of the story. Adults then become the active listeners in which their role is to ask the child questions and add information where appropriate. Children make inferences about the story based upon the pictures and use their oral language to describe what might be going on. Using this method of interaction encourages participation, personalization, and further use of children's oral and written language competencies (Whitehurst et al., 1994). Figure 2.1 can be used to help you to engage students in meaningful conversation using the dialogic reading format.

Oral Language Lesson 4: Text Talk

As children begin to learn how to read, *Text Talk* is a strategy that you can use to engage students throughout the process of reading. Text Talk is an instructional lesson that combines culturally responsive teaching, metacognitive questioning, and oral language as a means of improving students' verbal abilities through a more focused, meaningful, and personalized approach. "When children's real-life experiences were legitimized and when the curriculum was connected to their backgrounds, they were able to understand complex ideas even beyond their reading levels" (Conrad, Gong, Sipp, & Wright, 2004, p. 188; but see also Ladson-Billings, 1994; and Delpit, 1995). Asking open-ended questions and encouraging children to initiate their own questions about a story, as well as encouraging children to discuss these questions in small groups following the story, offers children the opportunity to draw from other people's experiences and consider ideas from diverse perspectives. Through the process of focused and purposeful discussion, children also begin

Figure 2.1   Storytelling Interviews

Storytelling Interview

Student 1 tells a story to Student 2; it is then the responsibility of Student 2 to report back to other group or class members what Student 1 said. Therefore, Student 2 has to be sure that he or she understands Student 1 completely. Filling in the following boxes can be a helpful tool in understanding what is important to know, question, and attend to in a story. Not all boxes may apply to all stories; the idea is to fill as many as possible. This can also be used when reading a story out loud to children. For example, stop halfway through a story and see how many boxes can be filled in before continuing on.

Possible Topics for Story Interviews

Tell a story about your favorite place.
Tell a story of your favorite day.
Tell a story about a pet or animal.
Tell a story about your favorite activity.

Tell a story about family.
Tell a story about your favorite
    time of year.

Title of Story:	
Main Character(s):	
Additional Character(s):	
What do you know about the characters so far? What do you think about them?	
What actions were taken?	
Was there a conflict? What was it?	
How was the conflict resolved?	
Was there another way the conflict could have been resolved?	
What do you (personally) know about the topic (background knowledge and information)?	
What is the main idea of the story?	
Does the beginning and ending of the story match? Or, were there differences?	
How did the story make you feel?	

to learn the democratic process in terms of valuing and respecting the ideas of others.

Oral Language Lesson 5: Readers Theatre

Readers Theatre as an oral language instructional technique has been well received by classroom teachers and students. Each student is assigned a character and reads this part aloud, taking appropriate turns as in a formal play. In lieu of a stage, the characters stand with their backs toward the audience until it is their turn to speak, at which point they turn to face their audience. Each student is to read with feeling and expression in the style of the character being played. The result is that students practice their reading and oral language skills simultaneously. Readers also develop varied emotional expression since they are enacting their interpretations of their characters. At times in a Readers Theatre, all students practice their oral language skills by reading a text together as a group and acting out their assigned characters.

In order to use Readers Theatre in the elementary classroom, it is best not to burden the very young with too many lines. Often, you will assume the role of the narrator. Stories with repeated lines are ideal because the children will start to expect what can happen next and get excited about knowing the answer. Children will delight in taking on the role of funny characters like vegetables, a tree, a stone, a weaver, a fisherman, a chief, a river, or a chair. Each student adopts the role of a character and mimes its actions. Readers can be assigned parts commensurate with their abilities. Poorer readers, for example, can be given small, easy parts in order to ensure their success, while not slowing down faster readers. Stories, plays, and poetry, which are useful in teaching elementary school literature, can be used. If the teacher is using Readers Theatre with very young children, the following adaptations have also proven to be of value:

- You can read to the children and allow them to provide sound effects, such as the wind blowing or the hooting of an owl.
- Children may read along with you or a student leader. This builds self-confidence, and the oral model teaches intonation patterns.
- Children may participate in a choral reading style by repeating refrains or by reading an easily remembered line as you point to the words on a chart paper.
- Older children may present their theatre production to younger schoolmates (Coger & White, 1982, pp. 180-181).

Literature that is useful for Readers Theatre for children is well written, has an absence of falseness and a personal vision, and describes a plausible world. These stories should create wonder and laughter, offer action and dramatic excitement, appeal to the imagination, and inspire a love of beauty both through the quality of the characters and through the beauty of the language. Look for repetition of sounds and actions, for verbal imagery, and for stories that show unfamiliar characters doing everyday things (Coger & White, 1982, p. 171). For many useful scripts appropriate for specific grades and skills, simply type "Readers Theatre" into any Web-based search engine. Numerous Readers Theatre scripts will appear for your use.

Oral Language Lesson 6: Conversational Opportunities

Most people who are trying to learn a new language enjoy having the practice of maintaining a conversation in an authentic situation. These conversational experiences are halting at first and the speakers may feel a bit foolish, but with a little patience and encouragement they can soon learn not only to translate their native languages into the new language but also to think about new comments to add in the non-native language or talk to themselves in that language (private speech, according to Vygotsky, 1978). Providing a few minutes for unstructured conversation with a peer is a good way to encourage natural dialogue, as well as provide opportunities for interaction with more- or less-skilled peers and give non-native speakers a chance to hone their skills (Anderson & Roit, 1996). Table 2.1 can help you increase students' information interactions with each other. The list in Table 2.1 can be adapted for a wide variety of grade levels with minimal modifications.

Table 2.1   Instructional Techniques Teachers Can Use to Increase Oral Language

Helpful Instructional Techniques

1. *Shared Reading.* Shared reading involves a teacher reading and sharing a book with students. Repeated exposures to text, a frequent aspect of shared reading, is a common way to increase comprehension. During the teacher reading, students should be encouraged to react freely to the text and to ask for clarification of any problems.

2. *Vocabulary Mapping.* In a semantic web, students graphically organize vocabulary from texts or other sources into related groups of words. Often this is carried out as a one-time activity, but it needs to be done frequently in order to provide both the consistency students need and the review process necessary to encode the information into long-term memory.

3. *Expanding Contexts.* After clarifying a word, students can discuss what it has to do with the selection, other selections, or their own experiences.

4. *Predicting.* It is important that students first talk about their understandings of story segments before they try to predict from them.

5. *Imagery.* Visualizing or creating a mental image of something in a text is believed to aid comprehension.

6. *Think-Aloud.* Students can think aloud, or talk about their thought processes while reading or completing other activities, and in this way clarify what was just learned through their oral language skills.

7. *Explaining Text.* Teachers could foster text explanation in students' native languages, English or otherwise. Having students explain or retell part or all of a text is good for comprehension and it also increases verbal elaboration and language flexibility as students share ideas (Anderson & Roit, 1996).

ADDRESSING LEARNERS WITH SPECIAL NEEDS

Learners Who Struggle

Learners who struggle with oral language often failed to develop oral-language knowledge during the early stages of development when children need to engage in oral language activities. For these students, extra time, often on an individual basis, will be necessary to build the foundation that these students need before more complex spoken and written language forms can be understood or duplicated. In addition to needing more instruction on a personal basis, such students also profit from older school mates who tutor them in learning to converse more fluently. These tutoring sessions can be informally structured around a topic of interest to both students so that the older student increases the younger student's background knowledge and ability to ask questions on a topic of personal passion. These tutoring sessions can be formally structured so that the older tutor writes stories told by the student who struggles with oral language, and these stories become a book that they read and reread together. You can also help struggling oral language users by assisting them to improve the prosody, melody, pitch, intonation, and vocal tones to communicate specific connotations that these students desire to express. One activity that you can use to do so enables these students to repeat prosodies that you model. A sample lesson for this purpose appears on page 27, and can be a valuable activity for learners who are learning English.

Learners Who Are Learning English

Why discuss learning English as a second language in the context of an oral language chapter? It is not adequate to simply immerse English learners in conversation and English literature. Teaching English as a second language is becoming a hot topic in reading instruction. With the demands on classrooms to have all students reading proficiently, more attention is being given to the non-native English speaker in the context of learning to read. The oral language skills of English learners can be greatly influenced by the amount of English vocabulary they have mastered and the amount of English spoken at home. In turn, the amount of oral language skill a student has will influence the student's ability to map the sounds of spoken language onto print or written text. If students come to school without exposure to English from birth, they will have a much greater challenge ahead of them when entering the English-dominant classroom. The reasons for this increased difficulty follow.

Speakers of different languages will come to school with different ideas of language structure (syntax), of how words are built (morphology), of sound systems (tones and phonology), of the variety of words from which to choose (lexicon), and of written symbols (orthography). Whether or not they come to school with any knowledge of print, such as what a book or what a word is, will vary dependent upon the exposures to these concepts in their home and community environments. Since there is a mismatch between the child's language and the language of the school, children will use the best strategy they have and will try to match the oral language they know with the written language they see. In sum, your ability to assist each English Language Learner (ELL) to become a proficient reader rests on your ability to use the oral language students know to learn the written language they must learn. The degree of overlap between these two language systems will vary with each ELL (Graves, Juel, & Graves, 2004).

Depending on the native language, and whether the culture of the home is a culture of literacy, ELLs will also vary in their understanding of language concepts. Some children do not know that print represents meaning. In other situations, the print concepts children bring with them from their culture may need to be altered in order to read English. For example, in English we read from top to bottom and from left to right, but in Arab nations, in Hebrew, and in India, this is not the case. It is also true that degree of language overlap will vary, depending on which language is spoken at home. For example, Spanish has a great deal of overlap with English in syntax, morphology, and orthography, whereas in Vietnamese none of the letters overlap with the English word. Pronunciation of certain sounds will also be affected if the native language has phonology and tones as opposed to just phonology, as in English. Certain sounds in English do not exist in other languages, such as the /r/ and /l/ sounds for Japanese speakers. Contrary to popular belief, these students don't just catch up to native speakers as a result of English exposure. "Research indicates that it takes English-language learners between six and eight years to reach the oral skill level of their English-speaking peers" (Collier, 1987).

So what can we do to instruct English language learners? First, we need to recognize children's strengths and guard against presuming that a student cannot think and comprehend simply because the student does not use English as a means of expression. We can also help children feel accepted by incorporating culturally familiar metaphors and experiences into the curriculum and allow them opportunities to showcase their native language skills in class. Building vocabulary and learning to identify objects and their uses in English is very helpful to developing later skills in reading comprehension. In addition, learning the high-frequency function word vocabulary of English is also vital. Often English language learners are able to break the reading code and decipher the written words, only to be stymied by the new words they have encountered that at that point hold no meaning for them. To assist ELLs, and other students, to learn to read the 100 most frequently appearing English sight words (such as *a, the, that, those, is, she,* etc.), you can write each on a separate card and mount them on the wall near the classroom door. As students line up, you say each, ask students to repeat them, and as the year progresses, have individuals say individual words without your prompting in a game-like format until all students can recognize each word unaided.

In order to experience success in reading comprehension, developing an oral language vocabulary is essential. For example, you can use books that feature children from the cultures represented by children in your classroom (Hispanic, Vietnamese, Somali, etc.). In doing so, you also honor specific culturally based language features and phrases that are commonly used by your children in home environments because the characters in these books will use them. Reading such books is one way to assist ELL students to feel welcomed and valued in the classroom and to begin to build upon what these children currently know. Another activity to encourage the oral language development of English learners can be a lesson where students learn key phrases in English that are used in the learners' native languages and practice using them in learning pairs or in conversational settings. Additionally, you could post a chart of everyday, high-frequency English words in one column and the equivalent words from the native languages represented in the classroom in the following columns. English learners, when asked to answer a question orally in class, may be able to answer a question quite fluently in their native language, but their limited English proficiency may mask their thinking abilities when it comes to oral expression. Students may need extra processing time in order to make the translation from the language spoken at home to answering in English.

Special Lesson to Improve Prosody in Oral Language

A Teacher Might Say: "Tell me about a conversation you had over the weekend!" The teacher should model exaggerated prosodic cues. If the child is confused about exactly what is being requested, the teacher could provide an example.

A Teacher May Want to Do: Praise children for using prosody in their language, as well as for using general language skills that are being focused on in the classroom (e.g., new words, complete sentences). Respond to the students' statements by connecting their oral language cues to specific emotions of the characters in the child's story. Ask the child to model *how* each speaker in their conversation spoke and to draw connections between how the character spoke, the emotion(s) the character was likely feeling at the time, and what the character wanted to emphasize.

A Teacher May Want to Have Students Do: In partners or in small groups, role-play conversations involving different types of emotions. Discuss these as a class. Ask children to point out what it is specifically about these conversations that conveys prosody, such as emphasizing a certain word, raising or lowering their tone of voice, or the pitches and melodies in their voices. Ask children to model for each other all of these aspects.

Lesson Could Be Assessed By: In small groups, have children choose a picture with a face expressing some sort of emotion. The children should be able to say a neutral sentence with varying types of prosodic cues as indicated by the picture. So, the child could say the sentence, "I went on a field trip yesterday" in an excited voice, identifying aspects of pitch, emphasis, and tone. Or they could say it in a sad, bored voice; again, followed by the group of peers identifying aspects of pitch, emphasis, and tone that established that interpretation.

Learners Who Excel

It should be noted that oral language ability is not predictive of later reading ability for all learners. For example, oral language is typically a strength for individuals with reading disabilities. In fact, these learners often excel in oral language. Many people with reading disabilities have excellent oral communication skills and are very effective orators. If you have exceptional orators in your class, you may be misled that learning to read should be easy for them. Such will not always be the case. Tom Cruise and Whoopi Goldberg, for example, are accomplished actors and have excellent oral language skills, despite persistent reading disabilities. Should you have excellent orators, you can ask them to tape record and then transcribe their one-on-one conversations with you. Then, you can use this transcription to build their vocabulary, decoding, and comprehension of written language. For other learners who excel in oral language, they may enjoy reading, enacting, and writing plays that they direct and display for classmates. They often enjoy reading orally and benefit by reading the words that one character says when you read the rest of the parts in a book to the class. Whether deciphering the written code for learners who excel orally is problematic or not, speaking and communicating aloud or in dialogue will be a great strength upon which you and they can draw to build other literacy skills.

SUMMARY

As you can see, oral language is a broad topic that involves many skills that are important for the development of skilled readers. This chapter reviewed some of theoretical forces that shape oral language development across infancy, childhood, and as a lifelong developmental process. Within that context and taking into account the diversity of experience and use of oral language among individuals, research-based practices such as (1) increasing the amount of daily production of their own speech, (2) storytelling, (3) dialogic reading, (4) Text Talk, (5) Readers Theatre, and (6) conversational opportunities are valuable lessons in developing oral language abilities that are beneficial to reading success. Learners who struggle need more one-on-one modeling by yourself or older schoolmates who become tutors. ELLs profit from prosodic book activities and sight word card practice. Learners who excel in oral language can increase their reading achievement by reading a character's part in a book that you read to the class, tape recording their orations to be read later, and writing plays to be performed. It was our goal that, armed with knowledge of the developmental processes of oral language and with research-based classroom lessons that support oral language skills, you can more successfully navigate Reading First and assist all your students to link their speaking knowledge, vocabulary acquisition, and reading skills together.

Prekindergarten and Kindergarten Literacy

Phonemes and Phonemic Awareness

With the Practitioner's Voice of Cynthia Reyes

Ms. Reyes tells us the sounds of words and teaches me how to say them. I paint letters with my fingers in finger paints, too. I'm learning to read real fast, better every day, thanks to Ms. Reyes!

—Wyatt, a preschooler

Phonemic Awareness (PA) is distinct from phonics. It is the ability to hear, identify, and manipulate individual sounds in spoken words. It is at ages three and four that the development of phonemic awareness becomes extremely important. For this reason, more and more high-quality preschools are incorporating phonemic awareness lessons into their curricula. Doing so has translated into increased academic and cognitive success for young learners (IRA, 2004; Dickinson & Tabors, 2001; Snow, Burns, & Griffin, 1998). While phonics, vocabulary, comprehension, and fluency development in kindergarten through Grade 3 has been emphasized across America and other countries, prior to 2001 there was not nearly as much emphasis on preschool literacy development. If all prekindergarten students experience the lessons and activities to be described in this chapter, every young child can come to a more rapid mastery of phonemic awareness and other basic concepts of print (NICHD, 2000). A child who has phonemic awareness skills also has an easier time learning to read and spell than children who have few or none of these skills (NICHD,

2004). In this chapter, we will describe how you can assist all students to attain these crucial skills for reading success.

WHAT TEACHERS NEED TO KNOW
ABOUT PHONEMIC AWARENESS

Phonemes are the smallest units of spoken languages. An advantage of teaching phonemes is that children can later recognize *onset* and *rime* relatively easily. Phonemes, themselves, are not marked by physical boundaries as are onset and rime in English, and this makes it difficult for most children to differentiate between individual phonemes without direct instruction. Given this difficulty, it is important that each of the components within phonemic awareness is taught (Ericson & Juliebo, 1998). The accompanying sidebar provides Reading First's definition of *onset* and *rime*, as well as the other components within the body of skills known as phonemic awareness (PA). Many teachers are not aware that most effective PA instruction develops each of these separate abilities for all students.

Terms That Relate to
Prekindergarten Literacy Development

Phoneme

A phoneme is the smallest part of *spoken* language that makes a difference in the meaning of words. English has about 41 phonemes. A few words, such as *a* or *oh*, have only one phoneme. Most words, however, have more than one phoneme: The word *if* has two phonemes (/i/ /f/); *check* has three phonemes (/ch/ /e/ /k/); and *stop* has four phonemes (/s/ /t/ /o/ /p/). Sometimes one phoneme is represented by more than one letter.

Grapheme

A grapheme is the smallest part of *written* language that represents a phoneme, or it is a letter that is used to represent a phoneme in the spelling of a word. A grapheme may be just one letter, such as *b, d, f, p,* or *s;* or several letters, such as *ch, sh, th, -ck, ea,* or *-igh.*

Phonics

Phonics is the understanding that there is a predictable relationship between phonemes (the sounds of *spoken* language) and graphemes (the letters and spellings that represent those sounds in *written* language).

Phonemic Awareness

Phonemic awareness is the ability to hear, identify, and manipulate the individual sounds—phonemes—in spoken words.

PREKINDERGARTEN **31**
AND
KINDERGARTEN
LITERACY:
PHONEMES AND
PHONEMIC
AWARENESS

Phonological Awareness

Phonological awareness is a broad term that includes nine skills, defined and modeled on the next page, that describe how phonemes can be identified and manipulated in the English language. In addition to phonemes, phonological awareness activities can involve work with rhymes, words, syllables, and onsets and rimes.

Syllable

A syllable is a word part that contains a vowel or, in spoken language, a vowel sound (e-vent; news-pa-per; ver-y).

Onset and Rime

Onsets and rimes are parts of spoken language that are smaller than syllables but larger than phonemes. An *onset* is the initial consonant(s) sound of a syllable (the onset of *bag* is b-; of *swim*, sw-). A *rime* is the part of a syllable that contains the vowel and all that follows it (the rime of *bag* is -*ag*; of *swim*, -*im*).

It is equally important that you know the eight groupings of phonemes in the English so you can teach them to students. These groups appear in Table 3.1 and represent the most common of the 38 phonograms that compose our language. You can teach students all of them by modeling how to say and manipulate one or two groupings at a time. Every PA lesson in this chapter instructs children to notice, think about, and work with (manipulate) sounds in spoken language to develop the nine skills that compose PA ability, as defined and demonstrated below:

Phoneme Isolation. Children recognize individual sounds in a word.

Teacher: What is the first sound in *van?*

Children: The first sound in *van* is /v/.

Phoneme Identity. Children recognize the same sounds in different words.

Teacher: What sound is the same in *fix, fall,* and *fun?*

Children: The first sound, /f/, is the same.

Phoneme Categorization. Children recognize the one word among several that has the "odd" sound.

Teacher: Which word doesn't belong? *Bus, bun, rug.*

Children: *Rug* does not belong. It doesn't begin with /b/.

Phoneme Blending. Children listen to a sequence of separately spoken phonemes and then combine the phonemes to form a word. Then they write and read the word.

Table 3.1   Most Common Phonograms in Rank Order Based on Frequency of
Occurrence in Monosyllabic Words

Frequency	Rime	*Example Words to Teach in Auditory Discrimination Lesson*
First most frequent: out of every 100 monosyllabic words, the number below will contain the rime in the next column.		
26	-ay	jay say pay day play
26	-ill	hill bill will fill spill
Second most frequent: out of every 100 monosyllabic words, the number below will contain the rime in the next column.		
22	-ip	ship dip tip skip trip
Third most frequent: out of every 100 monosyllabic words, the number below will contain the rime in the next column.		
19	-at	cat fat bat rat sat
19	-am	ham jam dam ram Sam
19	-ag	bag rag tag wag sag
19	-ack	back sack Jack black track
19	-ank	bank sank tank blank drank
19	-ick	sick Dick pick quick chick
Fourth most frequent: out of every 100 monosyllabic words, the number below will contain the rime in the next column.		
18	-ell	bell sell fell tell yell
18	-ot	pot not hot dot got
18	-ing	ring sing king wing thing
18	-ap	cap map tap clap trap
18	-unk	sunk junk bunk flunk skunk

PREKINDERGARTEN **33**
AND
KINDERGARTEN
LITERACY:
PHONEMES AND
PHONEMIC
AWARENESS

Fifth most frequent: out of every 100 monosyllabic words, the number below will contain the rime in the next column.		
17	-ail	pail jail nail sail tail
17	-ain	rain pain main chain plain
17	-eed	feed seed weed need freed
17	-y	ay by dry try fly
17	-out	pout trout scout shout spout
17	-ug	rug bug hug dug tug

Teacher: What word is /b/ /i/ /g/?

Children: /b/ /i/ /g/ is *big*.

Teacher: Now let's write the sounds in *big*: /b/, write *b*; /i/, write *i*; /g/, write *g*.

Teacher: (Writes *big* on the board.) Now we're going to read the word *big*.

Phoneme Segmentation. Children break a word into its separate sounds, saying each sound as they tap out or count it. Then they write and read the word.

Teacher: How many sounds are in *grab?*

Children: /g/ /r/ /a/ /b/. Four sounds.

Teacher: Now let's write the sounds in *grab*: /g/, write *g*; /r/, write *r*; /a/, write *a*; /b/, write *b*.

Teacher: (Writes *grab* on the board.) Now we're going to read the word *grab*.

Phoneme Deletion. Children recognize the word that remains when a phoneme is removed from another word.

Teacher: What is *smile* without the /s/?

Children: *Smile* without the /s/ is *mile*.

Phoneme Addition. Children make a new word by adding a phoneme to an existing word.

Teacher: What word do you have if you add /s/ to the beginning of *park?*

Children: *Spark.*

Phoneme Substitution. Children substitute one phoneme for another to make a new word.

Teacher: The word is *bug.* Change /g/ to /n/. What's the new word?

Children: *Bun.*

Rhyming. The rhythm and sound pattern of the English language that rhythmically groups together similar sounds so that they produce word associations.

Teacher: What words rhyme with *jay?*

Children: *say, pay, day, play*

In summary, when children work with phonemes in words, they are manipulating, blending, or segmenting the phonemes. Types of phoneme manipulation include blending phonemes to make words, segmenting words into phonemes, deleting phonemes from words, adding phonemes to words, or substituting one phoneme for another to make a new word. When children combine individual phonemes to form words, they are blending the phonemes. They also are blending when they combine onsets and rimes to make syllables and combine syllables to make words. When children break words into their individual phonemes, they are segmenting the words. They are also segmenting when they break words into syllables and syllables into onsets and rimes.

RESEARCH THAT TEACHERS CAN USE

Developing Phonemic Awareness

Exemplary preschool teachers use children's five senses as a powerful tool in teaching PA concepts and strategies (Block & Mangieri, 2003). These professionals turn to hands-on manipulation of letters and words as another instructional strategy whenever students do not learn a literacy concept initially. By teaching in this manner, they effectively relate students' orality directly to print. They also ask students to mimic their modeled sounds, blendings, segmentations, isolations, expressions, and emphases when they read words and text. These educators' skill in doing so enables preschoolers to use the beauty of fluent phrasing and the rhyme and rhythm of English to assist them to distinguish single sounds and learn all aspects of PA at a very early age.

Effective PA instruction also involves your creation of differentiated tones, pitches, and body movements to emphasize the variability, rhyme, and rhythm of English sounds. These movements play into some students' dominant learning input systems so that members of your class can experience a literacy-related learning episode together, regardless of their prior-to-preschool literacy-related experiences. Thus, within each of the following PA lessons, students experience single sounds through at least two of the following input systems: movement, touch, hearing, saying, air writing, scripting, single, chanting, and tracking words or environmental print as you read it aloud (Bus, van Ijzendoorn, & Pellegrini, 1995; Wells, 1986). The scientific research base

PREKINDERGARTEN **35**
AND
KINDERGARTEN
LITERACY:
PHONEMES AND
PHONEMIC
AWARENESS

concerning phonemic awareness also provides the following data to guide your instruction:

1. Each of the skills in PA can be taught and learned.

2. You do not need to spend large blocks of time each day on PA instruction. Ten to 15 minutes each day, for about 20 hours total in a year, has proven to be an effective amount of time for most students.

3. PA instruction is most effective when children are (1) taught to manipulate sounds in a word by pointing to, moving, seeing, or clapping to letters of the alphabet; and (2) asked to master only one or two (of the 38 phoneme manipulations) at a time. For example, you can play a game called "I'm thinking of something." Write down a word and hide it. Ask children to figure out your word by giving hints tied to letters, e.g., "I'm thinking of a word that begins with the sound of the letter *b*. What sound does the letter *b* make? Look around the room and see if you see anything that begins with the sound of the letter *b* and ends with the sound of the letter *l*."

4. PA instruction helps children learn to read. When children have an improved ability to distinguish sounds, they can more rapidly and accurately read words, which in turn better enables them to focus on a concept's meaning as they track its print.

5. PA instruction helps students learn to spell. The understanding that sounds and letters are related in a predictable way allows them to apply these same rules to spelling words.

6. The tests which appear later in this chapter (in *Tests to Assess Learning*) are effective as pre and post assessments upon which to base your instruction.

NEW CLASSROOM-PROVEN, RESEARCH-BASED PRACTICES

Teaching Phonemic Awareness

In this section, we will describe how you can have fun with words, teaching each PA component listed previously. These lessons enable you to build PA by using the words that children say, recognize, and/or write; by showing and posting the environmental print that they value; and by making rhyming games.

PA Lesson 1: Having Fun With Words

When children write and you say the words their scribbles are to represent, you can transform this activity using a "fun with words" PA lesson by isolating and blending single sounds in these words together. To have fun with words everyday, you can write the words that children said each scribble represented below each of their scribbles, and say each sound distinctly as you write it.

Then, to incorporate a second input modality, you and the student can clap when a new sound in that word is said by both of you. You can also let older preschoolers hold your hand as you write these words so they can feel the shapes that make up each sound's letter. You can also run your and their hands under each letter as you say the sounds of each letter together.

Another "having fun with words" lesson is to add additional sounds to the words that preschoolers say. A model that you can use to implement this valuable lesson follows.

Lesson to Teach Phonemic Awareness by Having Fun with Words

A Teacher Might Say: "Tell me about your weekend with your grandparents."

A Teacher May Want to Do: Praise children for using new words and complete sentences. Tell them to explain further what they are thinking, and ask them "why" questions.

A Teacher May Want to Have Students Do: Play games that involve new pictures to teach the sounds of the words the children used when they were telling about their weekend. Ask children to say the exact name for things and describe the objects in the new pictures that relate to the topic that the child has just described. Then, you can ask them to create a game as if they are doing the topic (in this case, a weekend with their grandparents) all over again. Ask the child to tell the class each step they would take to replicate the experience (i.e., the child would describe the sequence of events that occurred this past weekend in this example). Alternatively, students could tell a story that they created from a series of pictures that they bring to class or that you provide. As each step is described you write a summary word on a chart, or as a picture is shown, students say the word(s) it represents and you write the name of the picture beneath each one. After the child has finished the story, you ask all classmates to return to each word you wrote. As you point to each one, you ask them to perform one of the nine PA skills with that word. You can ask them to delete a beginning, medial, or ending sound; say a word that rhymes with that word; segment phonemes within that word; or substitute a phoneme for one that is contained in the word.

Lesson Could Be Assessed By: In small groups, have the students use the words from the stories or pictures to see if they understand the sounds of the words. Point to each picture in the order in which they were used in the story. Students should be able to tell the name of each picture and to identify the first sound of the name. (At a later date, they should be able to identify the last and then the middle sounds as well. Then, on subsequent days, they should be able to substitute phonemes and provide rhymes for each word.)

PREKINDERGARTEN **37**
AND
KINDERGARTEN
LITERACY:
PHONEMES AND
PHONEMIC
AWARENESS

PA Lesson 2: Teaching Individual PA Skills

To learn initial phoneme sounds, you gather four or five pictures that depict the initial (or ending) sound that you want children to learn. Children name each picture by slowly saying, blending, isolating, or substituting the initial sound in each word. Once students are fluent in initial phonemes, move to ending sounds, medial sounds, consonant blends, diagraphs, and word parts. Sample pictures that can be used in this activity are found in Figure 3.1.

PA Lesson 3: Using Environmental Print to Teach PA

Environmental print consists of the words that frequently occur in a child's environment, and it is often written in a distinctive font to instantly depict the concept it names, e.g., *Fruit Loops, Crest, Starbuck's Coffee.* You may already use environmental print to teach phonics or build vocabulary. Recent research has found that exemplary teachers have developed many new ways of using common logos to increase PA (Block & Mangieri, 2003). After reading the following description, you can add your own inventive activities to bring individual sounds to life in children's minds and speech. To begin this lesson, enlarge the home, billboard, and street graphic in Figure 3.2. Ask students to bring logos and environmental print from home. Then, you ask students to say (as you write) the words that their samples of environmental print represent. As you repeat each word, isolate, blend, or manipulate one of the nine PA skills described previously. Have students mimic your speech. Ask students to create stories using these words. When they say another new word that uses a PA concept that you are teaching in that lesson, write that word beneath the related environmental print word and have students employ their PA skill with that word as well. This activity can be turned into a rhyming game or song that you and students create spontaneously together. When environmental print lessons are used in each of these ways, students have reported to have enjoyed learning PA concepts significantly more than when this lesson was not a part of their instructional program (Block, Rodgers, & Johnson, 2004).

PA Lesson 4: Making Up Rhymes

To begin this lesson, read several rhyming phrases aloud emphasizing the rhyming work such as "The fat cat sat on a ___." Students are to finish the rhyme for you. Ask them to read all the words that don't rhyme in a whisper. Through this lesson, you can use rhymes and poems in a context in which students can use the dependability of English phoneme rules as clues to the sounds and meanings of new words (Mastropieri & Scruggs, 1991). Memory experts state that through such associations as these, children retain more of what they learn (Gans, 1994). To illustrate the power of rhyming as a learning aid, think of how many times in your life you have recited a verse to help you remember the number of days in every months: Thirty days has September, etc.

For older preschoolers, ask them to take turns making up lines for rhymes or sayings, using their classmates' names, e.g., Annie likes astronauts; Ben likes

Figure 3.1   Pictures That You Can Use to Teach PA Skills and on the Bingo Card (Figure 4.3)

to play baseball; Connor lives in California. These games can also be turned into book making projects. To do so, write down the rhymes that students create over the course of a few days, and let children illustrate and say the words pictured. Each illustration becomes a separate page in a class-created book.

When you read these rhymes and other poetry books, ask students to reread the rhyming words with you in a normal speaking voice. You can also sing jump rope chants, or sing and read nursery rhymes together such as the ones in the box on pages 39–40.

PREKINDERGARTEN 39
AND
KINDERGARTEN
LITERACY:
PHONEMES AND
PHONEMIC
AWARENESS

Figure 3.2   Teaching PA Concepts Through Environmental Print Games, Activities, and Songs

This Old Man

This old man, he played one. He played knick-knack on his thumb.

Refrain: With a knick-knack, paddy-wack, give your dog a bone. This old man came rolling home.

2nd Verse: This old man, he played two. He played knick-knack on his shoe.

(Continued)

(Continued)

3rd Verse: This old man, he played three. He played knick-knack on his knee.

4th Verse: This old man, he played four. He played knick-knack on his door.

5th Verse: This old man, he played five. He played knick-knack on his hive.

6th Verse: This old man, he played six. He played knick-knack on his sticks.

7th Verse: This old man, he played seven. He played knick-knack on his heaven.

8th Verse: This old man, he played eight. He played knick-knack on his gate.

9th Verse: This old man, he played nine. He played knick-knack on his spine.

10th Verse: This old man, he played ten. He played knick-knack once again.

The Spider

I'm told that the spider

Has coiled up inside her

Enough silky material

To spin an aerial

One-way track

To the moon and back;

Whilst I

Cannot even catch a fly.

TESTS TO ASSESS LEARNING

The following tests have been used successfully to assess PA.

Test 1: Knowledge of Individual Phonemes and Phonograms

You must assess the 38 phonemes and phonograms auditorily by asking every child to repeat phonemes independently. This test contains an item for each phoneme that you construct using the following format: "If I say *jay* and

PREKINDERGARTEN **41**
AND
KINDERGARTEN
LITERACY:
PHONEMES AND
PHONEMIC
AWARENESS

Table 3.2   Tests to Assess Phonemic Awareness Ability

Test to Assess Blending Abilities

Create a list of 10 one-syllable words. The first three contain only two phonemes (such as t-o; h-i). The next three have three or four phonemes that make two sounds (c-at; t-op). The last four are three or four phonemes that can be segmented into three parts (such as d-o-g; t-oo-k).

Test to Assess Rhyming Abilities

Select 10 pairs of words. Five of the pairs rhyme; five pairs do not. Randomize these. Then, read a pair and ask students if the two words rhyme (e.g., Does *boy* rhyme with *toy?*).

Test to Assess Segmentation and Isolation Abilities

Select 10 words that contain a variety of consonants and vowel sounds. Words should be common and in young children's listening vocabularies. Then say: "I am going to ask you to say some words in a special way. Words are broken apart so that each sound is said separately. For example the word *sky* is said /s/ /k/ /y/." Then, give a second example. Last, ask students to segment each of the ten words after you say each one.

---

change the *j* to *p*, what would that word be? And if I say *jay* and change the *y* in *jay* to an *m*, what would that word be?" This assessment checks for phonemic awareness for the first and final sounds in words. By separating all sounds in a word you can assess segmentation abilities. Similarly, by asking for the blending of individual sounds, you can assess phonograms, blending, and syllable recognition.

Test 2: Assessment of Nine Phonemic Awareness Skills

The second set of tests appears in Table 3.2. Some readers enjoy taking the pre and post tests in the table to see visible results of how much they have learned. Table 3.2 presents a nonthreatening format to use in pre and post assessments of each of the PA skills that compose phonemic awareness. You need not take long to analyze these test results. A score of 80 percent indicates that the student can independently initiate the PA skill tested and have a basic mastery of phonemic awareness.

ADDRESSING LEARNERS WITH SPECIAL NEEDS

Learners Who Struggle

Dr. Sally Shaywitz from the University Medical School of Learning and Attention Disorders at Yale University said that "very disabled readers deviated from very good readers in the brain activation patterns they used when reading required them to break up words into their underlying phonologic structure or sound pattern" (Shaywitz et al. 2004, p. 28). Soon we will be able to use brain imagery to diagnose individual students' brain activation patterns as a common course of action so that those with reading difficulties with PA can be detected early in a child's literacy learning. Soon we will also be able to actually examine the effects of specific PA instructional intervention on the brain. Already clinical studies have identified that the underlying problem in many students' auditory discrimination and in many reading disorders is the result of an incompletely developed *auditory conceptual function.* The primary cause of this faulty auditory conceptual function is neurophysical, and it occurs throughout the population, regardless of intellectual capacities, race, sex, or cultural factors—such as education and socioeconomic status. Secondary symptoms of this auditory discrimination difficulty are adding, omitting, substituting, and reversing sounds and letters in reading, spelling, and speech. It is often (incorrectly) thought that students make these errors because they are not paying attention. However, mispronouncing words or incorrectly seeing letters as inverted or scrambled symbols can be the result when students have not mastered PA. These students misjudge the sequence of phonemes (the sounds) within spoken words, or do not grasp how distinct letters or groups of letters represent words. You can obtain a copy of the Lindamood Auditory Conceptualization (LAC) Test to evaluate this difficulty from www.lindamoodbell.com.

One reason that this factor has escaped detection until recently is that a person can say a word without being conscious of its component sounds. It had been thought that if you could say a word, you could also discriminate its sequence of sounds. Whereas only four percent of the population is color-blind and cannot discriminate colors, 30 percent experience this auditory conceptual difficulty from a moderate to severe degree (Block, 2004; Stanovich & Cunningham, 1993).

The problem can be resolved with specific treatment. The solution is to stimulate a conscious input venue to the brain from another sense modality: *feeling.* When you alert students to the feeling of the actions of their tongue, lips, and mouth as they produce speech sounds, these tactile sensory inputs add additional information to the sounds that each letter, onset, and rime makes. The sequence of sounds and letters involved in reading and spelling can be reinforced with this additional feedback to the brain. Programs like the Lindamood-Bell Auditory Discrimination Program and the Elkonion Block method can be added to your curricula for students who experience difficulty developing PA. To receive information about these two programs as well as others, just enter "auditory discrimination programs" into Google and several recently revised and research-based programs will be revealed.

Learners Who Are Learning English

Phonemic awareness instruction is difficult for many English language learners (ELLs) unless they hear English phonemes in their home language and through culturally relevant literary experiences first. You can provide this cultural context by labeling objects in the classroom with all languages represented in the room. Then, you can ask students to read each of the words on the label orally as they run their hand under each letter. Next, at later times in the day you can ask students to walk in pairs to read each word. As student partners run their hands under each letter, ELLs read the words sound by sound in

PREKINDERGARTEN **43**
AND
KINDERGARTEN
LITERACY:
PHONEMES AND
PHONEMIC
AWARENESS

English and then in their native language. This lesson can be extended and modified in many ways to assist ELLs. You can read stories, sing songs, and chant rhymes in English and follow each reading by asking the class to repeat similar readings, songs, and chants with you, but these are recited in each of the home languages represented in the classroom.

Blending is often difficult for many ELL readers. Gliding individual sounds together in a word is an abstract concept. It is difficult to learn merely by watching someone else's mouth move as that person blends or by seeing the steady movement of a hand beneath a word as it motions the speed of blending individual letters that represent separate phonemes together. However, Rosenshine & Stevens (1984) found that spending additional time helping ELLs functioning at first- and second-grade reading levels to blend phonemes into a wide variety of words resulted in higher achievement and increased phonemic awareness than any other PA activity in which these students engaged.

Unfortunately, many of the past instructional approaches to blending were not as effective as desired. They asked students to say every sound separately, which resulted in unrecognizable words. For example, past blending programs would ask students to say the following sounds separately: /p/, /e/, /a/, and /t/. Now, say the sounds rapidly together. Did you say "puheeaht" instead of "peat" as in *peat moss?* The error in these programs occurred because many initial consonants end in the schwa sound (i.e., /uh/).

A more effective method is to teach students to say the ending rime first and then add the onset (Miller, 1993). For example, for the word *cat*, the student would say the sound /at/ and then add /c/ at the beginning to make a single, blended sound. You can extend this blending activity by using many words with the same rime, demonstrating that by changing one phoneme, ELLs can say an entirely different English word. (e.g., *cat* becomes *bat*). This repeated use of the rime to blend lesson also reinforces the sounds of common English phonemes.

Learners Who Excel

Parents often ask for research-based information to learn more about ways that they can help gifted young children's PA and literacy development. The International Reading Association recommends the following resources that you can suggest to them:

- *Your Gifted Child and Reading: How to Identify and Support Advanced Literacy Development*
- *Beginning Literacy and Your Child: A Guide to Helping Your Baby or Preschooler Become a Reader*
- *I Can Read and Write! How to Encourage Your School-Age Child's Literacy Development*

You can order these and other IRA publications by calling 800-336-READ, ext. 266. Or, visit the association's online bookstore at www.reading.org. Bulk pricing is available.

Other resources that have proven valuable for classroom PA instructional programs, as well as for parents, include the following parent brochures and television series (also available in Spanish):

- *Ready to Read: PBS Television Series and Parent Training Program* (KERA Television Station, Dallas, TX)
- *The Playground of Books: Tips for Parents of Beginning Readers*
- *Make the Reading-Writing Connection: Tips for Parents of Young Learners*
- *Making the Most of Television: Tips for Parents of Young Viewers*
- *See the World on the Internet: Tips for Parents of Young Readers—and "Surfers"*
- *Summer Reading Adventure! Tips for Parents of Young Readers*
- *Understanding Your Child's Learning Differences* (Barnes & Noble)

SUMMARY

It is important that you build all students' phonemic awareness. Doing so in the preschool years can establish the foundation for positive values for and attitudes toward reading, an understanding that sounds are represented by letters, and an understanding that print has meaning. In this chapter you read about several research-based lessons that will build PA, such as having fun with words, using environmental print to teach separate PA skills, and rhyming activities. Highly effective phonemic awareness instruction can also be provided to ELLs, gifted readers, and children who have difficulty learning. When you employ the scientifically validated lessons in this chapter, you will have taken a crucial step in our goal of leaving no child behind and making reading a preferred task for all children.

4

Phonics

The Building Blocks of Literacy

*My teacher always tells me to sound it out, but I don't know what that means.
I just move my finger and my lips cuz she does. Please don't tell her. I should
have learned [to sound it out] in kindergarten [but I didn't]. I don't think any of
the kids in Care Bears can sound the words out either.*

—Primary-grade student (Michael, 1994, p.55)

In this chapter, you can assess your present knowledge of phonic generalizations, learn what Reading First legislation requires relative to teaching these principles, and master several research-based lessons that have proven to significantly increase students' use of phonics to decode unknown words. A recent national study (Baumann, Hoffman, Moon, & Duffy-Hester, 1998) found that 98 percent of primary-grade teachers regard phonics instruction as a very important, regular component in their reading programs. Although there are many types of phonics instruction (e.g., intensive, explicit, synthetic, analytic, embedded), all effective lessons focus a learner's attention on the relationship between sounds and symbols as a valuable strategy to decode words. Teaching phonics, like all teaching, involves making decisions about what is best for children. Rather than engage in debates about whether phonics should or should not be taught, effective teachers of reading and writing ask when, how, how much, and under what circumstances phonics should be taught. Researchers agree that programs which constrain teachers from using their professional judgment in making instructional decisions about what is *best* in phonics instruction for every student simply gets in the way of good teaching practices (IRA, 1997, p. 2).

WHAT TEACHERS NEED
TO KNOW ABOUT PHONICS

Phonics is the ability to match speech sounds to printed letters. In 1986, Congress decreed that the Department of Education was to study the effects of phonics instruction on reading achievement. After four years of work, the study, *Beginning to Read: Thinking and Learning about Print* (Adams, 1990), was published. It recommended that programs for all children, good and poor readers alike, should strive to maintain an appropriate balance between phonics activities and the reading and appreciation of informative and engaging texts. "As important as it is to sound words out, it is important only as an intermediate step. Sounding words out should not be the end goal, but a way of teaching what [students] need to know to comprehend text" (Adams, 1990, p. 248).

Systematic phonics instruction is a way of teaching reading that stresses the acquisition of letter-to-sound correspondences and their use in reading and spelling words (Harris & Hodges, 1995). The National Reading Panel (NICHD, 2000a) encouraged a planned, sequential set of lessons in which phonic elements are taught explicitly. This guideline is based on empirical evidence from studies of students who did and did not receive phonics instruction. (See Goswami, 2000, for a summary of these studies.) Systematic and explicit phonics instruction "significantly improves kindergarten and first-grade children's word recognition and spelling" (NICHD, 2000b, p. 17). Reading First legislation states that phonics instruction should help students

- Understand why they are learning the relationships between letters and sounds
- Apply their knowledge of phonics as they read words, sentences, and text
- Use what they learn about sounds and letters in their own writing
- Adapt their next learning tasks to their individual needs, based on assessment
- Include alphabetic knowledge, phonemic awareness, vocabulary development, and the reading of text as tools for comprehension

Synthetic phonics lessons teach children individual sounds for letters. Then, students are taught how to blend those letters together to sound out words. In some synthetic phonics programs, the first text that children are asked to read contain only a few words so that single phonic principles can be practiced repeatedly. For example, the first two pages of an early story in a synthetic phonics text follow (Cassidy, Roettger, & Wixson, 1987, pp. 15–16):

Dad ran. Ann ran. Dad and Ann ran.

Decoding by pattern and analogy is a second type of phonics lesson. This method teaches students how to use the onset (initial letter sound) and the rime (medial vowel and ending consonants) to sound out words. Gaining knowledge of these riming patterns has proven to be particularly important as it helps students learn basic vowel patterns that compose English words. The most difficult part of using phonics as a decoding strategy is learning which vowel sound is represented by the letters *a, e, i, o,* and *u* when they appear in a specific word (e.g., *a* can represent seven different sounds). Decoding by pattern also sensitizes students to how vowel sounds are affected by other letters in the word. Such an approach has proven effective for many readers (Berent & Perfetti, 1995; Goswami, 2000).

The National Reading Panel (NICHD, 2000b) determined that explicit and systematic phonics is superior to nonsystematic or no phonics instruction, but that no significant differences in effectiveness exist among the various types of systematic phonics instruction. They also found no significant difference in effectiveness among individual, small-group, and whole-class phonics lessons when concepts to be learned are appropriate for students being instructed. Research has also shown that exemplary kindergarten teachers display exceptional talent in creating classrooms that are inviting, print-rich, and home-like, and in leading lessons in which children associated positive emotions with learning phonics (Block & Mangieri, 2003). Such kindergarten professionals teach phonics by writing notes and messages with students, so often that their students begin to ably rewrite them alone. These teachers are also intimately informed about developmentally appropriate practices and are always looking for new research-based practices to teach phonics and create even more print-rich classrooms. Letters, words, and sentences are taught together. For example, students make letters with their bodies on the floor, trace letters in the air, and clap to detect syllables in words. Classrooms are filled with charts that were constructed in answer to students' questions. In these rooms, children explore, question, and learn concepts about print in animated ways, using puppets and other physical objects.

Exemplary teachers also invite many adult assistants into their classrooms. They use these additional adults very effectively so that children have assistance immediately whenever they need help with phonics while they read. Outstanding first- and second-grade literacy teachers continue to teach phonics with more creative methods than do their counterparts at other grade levels. They take actions similar to those described above because they understand that for phonics concepts to be effectively learned at first- and second-grade levels, they must be taught in ways that students have not experienced before (Block & Mangieri, 2003).

RESEARCH THAT TEACHERS CAN USE

Teaching Phonics

Why do some students instantly recognize 95 percent of the words they hear and read while others cannot? During the last 15 years, more research designed to answer this question has been completed than ever before (Adams, 1990; Stanovich & Cunningham, 1993; Stahl, Duffy-Hester, & Stahl (1998). Through this research we have come to define *decoding* as language processes in which students construct meaning from spoken and written messages through symbol awareness, word analysis, strategic thinking, mental association, and personal reflection.

What do you need before you can teach phonics effectively? It has been demonstrated that teachers themselves must have a deep knowledge about the complexity of English orthography, or the science of how letters in any language are placed together to make meaning and phonology (IRA, 1997; Venezky, 1997). If you would like to improve your knowledge and teaching of phonic principles, there are two steps you can take. The first is to read the information in Table 3.1 in the previous chapter and learn basic phonic principles. In this table, you will find phonic rules that govern how students decode words to gain meaning. The second is to select phonics curricula that encompass all the generalizations in Table 3.1 that students must learn to become independent decoders.

What is the best way to teach children phonemic awareness and decoding skills? This question has been debated throughout the twentieth century. In response to this question, the International Reading Association has consistently maintained that *no single approach to reading and writing instruction can be considered best for every child* (IRA, 1997).

It will be important for you to develop the ability to teach all phonics principles defined in Table 3.1 through activities that students will have to perform independently in their lives beyond school. That is, such forms of authentic phonics instruction will include the reading of books that students enjoy, stopping to analyze words that may be unknown to students while you read a book aloud, writing about thoughts that students had after they finish reading, and answering students' questions about individual word meanings and pronunciations

If you want a phonics program to supplement your instruction, the most frequently used in school districts across America include Sequoyah Literacy Systems (100 Galleria Parkway, Suite 1340, Atlanta, Georgia 30309), the Advantage Program of Accelerated reading (P.O. Box 8036, Wisconsin Rapids, Wisconsin 54495-8036), Preparing Young Children for Reading Success (Debeck Education, P.O. Box 33738 Station D, Vancouver, B.C., Canada V6J 4L6), Preparing Young Children for Reading Success (Debeck Education, P.O. 33738 Station D, Vancouver, B.C., Canada V6J 4L6), the Benchmark Word Identification Program (2107 N. Providence Rd., Media, Pennsylvania 19063), and the Saxon Approach (Oklahoma City, Oklahoma), among others. (See Baumann et al., 1998, for additional program titles.)

What Are Phonics Generalizations?

Phonics generalizations are the rules of the English language that govern how letters, sounds, and syllables are placed together to create meaning. Theodore Clymer (1963) was among the first to analyze the usefulness of single rules to teach children about phonics and our language. Since that time, several studies have identified 45 rules that are usually taught to children about the English language, as shown in Table 4.1 (Clymer, 1963, reprinted 1996). Children must learn not only the rules of our language that apply to single letter sounds but also how sounds are blended together: (1)Anglo-Saxon letter-sound correspondences, and syllable and morphing patterns; (2) Greek and romance language letter-sound correspondences, and syllable and morphing patterns; (3) how *r* controls English vowel sounds; (4) rules for division of high-frequency words; (5) parts of words that have meaning, such as prefixes; and

(6) exceptions to English word patterns that arise when foreign words enter our language in their original spellings. By the end of second grade, most children should have learned the above phonic generalities and use this knowledge to decode unknown words at the second-grade level of readability.

In the past, phonics generalizations have been criticized by some because they were taught in an authentic manner, separated from real reading experiences, or overemphasized so that other important dimensions of reading instruction were not taught. As you may recall, when you were in elementary school teachers usually taught phonic principles as rules to be memorized, perhaps by asking you to remember as many as one hundred different rules. You may have also completed worksheets by matching sounds of letters and words you heard to pictures. Then, you may have learned exceptions to each of these phonic rules. Today, we know that students should not be taught so many rules, and they should have the opportunity to report which phonic generalizations they have learned and those which they want to learn, using self-reports similar to those shown in Table 4.1.

Because so many rules were taught, when you came to an unknown word, you may have either not remembered the rule it followed, or the word you needed to decode was an exception to that rule. Today, you will teach your students only those phonic generalizations that are most prevalent in our language, and these are shown in Figure 4.1. When you teach these generalizations, your students can decode English words with that pattern eight out of ten times because the letter-to-sound correspondence specified by these generalizations will appear in 80 percent of the phonetically regular English words. You can best teach these phonic generalizations in needs-based small groups just as you taught sight-word strategies. (The answer key is located at the end of this chapter, page 62.

NEW CLASSROOM-PROVEN, RESEARCH-BASED PRACTICES

Teaching Phonics

Phonics generalizations should be the first strategy that you teach in your phonics program and the first thinking processes that students use to decode an unknown word when that word contains a familiar English word pattern (e.g., phonics should be used to decode *hat* because it contains the /-at/ English word pattern found in many other words, such as *cat, rat, bat,* and *sat*). After you teach and give examples of a phonic generalization, demonstrate how you use that generalization in conjunction with context clues and structural analysis to decode many new words. Then read a sentence from a book and perform a think-aloud to decode one word in that sentence that adheres to the phonics generalization you are introducing. (Big books work very well for this section of the lesson because you can point to each phonetically regular word as you describe how you decoded it.) Next, ask one student to read aloud until he or she comes to the next word on that page that adheres to the same phonic generalization. Then, have this student explain the thinking he or she would use to decode that word if it was unfamiliar. Continue reading in this way until all

(Continued on page 53)

Table 4.1   Phonics Generalizations and Understandings About Words That Students Need to Learn

1. High-Frequency Words

2. Letter-Sound Relationships and Patterns
   a. Consonants
      - Consonant Clusters (e.g., s clusters: st, sp, sn, sm, sl, sc, sk, sw, spl, str, spr, scr, squ)
      - Consonant Digraphs
      - Alternative Sounds *r*
   b. Vowels
      - Long and Short
      - Vowel Combinations
      - Two Sounds of *oo*
      - Vowels With *r*
      - Silent *e*
      - Phonograms
      - Open and Closed Syllables

3. Word Structure, Word Meaning, and Other Categories
   a. Contractions
   b. Compound Words
   c. Affixes
      - Inflectional Endings
      - Prefixes
      - Suffixes
   d. Synonyms
   e. Antonyms
   f. Homonyms
   g. Plurals
   h. Possessives
   i. Clipped Words
   j. Abbreviations
   k. Syllabication
   l. Greek and Latin Word Roots

4. Phonic Definition
   a. Like single consonants, a *consonant*
      - *Cluster* can be the onset of a word, like *Spr* in *spring*
   b. Referred to as *consonant digraphs*, sometimes two consonant letters represent one sound that is different from either of the sounds alone (e.g., *cheese, where, shoe, this*).
   c. There are two common sounds for th (*thought and this*).
   d. The sound of *f* can also be represented by two other consonant clusters, *ph* (*phone, photograph*) and *gh* (*cough, laugh*).
   e. Sometimes consonants are doubled, as in *little, runner, summer, puffin, dress, bell*.
   f. Sometimes cluster of consonants may be referred to as final digraphs (a letter cluster at the end of a word) such as *ck, nk*, and *ng*.
   g. The sound of *k* can be represented by a c or a k as in *car* or *key*
   h. C and *g* make two sounds, as in *car, face*, or *giraffe, get*.
   i. Sometimes consonants are silent, as in *thigh, thumb, or thing*.
   j. *Qu* sounds like kw, as in quiet.

5. Syllable Rules
   a. Words have parts that you can hear.
   b. Some words have just one part and others have more than one part.
   c. You can clap and count the parts of words.
   d. Every syllable has a vowel sound.
   e. Usually, endings and prefixes are syllables in themselves.
   f. When you have a prefix, the spelling of the root word does not change (*reread*).
   g. When a word has two consonants in the middle, divide the syllables between the consonants (*bet-ter*).
   h. Syllables ending with a vowel have long vowel sounds (*ho-tel*).
   i. Syllables ending with a consonant have short vowel sounds (*mat-tress*).
   j. When a word ends with *le*, the consonant preceding it joins the cluster to make a syllable (*trou-ble*).
   k. Letter clusters such as *th, ch, wh, sh, ck, nk*, and *ng* usually stay together in a syllable.
   l. Affixes and endings are syllables that have meaning.

Figure 4.1   Phonics: Mastery Evaluation for Teachers and Gifted Readers

---

Phonemic Awareness

1. How many phonemes are in the word *umbrella?*   a. 1   b. 2   c. 5   d. 6   e. 7

2. How many graphemes are in the word *umbrella?*   a. 3   b. 4   c. 5   d. 7   e. 8

Vowels: Long and Short

Vowel sounds may be expressed in two ways: long and short. Mastery of each of these sounds will be evaluated in this section.

Long Vowel Sounds

Read each of the following sentences. Choose the word with the same vowel sound as the underlined word in each sentence.

_____ 3. The *raging* flood is destroying the beautiful homes.

      a. blue   b. clap   c. plate   d. mark

_____ 4. The old bus *broke* down on the way to the game.

      a. sport   b. cot   c. desk   d. pole

_____ 5. The *bright,* hot sun is shining on the window.

      a. quiet   b. perfect   c. thought   d. craft

_____ 6. The computer malfunctioned because it needs to be *cleaned.*

      a. crowd   b. poor   c. enough   d. class

_____ 7. The *cute* puppies were sleeping next to their mother.

      a. butter   b. mule   c. clasp   d. trick

Short Vowel Sounds

For each word listed below, underline the letter(s) that make the short vowel sound.

8. stamp	10. truck	12. humble	14. butter	16. crept
9. popped	11. dimple	13. intern	15. cotton	17. gamble

Vowel Generalizations: Sandwich Words (CVVC—Consonant-Vowel-Vowel-Consonant) vs. Layer Cake Words (CVCe—Consonant-Vowel-Consonant-silent *E*). The placement of vowels in a word determines the sounds that they represent. Mastery of ability to recognize these placements will be evaluated in this section.

Sandwich Words

For each word below, indicate with a √ the correct explanation of the vowel sound in that word.

18. **sail**   _____ long *a* sound   _____ silent *a*   _____ short *i* sound

                 _____ short *a* sound   _____ long *i* sound

19. **float**   _____ long *o* sound   _____ silent *o*   _____ short *a* sound

                 _____ short *o* sound   _____ long *a* sound

(Continued)

Figure 4.1 (Continued)

20. **please** _____ long *e* sound _____ silent *e* _____ short *a* sound

     _____ short *e* sound _____ long *a* sound

Layer Cake Words

For each group of words below, circle the words that represent the sound indicated at the top of each group.

21. *a-e*	22. *i-e*	23. *o-e*	24. *u-e*
pane	slide	loan	slug
tall	cliff	group	huge
sale	price	broke	blunt
crate	grim	pole	trust

Digraphs: Consonant and Vowel

Particular combinations of consonants and vowels create digraphs. Mastery of these digraphs and their sounds is evaluated in this section.

25. In the group of words below, circle the words that contain consonant digraphs. Underline the words with vowel digraphs. In the space to the right, write the digraph.

    beam _____ seam _____ charge _____ rough _____ brain _____ plead _____

    stain _____ phase _____ creed _____ throw _____ which _____ enough _____

Consonant Blends

Combinations of consonants create consonant blends. Mastery of your ability to recognize these blends is evaluated in this section.

26. Underline the consonant blend in each word below.

blanket	plow	strange	program	clock	standard
sprain	trauma	draw	smash	flock	drake

Diphthongs

Combinations of vowels create diphthongs. Mastery of your ability to recognize diphthongs is evaluated in this section.

27. Circle each word below that contains a diphthong. In the space to the right, write each diphthong for the word.

    couch _____ four _____ gray _____ spoil _____ train _____ crew _____

    convoy _____ own _____ plan _____ coat _____ fowl _____

(Continued from page 49)

students have had a chance to verbalize applications of the phonics generalization you introduced in this lesson. For each student to have this opportunity, you may need to continue this lesson for several days because one book may not contain enough words that follow the generalization being taught.

Teaching Individual Phonic Generalizations

An important phonics lesson is to teach students how to select from all the generalizations that they have been taught.

Lesson That Teaches How to Know Which Phonic Generalization to Use When

A Teacher Might Say: "Think about what you could do if you are unable to read a word in a story and do not understand the meaning of a word."

A Teacher May Want to Do: Make an overhead transparency of a page from a book, stop at a difficult word, and do a think-aloud of how you decoded the word. You can also model how you think about meanings of new words surrounding the one you know. For example, when reading the first page in *Miss Rumphius* by Barbara Cooney, you read the sentence, *"Once upon a time she was a little girl named Alice, who lived in a city by the sea."* You say, "I notice that the word city begins with the letter *c* and the word sea begins with the letter *s* but I hear the same sound at the beginning of each of these words. Can anyone tell me why?"

A Teacher May Want to Have Students Do: Students can discuss with a partner the reason why the two words begin with different letters but have the same sound. Students can also try to find others words on the page that might have the same sound but are spelled differently. Once students have generated their ideas, you can explain to them why the word *city* makes a soft *c* sound instead of a hard *c* sound like in *cat*. You can go back and review the meaning of the word city and how you realized the author was no longer talking about the sea.

Lesson Could Be Assessed By: Place in an envelope all the words from that story that being with soft *c* and hard *c* sounds. After reading the story, students could work together to sort the words from the book that begin with soft *c* sounds and hard *c* sounds. When students are done, they can be asked to verbalize and write other words that apply to this generalization and also words that do not apply.

Teach How to Apply Phonics Rapidly

Students need to learn to use the generalizations rapidly and independently. As Adams (1990) states, skilled reading is the result of a reader's speed and competence in perceiving the individual letters in words as well as the spelling patterns that make up words. To this end, researchers advocate sufficient practice in

- Learning letter names and phonemes, as well as developing phonemic awareness
- Learning recurring spelling patterns
- Learning the most common sequences of letters within words

When you teach this lesson, students are able to read words with greater fluency and more confidence. They will also be able to read unfamiliar words that contain similar basic spelling patterns they have been taught. For younger students, you can tape big letters to the classroom floor. During free time and before dismissal each day, you can ask your students, one at a time, to stand on a particular letter that you name or give a sound that the letter represents. The most dependable phonic generalizations appear in Figure 4.2, which you can use as a self-assessment of your knowledge. After you have answered each question, you can turn to the answer key at the end of this chapter to identify how many generalizations you know.

Realizing you must know phonic generalizations to teach them, you can learn any phonics rules from Figure 4.2 that you did not master by referring to one of the following books:

- *Teaching Phonics for Today: A Primer for Educators* by Dorothy Strickland
- *The Phonics Awareness Handbook for Kindergarten and Primary Teachers* by Lita Ericson & Moira Fraser Juliebo
- *Teacher's Guide for Evaluating Commercial Phonics Packages* by Jean Osborne, Steven Stall, & Mercy Stein

You can order these and other IRA publications by calling 800-336-READ, ext. 266. Or, visit the association's online bookstore at www.reading.org.

Teaching By Making Comparisons to Other Words

A highly effective, scientifically validated phonics lesson is to teach students to make comparisons between unknown words and other spoken or written words or word parts, a strategy know as *decoding by analogy.* For example, you can teach a key word, such as *catsup* for the /at/ phonogram in the words *hat* and *cup* which are displayed before them. Say: "If this word is *hat,* then this word part is (*cat*); if this word is *cup,* then this word part is (*sup*). Say the word parts together." Students will say "cat-sup" or "catsup." Later in the year, you can write five words that each represent a different phonogram, such as *day, flew, flag,* and *red,* and an irregular sight word, such as *the.* You can model the decoding-by-analogy process by reading a page from a book that contains a difficult word. As you read, pause to perform a think-aloud which demonstrates the analogies that students can use to decode a specific word that you are about to read. After you have told the parts of the word that you used to figure out the pronunciation and meaning of a particular word, read on. When you come to another word that can be decoded through analogy, you ask, "Is there any part of this word that you know, such as a meaning, sound, or spelling pattern?"

An example follows with the difficult word, *incumbent*, written in italics so as to emphasize the strategy being discussed in this section. This example occurred at Benchmark School in Media, Pennsylvania in a third-grade classroom (Gaskins, Gaskins, & Gaskins, 1991, p. 216):

> "The Senator was an *incumbent,* and so won the election easily." I can't think of a word that would make sense in this blank, so I think I'll try to decode it by analogy. I need to look for spelling patterns. I know a spelling pattern is the vowel and what comes after it. So, the first spelling pattern in this word is *I-n. I-n* is a word I already know, *in,* so I'll move on to the next spelling pattern. In this case that will be *u-m.* We have talked about the key word *drum,* so I will use that to help me with the second chunk. The third spelling pattern is *e-n-t.* I know the word *tent.* I already know the first chunk is *in.* And, if I know *d-r-u-m* is *drum,* then *c-u-m* is *cum.* And, if I know *t-e-n-t* is *tent,* then *b-e-n-t* is *bent.* The word is *incumbent.* Let's see if that makes sense in the sentence. "The senator was an incumbent and so won the election easily." Yes, that makes sense. I have heard that word on the news. I'm not exactly sure what it means though. I'll look it up. It says that in incumbent is a person who holds an elective office or position.

Teaching Phonics through Structured Language Activities

There are several structured language activities that have proven to significantly increase students' phonics use. The first is the structured language experience approach. In this lesson, students use five words you have introduced to compose a story that they write on chart paper. Next, students use all the words they know with word parts similar to those in the five you gave them to perform a chant and a spell-checking exercise. This exercise begins by students saying each word and spelling the word aloud as they point to the set of letters that make each sound. For example, *ball* would be said /bal/ and students would follow this chant by saying /b/, pointing to *b*, /ah/ pointing to *a*, and /l/ pointing to *ll*. The structured language activity that uses the five words that you introduce also reinforces students' awareness of the spelling pattern in the five key words. After students chant and spell-check each word that you introduced, ask the group to write these words from memory or copy them from the chart story that the group created. Then they write a word that has the same word part but one that they have not yet been taught. For example, after *cat* is written and taught, students must write *hat* without having been taught that word that day.

In like manner, children also profit from making their own alphabet books and books of favorite sounds and letters. They also learn phonic generalizations faster when you continuously highlight letters, sounds, word patterns, and basic phonetic rules throughout the day, as they arise in daily activities. You can engage this emphasis by (1) underlining the phonic element that appears most often in a chart exercise; (2) asking students to tell you the spelling of certain words before you write them in front of the group; (3) pointing out how two words begin with the same sound, letter, or blend after you say them; and (4) asking students to tell you what sounds a letter or word makes.

Tests to Assess Learners' Phonics Abilities

There are many types of phonic assessments. You likely use the ones prescribed by your statewide criterion-referenced test or the ones that benchmark students' progress in basal reading or supplemental programs. We want to introduce a newer form of phonics assessment: *Helping Students Think About Their Own Phonics Learning.* This self-assessment instrument has the advantage of helping students to independently apply and evaluate how well they use phonics to decode unknown words. This test can be modified to examine the instructional phonics components that you have taught by merely altering the number and content of the items listed on it. It is shown in Figure 4.2.

ADDRESSING LEARNERS WITH SPECIAL NEEDS

Learners Who Struggle

There are many research studies which validate the use of paired groupings, including learning pairs, dyads, study buddies, and peer-led tutoring in phonics instruction for less able readers (Block & Dellamura, 2000/2001; Jensen, 2000). In these groupings, readers are assigned or select a partner with whom they complete a certain literacy project. If students work as a pair, two different grades can be given and students can read materials at different levels of difficulty. If they work as a dyad (and read the same book or work using the same materials), students can receive the same grade and usually read the same reading selection. Two effective activities for pairs and dyads which can also be used as assessment methods are assisted reading and repeated readings. Assisted reading occurs when one student reads one page orally and his or her partner reads the next page. In repeated reading one student reads a page and then the second rereads the same page. (See Chapter 8 for additional methods for using repeated readings.) The teacher is present to assess students while they are reading with a partner.

Learners Who Are Learning English

ELL students can profit from games like Bingo and singing "The Alphabet Song" as you point to the capital letters and (later) lowercase letters as you say

Figure 4.2   Helping Students Think About Their Own Phonics Learning

Directions: Students can complete this assessment at the end of each week or at the end of each grading period. Teachers write all the objectives and literacy processes taught and practiced in class since the last self-assessment form was completed. Students write the specific objectives they need help to learn in the left column and the objectives that they judge that they can perform independently in the right column.

Name: _____   Date: _____

(Place a √ next to items that apply to you.)

Need Specific Help With . . .	*No Longer Need Help With . . .*
1. _____ Short vowels	A. _____ The letters of the alphabet
2. _____ Long words	B. _____ The sounds of consonants
3. _____ Meanings of words	C. _____ "I", "A," "the" and other sight words
4. _____ Remembering what I read	D. _____ Blending sound of letters together
5. _____ Recalling what I read yesterday	E. _____ Reading "ch," "sh," and "th"
6. _____ Writing longer sentences	F. _____ Meanings of lots of words
7. _____ Reading faster	G. _____ Understanding what I read
8. _____ Other: _____	H. _____ Reading a full book alone
_____	I. _____ Spelling
_____	J. _____ Handwriting
_____	K. _____ How to study
_____	L. _____ Concept of words
_____	M. _____ Concept of sentences
_____	N. _____ Concept of stories
_____	O. _____ Writing a sentence
Describe What You Want to Learn Next Week:	P. _____ Reading silently for five minutes
_____	Q. _____ Reading orally for one page without missing a word
_____	R. _____
_____	S. _____
_____	T. _____
_____	U. _____
_____	V. _____
_____	W. _____
_____	X. _____
_____	Y. _____
_____	Z. _____

them. Be sure that the letters are at students' eye level, not high above their normal range of vision, as such vantage points distort these letters' appearances. Emphasize the shape and size of single letters by asking students to wear nametags. Students group themselves together if the letter you say and write begins their name, ends their name, or appears in the middle. Then, students identify objects and labels in the room that have that letter and sound in them.

In the same vein, ELL students profit significantly by making letter folders, collecting as many pictures and words as they can find that contain a specific letter. These folders are presented by the child and then manipulated in many ways to guide various writing, story creating, and phonic center activities. Use flashcards and games (like Bingo, Tic-Tac-Toe, and Concentration) in which you say a word's or letter's sounds so you can build students' ability in matching and distinguishing letters, consonant blends, and word patterns. Pairs of students enjoy playing Go Fish, in which they ask "Do you have a word that starts with /c/, and at another time begins with the letter *s*?" A form that can be used to play Bingo and the letters that students can use to do so for this game and many others appears in Figure 4.3.

Learners Who Excel

Gifted students enjoy writing books that can be used in the paired sessions above. They also can generate large "writing word walls" on which content-area words are grouped by concepts and multiple-syllable words are listed beneath the word parts that they can be compared to, work in teams to increase the number of words that can be displayed, and work together to write more interesting and valuable books.

SUMMARY

The purpose of this chapter was to provide research-based, scientifically validated lessons and assessment tools for students so that they can learn phonics with ease. You also had the opportunity to assess your present knowledge of phonic principles. An underlying theme throughout the chapter is that no one method or approach to phonics is the best for every student. The only research-based finding is that the least effective program is to eliminate phonics instruction entirely. Your goal is to provide rich real-world reading experiences as students learn to use phonic generalizations to decode unknown words. The best phonic lessons involve several learning modalities, fun experiences where students enjoy putting sounds to words, and activities that enable students to assess themselves.

Figure 4.3   BINGO Game Boards for a Wide Variety of Uses

B	I	N	G	O

-am	-in	-ot
-en	-an	-et
-er	-est	-ing
-an	-on	-at
-it	-ea	-o_e
-i_e	-a_e	-ee
-ou	-es	sh-
ch-	th-	-op

Aa	Bb	Cc
Dd	Ee	Ff
Gg	Hh	Ii
Jj	Kk	Ll
Mm	Nn	Oo
Pp	Qq	Rr
Ss	Tt	Uu
Vv	Ww	Xx
Yy	Zz	

Answer Key

Figure 4.1   Phonics: Mastery Evaluation for Teachers and Gifted Readers

1. d

2. e

3. c

4. d

5. a

6. c

7. b

8. a

9. o

10. u

11. i

12. u

13. i

14. u

15. o

16. e

17. a

18. long a sound

19. long o sound

20. long e sound

21. pane, sale, crate

22. slide, price

23. broke, pole

24. huge

25. phase—ph, charge—ch, rough—gh, throw—th, which—ch, enough—gh

26. blanket—bl, plow—pl, strange—str, program—pr,—gr, clock—cl, standard—st, sprain—spr, trauma—tr, draw—dr, smash—sm, flock—fl, drake—dr

27. couch—ou, spoil—oi, crew—ew, convoy—oy, foul—ou

Vocabulary Development

Powerful Instruction for Reading Success

With the Practitioner's Voice of Phillip Todd Cupples

Andrea read quietly. She came to a word she had never seen before (Indian). *Softly, she tried to sound it out: "nn-duh-i-ah-nn." Her teacher heard her struggle and walked to her desk. Andrea said: "Can you teach me another way to learn words? I've tried sounding words out, and just knowing the sounds doesn't fill my mind enough to learn what the word means."*

—Block, 2004, p. 73

Vocabulary development is defined as "the growth of a person's stock of known words and meanings," and "the teaching-learning principles and practices that lead to such growth" (Harris & Hodges, 1995, p. 275). This chapter is designed to present the scientifically validated evidence and methods that you can depend upon in teaching vocabulary. The National Reading Panel (NICHD, 2000a) found that many studies "describe aspects of vocabulary without specifically addressing questions of how vocabulary instruction is conducted" (pp. 4–16). Recently, new research found that a comprehensive program of rich vocabulary instruction must teach four categories of skills, provide rich explanations of word-learning principles in action, and provide activities that encourage children to transfer word meanings to novel text (Block & Mangieri, 2005). These four categories of scientifically based lessons, as well as the scientifically validated principles upon which their success rests, will be described in this chapter.

WHAT TEACHERS NEED TO
KNOW ABOUT VOCABULARY

We also know that a lack of vocabulary is a key component underlying school failure for many students, especially children who are economically challenged (Biemiller, 2001; Biemiller & Slonim, 2001; Hart & Risley, 1995; Hirsch, 2001). For example, as early as age four, the typical student in an impoverished environment has been exposed to thirteen million fewer vocabulary words than the typical child in a working class family, and thirty million fewer total words than the typical child in a professional family (Hart & Risley, 1995). This creates an alarming situation. Moreover, expert readers know and use more reading strategies than less able readers (Block & Mangieri, 2003; Pressley & Afflerbach, 1995). All students should be taught that English words can be learned more rapidly if they are grouped into four categories: (1) words that occur often in everything they will read for the rest of their lives (high-frequency English words); (2) words that contain a basic, frequently occurring, phonetically regular English word pattern; (3) words that usually appear in a specific content area and describe some aspect of that discipline; and (4) words that have unusual historical origins, sounds, and spellings, or require inferential interpretations to determine their meanings, such as idioms and figurative language.

Research shows that without rich instruction, many students would not reach grade-level expectations in reading (Block & Mangieri, 2005; Snow, Burns, & Griffin, 1998; Snow, 2003). Direct vocabulary instruction should be delivered for 10-20 minutes daily in Grades K–3 for greatest student growth (Mangieri, 1972; Levin, Levin, Glassman, & Norduall, 1992). Without 10-20 minutes of daily focused instruction, most kindergarteners would need to have twelve years of reading words daily and learning by themselves approximately seven new vocabulary words every day to reach the level of reading vocabulary that most children of affluent parents possess by fourth grade (Block, Rodgers, & Johnson, 2004).

We also know that although some students acquire vocabulary on their own, many other children do not do so as well without instruction. As a result, the latter group does not learn the basic, most important, and most frequently appearing English words, and a negative cycle occurs. Because they lack the ability to derive meaning from words, they cannot read as well independently. Consequently, they are unable to acquire new word meanings as rapidly as independent readers, or to repeatedly practice and reinforce their vocabulary-building strategies and word-learning principles through multiple authentic reading experiences. As a result, these students frequently fall behind their peers in overall reading abilities, and they develop a negative attitude toward reading. Thus, wide reading and explicit instruction build vocabulary, language, and world knowledge (Beck & McKeown, 1991, 2002).

Instruction should begin in kindergarten. Before Grade 1, students can be taught through frequent journeys outside the classroom to learn precise names and descriptors of new objects and events. These actions teach students how a continuous searching for strong, "just right" words can increase their knowledge of the world, even before students seek to learn such vivid words through reading and writing (Stewart 2002a and 2002b).

VOCABULARY **65**
DEVELOPMENT:
POWERFUL
INSTRUCTION
FOR READING
SUCCESS

RESEARCH THAT TEACHERS CAN USE

One challenge that you will face as a teacher is to determine how to help your students master vocabulary strategies they need to be successful readers. The following research findings can guide your work.

All English Words Are Not of Equal Importance

Research shows that students should be taught words that they will encounter often in print (NICHD, 2000a). The more thoroughly students learn high-frequency vocabulary, the more able they will be at comprehending text that contains these or similar words. Students retain the meaning of high-frequency words if they are exposed to them repeatedly in print (NICHD, 2000a; NICHD, 2004). No more than ten words should be taught per week in Grades K–3 (Block & Mangieri, 2005; NICHD, 2004).

Teach Important Words That Transfer

Generalizable core words need to be taught so students can learn how to transfer newly learned word-learning principles to new words automatically (RAND Reading Study Group, 2001; Snow, 2003; NICHD, 2000a). Students should be taught words that represent major aspects of the English language (i.e., high-frequency words, words with special word parts, words that describe specific content area ideas, words that sound alike). They should also have many effective learning opportunities with these core words so they can rapidly deduce the meanings of a wide array of similar words in our language. Since the words you will teach are characteristic of a core of word families, the learning of one word creates a key to unlocking the meaning of several dozen other new words. When you teach vocabulary, begin with nouns students can picture in their minds and concrete-referent words (words that describe objects, events, and things that are prevalent in a child's world, such as *television, holidays,* and *recess*). Teach these words at the beginning of the year because students learn these words most rapidly (Snow, 2003; NICHD, 2004).

Students Retain Newly Taught Words When They Understand Their Meaning

In order for most students to understand a word's meaning, they must experience rich, effective instruction around that word (Beck & McKeown, 2002; Block & Mangieri, 2005). You go beyond asking your students to merely say and memorize important words. Instead, you teach students the meaning of words through a series of targeted, varied, and research-based lessons. This instruction should provide tactile, dramatic, kinesthetic, oral, and written exposure to a word's meaning. For example, a teacher who is teaching the word *freezing* to first graders would not only say the word and have the students repeat the word but would also have the students make and handle ice cubes, go for a walk outside on a cold day, and talk together about what being much colder would feel like. The class could bring in pictures from magazines of snow and ice. They could dramatize being cold by shivering.

Give at Least Six Exposures to a
New Word and Its Meaning in Succession

When students first encounter a new word, they recognize its appearance letter by letter. Repeated exposures increase the size of the visual unit they recognize so that they can eventually know many words with the same letter or meaning-based patterns automatically (Samuels, 2002, see page 30). You can provide such exposure by giving your students a range of 10 to 15 research-based, highly effective vocabulary-building learning experiences for each word (and the family of words it represents). This repeated, successive work with a word is called *fast-mapping* (Block, 2004). Fast-mapping is an instructional schedule that enables students to have at least six consecutive opportunities to independently apply the word-learning principle just learned so that its use becomes automatic.

Teach Word-Learning Principles
and Vocabulary-Building Strategies Together

Students increase their vocabularies more rapidly when they learn word-learning principles and a vocabulary-building strategy together (Block & Mangieri, 2005). This enhanced instructional method builds fast-mapping and has been proven to also develop students' abilities to transfer the thought processes used to gain the meaning of a core word immediately to new words within that word's core family. Such fast-mapping and transfer ability also builds students' word consciousness (Block & Mangieri, 2005; Block, 2004). Word consciousness is a person's ability to think about words and use them in meaningful contexts.

Link Vocabulary to Common Themes

Word consciousness develops even more deeply when vocabulary words are tied to a common theme. Your lessons should relate to high-interest themes and topics with words that students experience daily in content area and language arts classes. For example, words like *star, comets, meteors, galaxy,* and *cosmos* would all connect to the theme of universe. As a result, when students confront an unknown word, the deep understanding of the word-learning principles, vocabulary-building strategies, and word consciousness that has been created by direct instruction enables them to independently initiate the thinking processes necessary to unlock the meaning of it and other theme-based words not taught.

Vocabulary and Comprehension
Skills Build Simultaneously

Direct instruction should be given in context so students can learn how to derive meaning independently. Context activities are best (NICHD, 2000b), too, as a means to use vocabulary instruction to build students' inference abilities (NICHD, 2000b; Levin, Levin, Glassman, & Norduall, 1992). When you teach

VOCABULARY **67**
DEVELOPMENT:
POWERFUL
INSTRUCTION
FOR READING
SUCCESS

words in context, vocabulary and comprehension build simultaneously as well as students' positive attitudes toward reading (Block & Mangieri, 2003). The more motivated students feel to learn words, the more words they will learn (Brabham & Lynch-Brown, 2002). As they learn more words, their reading abilities advance to higher levels. As you teach vocabulary using the activities in this chapter, you will be developing a continuous, upward spiral of reading power for your students that can add greater pleasure to their reading experience.

NEW CLASSROOM-PROVEN, RESEARCH-BASED PRACTICES

Teaching Vocabulary

Expert readers do not approach the learning of vocabulary by calling upon the same word-learning principle or vocabulary-building strategy for every word. They have been taught, or deduced independently, that certain word meanings can be obtained most rapidly when they think about which category the word falls into. What set of strategies and principles best match each individual term they must learn? With the following lessons, you can pass this wisdom on to all students. They can learn that some words can be learned best through (1) thinking about the part of speech that the word represents in a sentence as they add all the semantic and syntactical context clues that come from the words that surround that word; (2) recognizing the meanings of distinct word parts and adding the individual prefix, root, and suffix meanings together to deduce an unknown term's unique meaning; (3) recognizing that a word does not appear frequently and really is content-specific so its meaning relates to the big topic being described in the paragraph in which this word appears; or (4) knowing that none of the above learning clues applies to a specific word, so it must have an unique history, sound, or inferential meaning that can be learned through a mnemonic device or associative memory clue that they create themselves. The following lessons develop students' abilities to use the first set of thinking processes for the appropriate words.

Teaching the First Category of Words: How and When to Use Semantic and Syntactic Context Clues and Parts of Speech

The first skill that students need to learn is how to use the role that a word plays in a sentence, such as whether it is a noun or verb, and the syntax and semantic context clues from all the other words in the sentence to determine an unknown word's meaning. Context clues include definitions, paraphrases, restatements, examples, parenthetical expressions, descriptions, and synonyms. You should couple those clues with instruction on parts of speech and model through several think-alouds how these word-learning principles and strategies help you learn words that you see frequently in several subject areas.

**Lesson to Teach Students to Use
Context Clues and Parts of Speech**

A Teacher Might Say: "I am going to read you two sentences. In the second sentence there is a word I do not know the meaning of and I need your help. 'The car started the trip when it was low on gas. After an hour's drive the care sputtered to a stop.'"

A Teacher May Want to Do: Show students how to look at syntactical context clues and determine that *sputtered* is a verb. Then, by using semantic context clues, they can predict what the word means in reference to a car that is low on gas. Last, through rereading the sentence, they can say the sounds of the first letters in the word *sputtered* and think of words heard in the past as well as a meaning that would make sense in that sentence.

A Teacher May Want to Have Students Do: Students can practice using context clues to understand the meaning of unfamiliar words by finding sentences with difficult words and writing them down. Students should underline the unfamiliar word. After rereading the sentence, they can use a highlighter to highlight all of the clues in the sentence that may help with word meaning. Students can then say or write the meaning of the word.

Lesson Could Be Assessed By: After several unfamiliar words have been identified in a sentence and the meaning of the words determined using context clues, students can pair with a student who is also finished. While taking turns reading the sentences and determining the meaning of the unfamiliar words, students can work together to confirm or disconfirm the correct meaning of the words.

It is important to teach readers that semantic context clues are valuable decoding tools, but when used as the sole decoding tool they can predict only about one-fourth of all content-specific words (Gough, Alford, & Holly-Wilcox, 1981). In addition to the lesson described above, you can help younger and less able readers learn how to use context clues through a shared reading of a big book. Cover with a self-stick note all but the first consonant and vowels in a semantically rich word. You can cover several words in distantly spaced sentences throughout a book, so the chance that students can guess each word from the preceding semantic clues is high. For kindergartners, you can

VOCABULARY **69**
DEVELOPMENT:
POWERFUL
INSTRUCTION
FOR READING
SUCCESS

cover four words; for first graders, five words; for second graders, six words; and for third graders, cover seven words. Then, you can model how, when students come to a word they don't know (the word that is covered with the self-stick note), they can say the sound of the first letters, pause, and then continue reading. Your intent is to use the sounds of the first letters, along with syntactical, semantic, and parts-of-speech meanings of the unknown word in connection with the meanings of other words in the sentence, to derive the meaning of the unknown word. An example of such a modeling session that was used by Mr. Evans, an exemplary first-grade teacher, is described below.

(All the letters in the word *queen* are covered but *que*). "I have covered a word on this first page to illustrate what you can say to yourself and think when you come to words you don't know. You can put together the meaning for all the other words in the sentence to figure out a word, which is called using context clues. Then, you think about the part of speech that the unknown word plays in that sentence. I'll show you how to do it. If I didn't know this word, I'd say to myself: 'Once upon a time there was a handsome king and beautiful /que/ [pause] who lived in a large castle on the top of the highest hill in all the land.' By reading to the end of the sentence, using what I know from previous stories, the sound of the first letter of my unknown word, and the fact that the word has to be a noun, I know that a noun that would make sense in the context is *queen*. When we come to the next covered word, I want you to use context clues and parts of speech with me to learn the word's meaning. Then explain to me what you thought to figure out that word's meaning. . . . "

The Vocabulary Teacher's Book of Lists (Fry, 2004) is a valuable book that can become an instant reference to use in fast-mapping nouns, verbs, and other parts of speech. It contains countless vocabulary lists that you can use to build such lessons. After students are introduced to *The Vocabulary Teacher's Book of Lists* they can make their own book of lists which contain words that they have learned.

Naming Words, Doing Words, Painting Words

Another lesson that explicitly teaches students how to use context clues and parts of speech follows. Students dictate stories as a class. After a story or a series of sentences has been dictated, you can teach how nouns can be found in specific spots in sentences. Then you can note that nouns are often known as *naming words.* When you have written *naming words* in a column to the right of the sentences the students have dictated, you can go back and ask the children to tell you each word in the sentences that names an object, person, place, or a thing. As each word is identified, you circle it in a color such as yellow.

Then you can teach students that certain words—adjectives and adverbs— are called *painting words,* which enable us to draw pictures in our minds of what we are discussing. Again, we turn the students' attention to the sentences they dictated and ask them to point out the different words that help them to paint

Figure 5.1   Examples of the Naming, Doing, and Painting Words Activity and the Rebus Activity to Teach Syntactical Context Clues

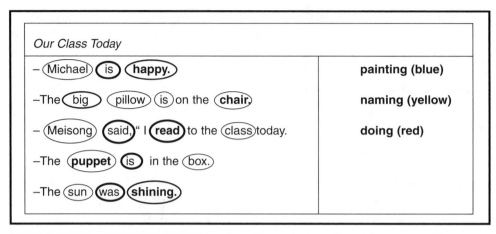

Our Class Today

– Michael is **happy.**

–The big pillow is on the **chair.**

– Meisong said, " I **read** to the class today.

–The **puppet** is in the box.

–The sun was **shining.**

painting (blue)

naming (yellow)

doing (red)

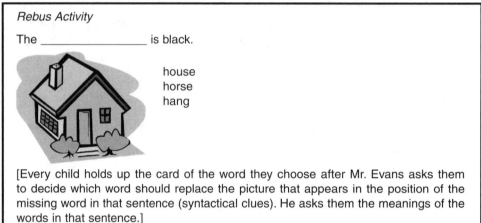

Rebus Activity

The _____ is black.

house
horse
hang

[Every child holds up the card of the word they choose after Mr. Evans asks them to decide which word should replace the picture that appears in the position of the missing word in that sentence (syntactical clues). He asks them the meanings of the words in that sentence.]

clearer pictures of objects in their minds. As they tell you a painting word, circle that word in blue. An example of this activity appears in Figure 5.1.

Next, you can teach students that verbs are sometimes called *doing words* because they tell us what people are doing. Again, return to the paragraph and ask students to tell you which words are doing words and circle those in a third color like red. When students examine the sentences with painting, naming, and doing words circled, they can notice that some words between these circled words remain uncircled. These uncircled words are usually sight words, and, for the first time, sight words become easier for students to identify because of syntax clues. Specifically, as shown in Figure 5.1, sight words stand out when all other words are circled, and their repetitive nature becomes a clue to learning them. That is, when this repetition is revealed, less able readers find that reading need not be the arduous task they once envisioned: they do not need to decode every new word that is unveiled to them in a sentence. With this knowledge in mind, students are ready to read, or to have books read to them in which many naming, doing, and painting words appear. See Table 5.1 for a list of recommended titles. These books were specifically chosen because they repeat common phrases and use the same naming, doing, and painting words repeatedly. By having students pick out

VOCABULARY **71**
DEVELOPMENT:
POWERFUL
INSTRUCTION
FOR READING
SUCCESS

Table 5.1   Books That Increase Students' Abilities to Use Semantic and Syntactic
Context Clues

The numbers in parentheses following each entry indicate how many words are contained in the story.

A Woggle of Witches by A. Adams, 1971, New York: Scribner (139)

Animals Should Definitely Not Wear Clothing by J. Barrett, 1970, New York: Atheneum (65)

Arthur's Christmas Cookies by M. Brown, 1995, Boston: Little, Brown (150)

The Fireflies by E. Carle, 1995, New York: Harcourt (107)

May I Bring a Friend? by B. S. DeRegniers, 1964, New York: Atheneum (151)

Drummer Hoff by B. A. Emberley, 1995, New York: Simon & Schuster (30)

One Fine Day by N. Hogrogian, 1971, New York: Macmillan (150)

Good-Night, Owl by N. Hogrogian, 1995, New York: Simon & Schuster (51)

The Snowy Day by E. Keats, 1962, New York: Viking (157)

Peter's Chair by E. Keats, 1967, New York: Harper & Row (153)

Goggles by E. Keats, 1969, New York: Macmillan (149)

Leo, The Late Bloomer by S. Kellogg, 1973, New York: Dutton (78)

The Mystery of the Missing Red Mitten by S. Kellogg, 1974, New York: Dial (128)

The Comic Adventures of Old Mother Hubbard and Her Dog by A. Lobel, 1968, New York: Bradbury (91)

The Bear's Toothache by D. McPhail, 1972, Boston: Little, Brown (111)

Where the Wild Things Are by M. Sendak, 1963, New York: Harper & Row (139)

Noisy Nora by M. Sendak, 1973, New York: Dial (103)

the naming, painting, and doing words, syntax clues become almost automatic for many children. In the process, sight words become manageable and new words become less difficult to decode.

For younger children, *rebus stories* serve the same function. A rebus story contains pictures or drawings inserted in place of the words that you want to teach children. For example, Mr. Evans was introducing rebus stories to his children. First he passed out three word cards. On one card was the word *house*, on a second card was the word *horse*, and on the third card was the word *hang*. Then he wrote this sentence on the board: *The* (and then he drew a picture of a house) *is black* (see Figure 5.1). When Mr. Evans read the sentence aloud, he put his hand under the house and didn't say anything. He asked the children to hold up the card that would fit in that sentence. Because each child held up one of the three cards he had given them, he easily determined which children recognized the word *house* and matched it with the picture that depicted its meaning.

Teaching the Second Category of Words: Adding the Meanings in Word Parts Together

When students learn the meaning of common prefixes, suffixes, and root words, they will have mastered the invaluable vocabulary-building strategy of learning how longer words in our language are built. If you teach the four most

Figure 5.2   Book Page for Teaching How and When to Add Word Parts Together

_____
(Student's Name)

My Vocabulary Book of Inferences About Learning Important Words

Page I inside the book could look like this: When and How to Add Word Parts Together

Beginning of a Word's Meaning (Prefix) +	Meaning of Base or Root =	Infer Whole Word's Meaning

(Continued)

VOCABULARY **73**
DEVELOPMENT:
POWERFUL
INSTRUCTION
FOR READING
SUCCESS

Figure 5.2 (Continued)

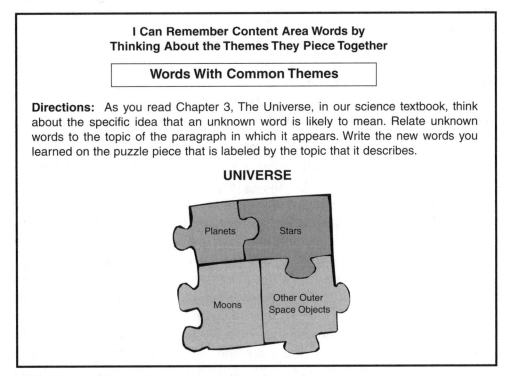

I Can Remember Content Area Words by Thinking About the Themes They Piece Together

| **Words With Common Themes** |

Directions: As you read Chapter 3, The Universe, in our science textbook, think about the specific idea that an unknown word is likely to mean. Relate unknown words to the topic of the paragraph in which it appears. Write the new words you learned on the puzzle piece that is labeled by the topic that it describes.

UNIVERSE

Planets | Stars

Moons | Other Outer Space Objects

common English prefixes (*un-, re-, in-, dis-*), students will have a strategy to unlock the meaning of about two-thirds of all English words that contain prefixes (NICHD, 2000b). Prefixes should be the first vocabulary-building strategy that you teach for this second category of words. You can teach this strategy as early in a child's educational career as kindergarten. Prefixes should be taught before suffixes and root words because they are easier to learn. They have clear, consistent meanings (e.g., *re-* means *again; dis-* and *un-* mean *not*). They are usually spelled exactly the same every time they are used to build a long word. They always occur at the very beginning of every word in which they appear.

After students have learned prefixes, they are ready to learn base or root words. Base words are the main meaning-bearing section of a word. For example, in the word *prehistoric, -histor* is the main meaning-bearing section of the word and is the base of that word. Students taught how to use base and root words to learn more words become better readers (Brabham & Lynch-Brown, 2002; Mangieri, 1972; Yopp & Yopp, 2003). For example, after students are taught that *hand* is the base word in *handy, handkerchief,* and *underhanded,* they become more aware that words with common base words will have meanings that relate to each other.

Root words are similar to base words in that they provide the dominant meaning for words to which prefixes and suffixes are attached. They differ from base words in that they have come from other languages, with 60 percent having Latin or Greek origins. An effective lesson to teach root words, Word Architecture, is shown in Figure 5.2. This figure shows a page of a book students can compile to learn this category of words. It will enable students to keep a vocabulary book in which they create their own connections and graphics to learn how to add word meanings together.

Teaching the Third Category of Words: Learning Less-Frequently Appearing Content Area Words

Long, unfamiliar words usually name something specific about the content of the topic being read. To learn these words we must think about what the word could do to connect to the subject being discussed in the paragraph in which it appears. Perform a think-aloud to show the thought processes you use to apply this principle and strategy together in a content area book. Point to another content-specific word in that same textbook and ask a student to describe what principle and strategy can be used to derive its meaning. Last, let students spend several days practicing these processes independently, raising their hands when they come to unknown words. Listen to their thoughts about what they are doing to try to learn the unknown words, and scaffold (provide support, questions, and prompts to help students complete the thought processes you demonstrated) until they can create these thought processes automatically and independently. Graphics, such as semantic maps and charts that show the relationships and links between the words within a content area text, are another valuable tool that can assist students to deduce the meaning of content area words.

Teaching the Fourth Category of Words: Unique and Unusual Words

You can teach students that some less-frequently appearing words are not particularly long, are not content-specific, and do not follow traditional English spelling patterns. To learn these words, students must identify a special, distinct feature in the word. Often these features relate to (1) that word's history, such as containing a spelling or sound that carried over from the word's original language (e.g., *Chevrolet*), (2) the unusual sound a word is designed to convey (e.g., zzzzzzzzz), (3) only one meaning or spelling that a word could have, such as homophones, or (4) special inferential meanings that a word or phrase means that is not represented in the individual words' literal meanings, such as idioms and figures of speech. To learn this classification of words, you can teach students to use the origins and history of the word, the unusual sounds made by the letter combinations in the word, mnemonic devices that have personal meanings to memorize the unique features and meaning of the word, and to think at an inferential level to visualize what a series of words could mean, if they were not interpreted literally. Use of meaning-based images and mnemonic devices increases vocabulary acquisition (Block & Graham, 2000; NICHD, 2000b; Levin, Levin, Glassman & Norduall, 1992). A sample lesson of this type follows.

VOCABULARY 75
DEVELOPMENT:
POWERFUL
INSTRUCTION
FOR READING
SUCCESS

Teaching Idioms, Figurative Language, Metaphors, and Similes

An idiom is a complex expression, the meaning of which cannot be derived from the meanings of its individual words (such as "raining cats and dogs"). There are several types of idioms. *Figurative language* refers to phrases that convey a feeling or thought that is characterized by painting an image (such as "so nervous that my stomach has butterflies in it"). *Metaphors* are figures of speech that make a comparison between two things that have something in common, but the words *like* or *than* are not used to make the comparison (such as "clouds are billowy pillows"). *Similes* are metaphors that make comparisons between two things with the words *like, as,* or *than* (such as "soft as silk"). *Personification* is a figure of speech in which nonhuman things are given human qualities (such as Meisong's story about frisky feet in Chapter 8). *Proverbs* are sayings that describe a truth about life (such as "You can't judge a book by its cover").

These advanced grammatical structures occur frequently in literature and in conversational speech. This lesson can help students to better understand other people's literal and implied meanings and to write and speak more precisely and vividly. Each of these literary devices differs in the extent to which its literal meanings relate to its implied meanings. As you would expect, students have an easier time when introduced to a device whose literal meanings are more closely related to their personal experiences. Once you have read a book that contains several of these devices, you can develop students' awareness of their power and build up their self-selected use of each type by using the idioms in Table 5.2 to write class stories and by asking students to define what the idioms mean in the context of their stories. You can also write a different idiom, proverb, or example of figurative language on the board every day for two months. Ask students to reflect on its meaning and discuss it, in a half-minute activity at the end of school as everyone prepares to leave for home. Then you can encourage students to use the device in a writing assignment the next day, or you can use it in the next day's morning message.

Another effective lesson is to guide students to reconcile opposing positions in proverbs, idioms, and figurative language. As Manzo (1981) found, "Most often this . . . step has the most profound effect upon intellectual growth. Through it students come to realize that most things are set in a dynamic tension to one another. Life and learning are a process of reconciling seemingly opposing positions" (p. 414). Many books that list proverbs and other frequently appearing English figurative languages are available in libraries and bookstores.

If students wish to learn more about idioms, the following books can be helpful.

- *Hog on Ice and Other Curious Expressions* by Robert Funk
- *Tenderfoot and Ladyfingers* by Robert Funk
- *Eight Ate: A Feast of Homonym Riddles* by Robert Funk
- *In a Pickle and Other Funny Idioms* by Marvin Terban
- *Put Your Foot in Your Mouth and Other Silly Sayings* by Marilyn Cox
- *From the Horse's Mouth* by Mark Nevin & Mary Nevin
- *Chin Music: Tall Talk and Other Talk* by Sally Schwartz

Table 5.2   Examples of Proverbs, Idioms, and Figurative Language That Can Be
Used to Increase Students' Vocabulary

Proverbs

Stretch your feet only as far as your
   sheet will permit. (Spanish)
Look before you leap. (Greek)
You can't judge a book by its cover.
The genius, wit, and spirit of a nation
   are discovered in its proverbs. (English)
There is no proverb which is not true.
   (Spanish)

A stitch in time saves nine.
You do not teach the paths of the
   forest to an old gorilla. (African)
Lend to one who will not repay,
   and you will provoke his dislike.
   (Chinese)
Only in the grave is there rest.
   (Yiddish)

Idioms and Figurative Language

hold your horses
hit the ceiling
killing two birds with
   one stone
don't beat around the bush
you don't have a leg to
   stand on
he had me in stitches
all ears
at the end of one's rope
bend over backward
cat got your tongue?
dressed to kill
elbow grease
eyes bigger than your
   stomach
for the birds
go to bat for someone

if the shoe fits, wear it
keep something under
   one's hat
knock someone's socks off
let the cat out of the bag
monkey business
out of the woods
play it by ear
raise a stink
shake a leg
smell a rat
spill the beans
spread oneself too thin
tongue-in-cheek
wet blanket
straw that broke the
   camel's back
wet behind the ears

under the weather
between the devil and
   the deep blue sea
give someone the cold
   shoulder
keep your shirt on
bury your head
   in the sand
in one ear and out
   the other
white elephant
straight from the
   horse's mouth
chip off the old block
get into someone's hair
paint the town red
thinking cap
feather in your cap

- *A Surfeit of Similes* by John Juster
- *Napping House* by Audrey Wood
- *Quick as a Cricket* by Audrey Wood
- *Thirteen* by Remy Charlip & Jerry Joyner

Native American books like *The Girl Who Loved Wild Horses* and *Dancing Teepees: Poems of American Indian Youth* by Virginia Driving Hawk Kneve also contain many metaphors and can be used as models of their use in clarifying meaning.

TESTS TO ASSESS LEARNING

Timed vocabulary quizzes have been demonstrated to build automatic transfer of new words to authentic reading situations (Tan & Nicholson, 1997). You can

VOCABULARY **77**
DEVELOPMENT:
POWERFUL
INSTRUCTION
FOR READING
SUCCESS

assess this ability through individualized tests. Such tests begin when you ask a student to read silently. Stop the reading at four specific times. First is when you come to a Category One word that the student may not know. Ask what word-learning principle and vocabulary-building strategy the student could use to deduce that word's meaning. If the student answers correctly, indicate this ability on a class assessment record form. If the student misses it, teach these processes again, and mark on your form that you will place this student in an instructional group to reteach these processes. Stop the reading for the second, third, and fourth times when you come to words from Categories Two, Three, and Four that the student may not know. Repeat the above actions using each of these words.

ADDRESSING LEARNERS WITH SPECIAL NEEDS

Below are some ways that you can help assure that the practices and strategies explained in this chapter can be learned by students with special learning needs. Through these special adaptations, most students can come to understand the word-learning principles and vocabulary-building strategies in this chapter. You will see their transfer to novel words and state criterion-referenced literacy achievement tests as well as to standardized norm-referenced tests (Block & Mangieri, 2005).

Learners Who Struggle

Flashcards, when used judiciously, and as one among varied teaching aids, significantly increase the vocabularies and reading comprehension of students with learning difficulties. (Biemiller, 2001; Gorman, 1993; Nichelson, 1998; Taka, 1997; Tan & Nicholson, 1997). Reproducible flashcards provide extended and varied practice opportunities. The key to the success of the flashcards is that, used purposefully, they add a manipulative practice opportunity to help students with special learning needs develop automaticity with their learning of new words. Flashcards can be used by students in pairs (where students teach each other the words missed) and in games such as Concentration, Bingo, Tic-Tac-Toe, or Candy Land, where a word and its meaning must be matched before a square can be claimed. A game board that can be used with a spinner for these lessons appears in Figure 5.3.

Learners Who Are Learning English

Teaching ELLs not more than ten new vocabulary terms, using three different VAKT (*Visual Auditory Kinesthetic Tactile*) methods of teaching during a 30-minute period, has been demonstrated to significantly increase ELLs' vocabularies (Moll, 1997). For example, you can introduce a word by saying it, pointing to it in a book, writing it and its definition, and doing a think-aloud about how you knew the word. For a second exposure during the same 30-minute time frame, you can teach by reading a book aloud, stopping at the word, and

Figure 5.3   Spinner and Candy Land Game Board

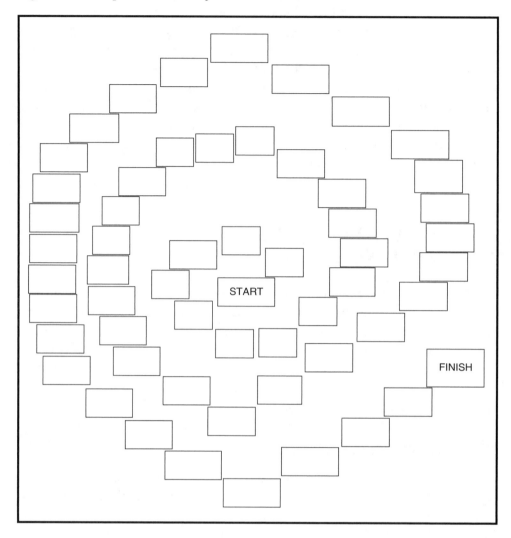

asking students to do each of the above actions. For the third teaching exposure, students could reread the book silently (if it is a very short book) or read a different book that contains the words just taught. While the children read silently, you complete the steps described individually.

Books and Online Resources for Building Vocabulary

- The *Vocabulary Teacher's Book of Lists* by Edward B. Fry, Ph.D., will assist reading and language arts teachers with vocabulary-building lessons.
- Vocabulary lessons and research from the Vocabulary Acquisition Research Group–Centre for Applied Language Studies, University of Wales, Swansea can keep you up to date on the latest vocabulary research and methods, www.readwritethink.com.

Learners Who Excel

Gifted learners enjoy working together to create spinner games, flashcards, bingo cards, matching games, word search puzzles, and crossword puzzles

VOCABULARY **79**
DEVELOPMENT:
POWERFUL
INSTRUCTION
FOR READING
SUCCESS

using words you taught. They enjoy leading their games when they present them to their peers. They also profit from working in pairs to challenge other pairs to learn words that are similar to, but more difficult than, the examples you've used in the category you've just taught. The following Web sites can be used for these purposes, to inspire gifted learners to attain richer and deeper vocabularies, and to enable gifted learners to work with a teaching aide when you are working with other students.

- *Vocabulary.com.* Puzzles and games, www.vocabulary.com
- *The Word Detective.* E-zine with column about words and their meanings, www.word-detective.com
- *Super Kids.* Vocabulary section includes hangman games, word-a-day, make your own word puzzles. Elementary-school level, also advertises software for sale, www.superkids.com
- *EnglishCLUB.net.* Features grammar and vocabulary activities, word games, pen pal listings, and question-and-answer service. Includes free classroom handouts for ESL teachers, www.englishclub.com
- *Interactive Audio-Picture English Lessons.* Offers interactive ESL with pronunciation and pictures, www.web-books.com/Language
- *a4esl.org.* Aimed at ESL but good for any student mid-elementary level up, a4esl.org

SUMMARY

The purpose of this chapter was to provide research-based and scientifically validated practices that you can use to significantly increase students' vocabularies. We described eight vocabulary-learning principles. You can use these as you design your own vocabulary-development program. The lessons that have been demonstrated to be particularly successful in vocabulary development are (1) shared reading; (2) assisted reading; (3) repeated readings; (4) teaching semantic and syntactical context clues; (5) definitions, idioms, figurative language, metaphors, and similes; (6) teaching unusual, low-frequency words; (7) showing how words are built; and (8) teaching content area words. Timed vocabulary quizzes, standardized vocabulary tests, and an informal test involving the deduction of unknown word meanings in the process of reading authentic text are three of the most valuable and reliable measures of students' independent vocabulary-building abilities. A special lesson was described that helps students think about their own learning processes. ELLs need lessons that enable them to see and learn a word at least three times in succession within a 30-minute period, whereas students with learning disabilities profit from judicious and varied uses of flashcards. Gifted learners enjoy working in pairs and using the Web sites described in this chapter to broaden their own vocabularies and challenge their equally able peers. In the next chapter, we will describe how students can move from the more laborious tasks of decoding words and deducing word meanings to become highly fluent silent and oral readers.

Achieve and Measure Reading Fluency

Expanding the Opportunity

With the Practitioner's Voice
of Theresa J. Palumbo

Ms. Hulsey is reading Nicholas Cricket. *Allison and her second-grade friends are engrossed in the story's beautiful melody created by many words that they have never heard before. This is the first day of a fluency unit that Ms. Hulsey, their teacher, developed after a conversation she had with Allison yesterday:*

Ms. Hulsey: *Would you like to read a few pages for me?*

Allison: *Okay. [She plods slowly through each word, pausing before each one.] I didn't do real good, did I?*

Ms. Hulsey: *Why do you think you are having problems?*

Allison: *I don't know how to read fast. When I read this slow, I can't remember what I read.*

Ms. Hulsey: *Tell me about the times when it is easy for you to read and you enjoy it.*

Allison: *When I read books over and over again and when I know the things in it, like when I read the* Curious George *books.*

> *Ms. Hulsey:* *I understand. What if I began a unit to help you? We can begin tomorrow.*
>
> *Allison:* *Thank you, Ms. Hulsey. I don't want people to think I'm dumb just because I read slow.*

The fluent reader is one who can perform multiple tasks—such as word recognition and comprehension—at the same time. In this time of high-stakes testing it is imperative to label terms appropriately so there is no confusion regarding reading achievement. Reading quickly, without comprehending the passage, is a futile effort. Therefore, the purpose of this chapter is to increase students' fluency so that optimal comprehension occurs. Reading fluency characteristics include accuracy and ease in decoding, speed of reading, simultaneous comprehension and decoding, and expression in oral reading prosody—tone sequences, stresses, and pauses. In this chapter, you will learn research-based lessons and assessment strategies that have proven to advance beginning readers' abilities to achieve proper speed of reading from the first stages of reading development.

WHAT TEACHERS NEED TO KNOW ABOUT FLUENCY

Fluent reading has several characteristics. For instance, ". . . the multitask functioning of the fluent reader is made possible by the reduced cognitive demands needed for word recognition and other reading processes, thus freeing cognitive resources for other functions, such as drawing inferences" (NICHD, 2000, p. 233). These findings of the National Reading Panel are a natural extension of the theoretical rationale and research work by LaBerge and Samuels (1974) and Samuels (1976) on automatic information processing in reading. Reading fluently is a learned activity that becomes better with practice:

> To perceive an entirely new word or other combination of strokes requires considerable time, close attention, and is likely to be imperfectly done, just as when we attempt some new combination of movements, some new trick in the gymnasium or new 'serve' at tennis. (Huey, 1908, p. 36)

Fluency development is analogous to learning to play tennis. A tennis player is tested to determine her level of play and then placed in a category with players at this same level. On occasion she'll play down a level to get in a quick game without the need to exert a lot of effort, or play up a level in order to challenge herself and determine where she needs practice. To be the best one can be and to develop skill level most efficiently, one needs to play (or read in this case) within the range of skill level where frequent successes will be obtained.

ACHIEVE AND **83**
MEASURE
READING
FLUENCY:
EXPANDING THE
OPPORTUNITY

Repeated reading—repeated tennis, read a lot at the right level—play a lot at the right level. This is the theory behind *Repeated Reading,* a practice that has been demonstrated to increase fluency, as will be described later in this chapter.

Research has also demonstrated that a person can be fluent at one readability level, yet not have achieved fluency at the next higher readability level. As Logan (1997) found, "automaticity should be viewed as a continuum rather than a dichotomy." For example, if a second grader has recently become fluent at the second-grade readability level, she likely is not yet fluent at the third-grade readability level. Thus, it is incorrect to say that a child is a "fluent" or "not a fluent" reader, unless this is clarified by which readability level one is referring to. Adults that are good readers would likely be fluent on many passages but still may not be fluent on difficult topics that are not in their areas of specialty.

RESEARCH THAT TEACHERS CAN USE

Fluency is a reading skill that is often neglected in classroom reading instruction. The National Assessment of Educational Progress conducted a large study of fluency achievement status in American education (Pinnell et al., 1995). This study found that in a nationally representative sample of fourth graders, "44% of the students were disfluent even with grade-level stories that the students had read under supportive testing conditions." Furthermore, Pinnell's study found a close relationship between fluency and reading comprehension. Students who are low in fluency may have difficulty getting the meaning of what they read, as Allison verified from personal experience in the opening scenario.

Fluency and comprehension are closely linked because to infer and understand text, readers must create a flowing, coherent mental representation of what is read, "especially if the text itself is faulty or inadequate" (Samuels, 2003). Fluency probes are needed before students can realize greater reading power, and Samuels suggests that such data cannot be obtained through comprehension and vocabulary checks. Similarly, Kuhn and Stahl's (2000) review of fluency research concluded that although assisted reading, Repeated Reading, or other approaches that integrate a number of fluency-building activities into a classroom were effective, it is not clear why they were. Were the observed effects due to a particular instructional activity, or could they be accounted for by the mere increased volume of reading that children do relative to the amount of time spent in teacher-directed, traditional instruction (Rasinski, 2003)?

Instructional supports, such as those that will be described next, appear to be essential in the development of fluent reading for most students. Whether it is provided through Repeated Reading, modeling, taped narrations, another individual, computer-based assistance, or repeated practice seems to be less critical than the fact that some instructional supports exist. Such support seems to allow learners to work within their zone of proximal development (Vygotsky, 1978), offering the scaffolding they need to move from laborious to flowing reading (Kuhn & Stahl, 2000).

Figure 6.1   Model to Achieve and Measure Reading Fluency

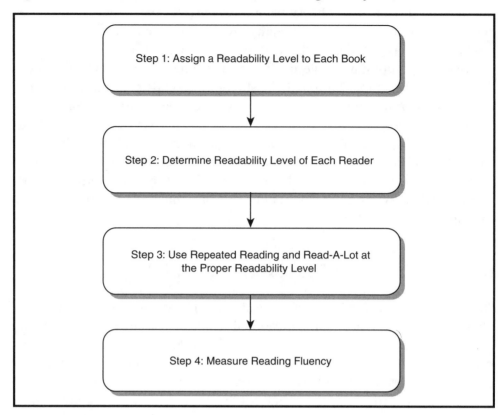

NEW CLASSROOM-PROVEN, RESEARCH-BASED PRACTICES

Scientifically validated fluency instruction and assessment is summarized in the *Model to Achieve and Measure Reading Fluency* shown in Figure 6.1. This comprehensive model contains four steps, which will be described in this section.

This model was created with the interest of increasing the number of children that will learn to read fluently by making accessible the right reading resources. It is intended to complement the Repeated Reading and Read-A-Lot instructional methods *at the proper readability level*. It provides a suggested measurement of fluency that includes a comprehension component. This model may be particularly helpful to struggling ESL readers or readers from low socioeconomic groups because these citizens may have more difficulty locating the proper resources.

Step 1: Assign a Readability Level to Each Book

Reading at the proper readability level is important because new words are encountered and practiced systematically. Repeated Reading and Read-A-Lot instructional methods *at the proper readability level* each require an availability of an assortment of books at each readability level. The problem we have in America today is that children are not able to readily acquire books at their readability level. This holds true in many libraries across the country, in

ACHIEVE AND **85**
MEASURE
READING
FLUENCY:
EXPANDING THE
OPPORTUNITY

bookstores, in schools, and in learning centers. In a recent conversation, one mother mentioned, in surprise and regret, that any two books and associated materials that came home from school as part of a reading package had many different reading abilities within the same reading level designation. In order for children to learn to read fluently, they should have easy access to many books, articles, and stories *at the proper readability level.* Many young readers try to read above their abilities too early, become frustrated, and tend to give up. Children should read many books, at least 20 per year, at their independent readability levels. There are three levels of challenge of readability: independent (98–100 percent known words), instructional (93–97 percent known words), and frustration level (below 93 percent known words).

One of the largest bookstores in town has a very limited numbers of books with designated readability levels assigned. Only one small section has books with readability levels printed on the bindings, and this is only for the youngest readers. Unfortunately, there's even a problem within this section. The readability levels vary because each publisher assigns its own readability levels. For example, a level three for one publisher is not the same readability level as a level three for another publisher. Take a look at your local library, school, or bookstore and see if this is true in your community.

The process of printing readability levels on each book is easy, but there will need to be a concerted effort to get this done. Advances in technology greatly increase the ability to assign readability levels to each book. There are word processing computer programs that have the programming to give a readability level for any selection. Simply select a paragraph from the beginning, middle, and end of the selection and type these into a word processing software package for analysis. An add-on to your software may be required. Inputting just one paragraph will also give a good idea of the readability level. Teachers often would like to check the readability of a piece of writing. Edward Fry, formerly of the Rutgers University Reading Center, created one of the most widely used and easy-to-use readability graphs for educators. These graphs are available online.

What levels should be assigned? Readability levels should be assigned starting just beyond picture books, containing no words, up to the readability level around the eighth grade. All books could have a readability level assigned, but preschool through eighth grade is the range in greatest need for this designation. Since consistency of all books is of the utmost importance, the designating function will have to be done by one organization rather than by each publisher. The Library of Congress will likely need to require that the readability level be printed on the copyright page of each book. There is great benefit in having the readability levels printed on the binder of the books so that parents, teachers, and children can quickly obtain the most efficient reading resources. Color-coding the books, rather than assigning a number indicator from lower to higher, can also be a benefit children because it's less indicative that one student is reading at a lower level than another. Another benefit to color-coding is that students may be less likely to be tempted to read at the higher levels before they are ready. The color-coding should only be implemented on a national scale once there is complete uniformity; otherwise, there may be more confusion generated. Readability levels should be printed on books as soon as possible. Once this task is complete, a discovery may be made that there are a greater number of books needed at particular readability ranges. My guess is that there may be a need for more books at the first- and second-grade readability levels, but we'll have to wait to see if this speculation is correct. With each day that passes, children are missing out on the opportunity and pleasure that comes by acquiring reading fluency.

Surprisingly, there will be dissenting opinions to printing readability levels on each book; and this is likely why this task has yet to be accomplished. Therefore, the following answers will be readily available.

Concern Number One: One part of the book may be at one readability level and a different part at a different readability level. Answer: Then assign a range to this book; for example readability levels 2.5–3.5.

Concern Number Two: Who will make the assignment of the levels? One professor said, "This is very political; many companies will want to obtain the contract to assign the readability levels." Answer: This professor is right. There is a need to have one company make all the readability level assignments for all the books so that there is consistency. A commission can be formed to determine the proper guidelines for implementation. Interested parties may include academicians, teachers, and politicians. Maybe the Library of Congress will need to initiate this.

Concern Number Three: The right readability levels will be designated, but they won't get assigned to books. Answer: That's okay too; in time the coding of the books will improve, but it won't get better until it's started!

Concern Number Four: Assigning readability levels and encouraging children to read at their appropriate level will stifle creativity. Answer: (Be prepared because this is where you'll hear the greatest and most forceful disapproval.) The proposed idea does not require that every library and bookstore sort their books for younger readers by readability level. If libraries, schools and bookstores want to continue to sort their books by author or publishing company or topic, that's fine. For parents who want to have access to books that will help their child acquire reading fluency, the readability level needs to be available somewhere, and it needs to be consistent for all books. There may be resistance from authors because they will not like that libraries and bookstores will have the option to sort their books other than by author. The best answer to this concern is, "So what!"

Step 2: Determine Readability Level of Each Reader

The second step in this model, after the readability levels of the books are easily identifiable, is to determine the readability level of each reader. This is an important step, and it is much easier to obtain than one might think. Therefore, completing this step should not slow down the process to achieve reading fluency. This may sound too unscientific, but all that is really necessary in order to begin is an educated guess. In this process, the readability levels are readily assessable, so if one were to guess a readability level of 3, and chose books accordingly, but were surprised that their child or student couldn't handle these books, then the next selection would be at readability level of 2.5. It doesn't need to be any harder than that.

ACHIEVE AND **87**
MEASURE
READING
FLUENCY:
EXPANDING THE
OPPORTUNITY

Since the No Child Left Behind Act requires instructional practices to be empirically based, teachers should obtain a precise readability level for each child by using a computer software package that has been tested for reliability and validity. One such program that currently is available is a computer-based, norm-referenced reading test that provides readability levels for students in Grades 1 through 12. A program such as this will likely be necessary in the school setting.

On occasion, allow a child to read up one level if a particular book catches his attention. This will challenge and maintain enthusiasm for the young person without conflicting with the benefits of the system. This should be a rare occurrence and should not be necessary too often assuming there are enough books in each category. If the library doesn't have enough books in each category, then go to a bookstore and invest in your child's future. Just a warning; once at the bookstore, it will be tempting to allow your child to choose any book he wants. Once the readability levels are published on each book, it will be the responsibility of the parent or teacher to have most of the reading *done by the child* at his appropriate level. If there are enough books in each designated category, the child will be exposed to many different words and ideas. This will allow the developing child to enhance and expand his vocabulary and continue to spark interests in various ideas and topics. If a parent is choosing a book to read to the child, then the range of readability levels greatly expands.

Step 3: Use Repeated Reading or Read-A-Lot at the Proper Readability Level Instructional Strategy

Samuels (1979) and Chomsky (1978) developed the methods of *Repeated Reading* and *Modeled Repeated Reading*, respectively, nearly three decades ago. The Repeated Reading technique was based on LaBerge and Samuels's automaticity theory, which showed that fluent readers are those who decode text automatically, leaving attention free for comprehension. Samuels looked at the way reading was taught and determined that teachers often rushed though an entire basal workbook in one school year. For the slower readers, this was difficult because the pace was too fast. Each day was another day of frustration for these students because they could never catch up. Samuels and others (NICHD, 2000; Dowhower, 1987; O'Shea, Sindelar, & O'Shea, 1985, 1987) have shown through empirical studies that Repeated Reading increases fluency by having children re-read a short passage several times until satisfactory levels of word recognition accuracy, speed, and comprehension are achieved. Research by O'Shea et al. (1985) has shown that most of the gains in reading speed, word recognition, error reduction, and expression in oral reading are acquired by the fourth reading. They concluded that, "Four readings appear to be optimal since, after four readings, 83% of the fluency increase between one and seven readings is achieved" (p.138). Based on this research, if a child has read a book four times, it may be a good idea to begin to encourage him or her to gain interest in other books. On the other hand, if a child takes a strong interest in a book and gains strength and comfort, liking this to a blanket for a younger child, it is recommended that the child be allowed to continue to read this book as other books are introduced. A lesson to accomplish this goal follows.

Lesson to Develop Fluent Readers:
Beyond Accuracy to Automaticity

A Teacher Might Say: "Tell me how a person becomes really good at a sport, such as tennis or wrestling, or a musical instrument, such as the piano." Students will know what is required to be good. They will know that a coach is helpful to become accurate in the skill. The students also know that it takes a lot of practice to move beyond accuracy to become automatic at the skill.

A Teacher May Want to: When a complex skill is done with ease and can be done without conscious awareness, we say it is automatic. Encourage students to go beyond word recognition skills to automaticity. (1) Teach the basic skills so that the students can be accurate. (2) Provide practice time so the student goes beyond accuracy to automaticity (i.e., fluency). (3) Because the first two tasks are hard, and students often want to quit when tasks are hard, motivation is essential to keep them on task until they become fluent at their respective grade leveled readability levels.

A Teacher May Want to Have Students Do: Practice Repeated Reading in pairs. Have one student read the text orally while the other student listens; then have the other student take a turn. Students benefit by hearing other students read, and they benefit by hearing the story read numerous times. Prosody improves with each reading, and as prosody improves, comprehension does also. Have the students read many books silently at their instructional and independent reading levels. When students read extensively, they encounter the same high-frequency words over and over again in numerous contexts. As the students see the same words repeatedly, they develop the ability to recognize them as single holistic units.

Lesson Could Be Assessed By: The construct of reading fluency is defined as "simultaneous decoding and comprehension." The indicators of reading fluency are speed of reading and comprehension. The most common method to measure speed of reading is with Curriculum-Based Measurement (CBM) (Deno, 1985). One measure of the comprehension portion of fluency is to have a student read a short passage and immediately have the student retell what was just read.

Repeated Reading is being used today successfully by many children across the country and is being enhanced by technology to deliver the Repeated Reading and Modeled Repeating Reading opportunities that did not exist previously. Technology has made this proven reading method easier to implement by letting the computer do the work of the teacher. Torgeson (1986) states that

ACHIEVE AND **89**
MEASURE
READING
FLUENCY:
EXPANDING THE
OPPORTUNITY

computers have the capacity to deliver motivated, carefully monitored, individualized, and speed-oriented practice in concentrations far beyond those available in traditional assessment. One instructional tool has the children listen to a modeled reading of a passage, and then the children read the passage aloud until they've achieved fluency of this passage. A beneficial aspect of this technique is that during this process, children hear themselves read and are part of the process of determining if they believe they've mastered the passage. Aspects of these programs that help to increase reading fluency include

- Repeated oral reading
- Listening to modeled reading
- Self-monitoring
- Information feedback

Some children are embarrassed to read aloud to others but don't mind reading into a tape recorder and subsequently hearing their own rendition of their favorite story. Students still can read to each other in the classroom since many will enjoy doing this, and enjoyment is always a desirable byproduct of any activity. I've heard the latest idea being practiced in Florida is to have children read to dogs. Apparently the dogs don't laugh when mistakes are made. Maybe that's why dogs are man's best friend.

Sustained silent reading is often used in the classroom setting. Exclusive use of this method is generally not sufficient to obtain reading fluency. The method of Read-A-Lot may seem trite; however, there is a component that can be added to this method that will make this tool quite effective. To be comprehensive, Read-A-Lot should include the phrase *"at the proper readability level."* In addition, if there is a component of comprehension included, this is a great benefit. This can be accomplished by having children answer questions about the story they've just read. This should be done without the opportunity to look back at the passage to locate the answers and should be done prior to going onto the next story. When children read the passage fluently, including answering questions about the story at a satisfactory level, they can move up a readability level.

Tests to Assess Fluency

Step 4: Measure Each Student's Reading Fluency Level

To do so, ask each student to read for two minutes. When finished, count the total number of words read and divide by two. These actions will provide you with the rate of speed at which students can read silently or orally (if the test was an oral reading test).

Consider this scenario. A boy decides that he is a little behind the others in his reading skills. He's confused as to why the boy across the street enjoys reading, and he begins to wonder if he's possibly missing out on something. It's nearing the end of the school year, and he makes the following statement to his teacher: "I'm going to read a lot this summer and be a good reader by the end of the summer." His teacher, who is constantly being asked to prove that her students are successful, responds, "How will you measure it?"

In these times of high-stakes testing, the measurement of fluency is of utmost importance. "Because the ability to obtain meaning from print depends so strongly on the development of word recognition accuracy and reading fluency, both should be regularly assessed in the classroom, permitting timely and effective instructional response when difficulty or delay is apparent" (Snow, Burns, & Griffin, 1998). Measurement of fluency should include the components that make up fluency: ease in decoding (speed of reading), expression in oral reading (prosody), and simultaneous decoding and comprehension. Some students decode text quickly but do not necessarily comprehend what they've read. In this case, they're having trouble defining words and comprehending the story, which includes making inferences from the text, as shown in Figure 6.2.

Fluency is measured currently throughout the country by the Curriculum-Based Measurement (CBM) method (Deno, 1985). This method captures an important aspect of reading, which is to read quickly. This method has the child read aloud for one minute. The number of words *read correctly* is considered to be that child's fluency level. Teachers know that reading fast, without necessarily comprehending, is not what their goal was when they set out to teach children how to read. Therefore, teachers are frustrated by the use of CBM as a measure of a child's reading ability. The reason CBM is used is because it is quick and easy to obtain a gauge of students' reading levels. These characteristics are not to be taken lightly. Part of the reason there is not a better measure of fluency, that includes comprehension, is because adding a comprehension component tends to make the test less quick and less easy, and this is important since there are so many students to be tested. Teachers and parents often lament over the true statement that testing time takes away from teaching time. CBM does correlate well with reading achievement that includes a comprehension component, but in many cases CBM alone is insufficient.

CBM is not telling the whole story; therefore there is a need to explore other measures of fluency that capture the comprehension component. A new measure of reading fluency, or an additional measure that can be given along with CBM to capture the comprehension component, will help to ensure that "no child is left behind," and it will also give teachers one less issue to worry about.

ADDRESSING LEARNERS WITH SPECIAL NEEDS

Learners Who Struggle

Poor readers that received an intensive reading intervention increased their reading fluency. Functional magnetic resonance imaging revealed that the activity in the brains of the previously poor readers "demonstrated increased activation in left hemisphere regions, including the inferior frontal gyrus and the middle temporal gyrus." These are areas of the brain used by good readers (Shaywitz et al., 2004, p. 13). Thus, after the intervention, the brains of children who read poorly began to function like the brains of good readers. This illustrates that if the right reading instruction is presented and the proper resources are available, there is the potential for many more people to become fluent readers than in our current less-than-optimal situation. There is also a

ACHIEVE AND **91**
MEASURE
READING
FLUENCY:
EXPANDING THE
OPPORTUNITY

Figure 6.2   Model to Achieve and Measure Reading Fluency

The goal of this activity is to build fluency for students.

These are the steps necessary to accomplish this goal:

1. Determine readability level of each student.

2. Acquire materials that are at each individual student's readability level.

3. Provide a model of what the selection should sound like. Provide this model in three speeds: slow—have the student point to the words as the selection is being read; medium—have the student visually follow along as the selection is being read; fluent—have the student listen, and visually follow along if possible, while the selection is being read. There are software programs that can be purchased that will do this for the teacher, but otherwise the teacher can read to the children.

4. Record the children as they read the selection at slow, medium, and fluent speeds. Have the children listen to their recordings. Students benefit from hearing their own recordings.

5. Measure each student's comprehension of the article. Use the same questions for each selection. Stories written in America follow the same pattern and children should learn this pattern. This is called a *story grammar.* Ask the students the following questions:

   • *Setting.* What are the place and environment in which the story takes place, and who are the characters? (i.e. "Once upon a time. . .")

   • *Initiating Event.* This establishes a goal. Something happens in the story that creates a goal.

   • *Attempts.* The characters in the story want to reach the goal.

   • *Outcome.* Was the goal reached?

6. Student and teacher determine when the student should leave this passage and move to another passage within the same readability level or the next readability level. This judgment is based on the two components of reading fluency: speed and comprehension. Once a student is reading quickly, with proper prosody and answering a high percentage of the questions correctly, she or he may move to the next passage or level.

gap in reading levels in our country. In Minnesota, and likely throughout the country, there is a socioeconomic distinction where many children from families at lower socioeconomic levels learn to read later and have poorer reading skills than children from families at higher socioeconomic levels. This may partially be due to the inability to acquire the proper reading materials.

Learners Who Are Learning English

Some learners who are learning English as a second language are also falling behind in their reading fluency. Parents not speaking English at home are less able to read stories to their young children or to help their older children learn to read stories written in English. It's beneficial to read to young children and expose them to various types of literature. If a parent is unable to do this, obtaining fluency for the child is more difficult, but it is still possible. To become fluent readers, children need to transition from being read to, to reading by themselves. Current reading technology that requires students to read into a recording device is very helpful to these learners because they can listen to these recordings to improve their fluency. They can hear a modeled reading that has a slow speed (so that each word can be followed on the screen), a medium speed, and a high speed at which students can hear the story read fluently. Students that imitate this, and then hear their own reading of the story, can make significant developmental increases in their word formations and reading fluency.

Learners Who Excel

The methods described in this chapter to increase fluency will be applicable to the students who excel also. These students also need to decode and comprehend at the same time in order to be fluent readers. One strategy for incorporating more difficult curriculum into a classroom, without separating reading groups into ability levels, is to have each group read about the same topic but with different challenging materials. For example, students read about the *Titanic,* but two texts are used. The text for readers who excel has more difficult words, phrase structures, and concepts. For these readers, there likely will be more ideas that are off the causal network. This means that there are more ideas that do not have a pertinent role in the story, but they are ancillary instead. For example, in this sentence, "The boy, wearing the blue hat, ran across the street without looking." The ancillary phrase is "wearing the blue hat."

Thus, the more advanced learners will read stories that are more difficult, and associated questions will also be more challenging. Learners that excel may be able to comprehend well but still may not be reading at a fast enough speed. In this case, reading many books at the student's independent reading level will increase the speed while maintaining good comprehension. If the student's interests can be determined, it is beneficial to help the student locate books on these topics. Students who excel often have interests that are more unusual than those of the typical student.

SUMMARY

To improve reading fluency for many children, readability levels must first be printed on each book from the preschool through eighth-grade level. Next, determine the readability level of each reader. Use Repeated Reading or Read-

ACHIEVE AND **93**
MEASURE
READING
FLUENCY:
EXPANDING THE
OPPORTUNITY

A-Lot *at the proper readability level* instructional strategy to increase fluency. Last, appropriately measure reading fluency by including a comprehension component. If this process is implemented, reading fluency should increase for many children and proper measurement of reading fluency can be obtained.

Our goal is that, through reading this chapter, you can better appreciate the benefits of building every young reader's fluency. Methods of doing so include printing readability levels on each book, repeated readings, and assisted reading. You can teach effective phrasing. May your hard work reveal itself in the manner that occurred for Ms. Hulsey. When she had taught several fluency lessons, she received a note from Allison's mother. It said: "Thank you for all you have done to change Allison's attitude toward reading and herself. She can now read as rapidly and remember as much as her friends, and she is so proud. As a matter of fact, I shed tears of joy upon receiving my Mother's Day present yesterday. Allison ran up to hug me, and said: 'I want to read a couple of my favorite stories that I wrote just for you, and then a book that I've been reading at school just for your Mother's Day. Happy Mother's Day!'"

7

Comprehension Instruction

Scientifically Validated Effective Methods

I never liked reading when I was in first grade. I could never understand or remember anything. Then, Ms. Morton taught me how to understand what the author was saying and why he was saying it. Because of Ms. Morton, I love to read now. I love it so much that I can't stop! I like to come to the end of a book and already know what the ending is even before I get there, 'cause I'm comprehending so good, that's what Ms. Morton says about me. Do you know what? Now that I'm with Ms. Morton, I'm right about the ending too, almost every single time!! I can set my own purpose for reading and I stop a lot to think about what I just read and why it is important to me. Get me another book, quick, Ms. Morton!!!

—Roberto, a second grader whose
parents do not speak English

Reading First defines reading comprehension as the thinking processes used to obtain meaning from print, media, or graphic communications. Reading First legislation also clearly states that "comprehension is the reason for reading" (NICHD, 2000, p. 48) and that all students should become good comprehenders by Grade 3. The qualities of a good comprehender, and the evidence-based instruction that best supports their development, have been identified through 38 high-quality studies. These findings, upon which Reading First legislation was based, are described below.

WHAT TEACHERS NEED TO
KNOW ABOUT COMPREHENSION

Comprehension was judged by the National Reading Panel (NICHD, 2000, pp. 34–39) to be a process that requires continuous attention and instruction (from preschool until the end of students' education) to mature. Unlike the reading skills of phonemic awareness, phonics, and decoding, comprehension abilities are not skills that, once mastered, never need to be relearned. Rather, comprehension is an ability that, with high-quality instruction, constantly deepens and broadens over time, enabling students to appreciate more sophisticated and subtle meanings. In this chapter, we want to add to your repertoire of teaching tools so that all students can comprehend with greater ease, pleasure, and speed.

As Duke and Pearson's (2002) synthesis of comprehension research reported, comprehension instruction must include both explicit, teacher-directed instruction in specific comprehension processes and a great deal of time and opportunities to read silently, write, and discuss text. Exemplary educators teach students *when* and *how* to use each comprehension process. They model how and why students' use of a specific comprehension process, at a specific point in a text, will be successful in obtaining meaning (Block, Rodgers, & Johnson, 2004; Hattie, Biggs, & Purdie, 1996).

The National Reading Panel (NICHD, 2000) reviewed 38 research-based studies concerning comprehension instruction in Grades K–3. The panel found that even the youngest readers should be taught how to comprehend by connecting their thinking processes to the text and their own knowledge, expectations, and purposes for reading. The quality of a teacher's instruction as well as each lesson's instructional goal influences how much students learn. When excellent teaching occurs in the classroom, teachers, administrators, students, and parents should recognize that pupils are reading text with understanding, constructing memory, making mental metacognitive representations of what they understand, and putting new understandings to use when they communicate with others.

Prior to 1990, many teachers taught comprehension by merely giving directions, telling students to "read carefully," assigning workbook pages, or orally asking literal questions after a text was read. Today, however, more effective lessons are being developed by researchers and used by exemplary teachers (Block & Mangieri, 2003; Block, Oakar, & Hirt, 2002). During this past decade, reading researchers have painted a more valid portrait of how instruction can improve students' comprehension. We have learned that effective lessons must meet multiple students' pre-instructional levels of comprehension competence. Such lessons must include ample silent (but teacher-monitored and assisted) reading time and rich student-generated questioning, thinking, discussion, and application of material read. Regardless of the grade level taught, comprehension lessons should include modeling, think-alouds, scaffolding, guided practice, and independent silent-reading opportunities to use comprehension processes independently.

COMPREHENSION **97**
INSTRUCTION:
SCIENTIFICALLY
VALIDATED
EFFECTIVE
METHODS

RESEARCH THAT TEACHERS CAN USE

Research indicates that teachers should divide their comprehension lessons into three types. These strands of highly effective, research-based lessons teach the thinking processes that expert readers use to comprehend (Block, 2003; 2004; Block, Rodgers & Johnson, 2004). Six research-based findings follow.

Good Readers Set a Purpose for Reading and Apply What They Read to Their Lives

Good comprehenders identify reasons for reading fiction, nonfiction, magazine articles, current event items, technical manuals, and technologically based text. Exemplary comprehension lessons should provide time for students to be taught from, and have time to practice reading, a wide variety of high-quality genres every year. Expert readers also stop and reflect while they read, apply what they read, and put important ideas into their own words for themselves and others through rich classroom discussions.

Good Readers Initiate Their Own Comprehension Processes to Overcome Confusion in Texts

These processes include (1) predicting, (2) looking for important information, (3) recognizing authors' main ideas, (4) drawing conclusions, (5) putting themselves in the book to obtain a complete understanding, (6) summarizing, (7) inferring, (8) using details, and (9) identifying causes and effects, comparisons and contrasts. Each year, as students proceed through school, the instructional methods that teach these processes should become more advanced. When such graduations occur, students' comprehension abilities keep pace with the depth and density of text at subsequent grade levels.

Good Readers Infer, Draw Conclusions, Image, and "Think About Their Own Thinking" While They Read

Expert comprehenders have been taught how to control their own reading, adjust their speed to match the difficulty of the text, and to set a purpose for the reading. While reading, they infer, draw conclusions, and image. After reading, they check their understanding, reflect on what they have learned, and apply it to their lives. Research has demonstrated that younger readers who image or visualize while they read comprehend and remember more than peers who do not visualize (Pressley & Afflerbach, 1995). Before most students can reach this level of independent reading ability, they have to be taught how, when, and why to use each of these comprehension processes.

Good Readers Make Use of Prior Knowledge to Make Meaning

Expert comprehenders use their experiences, knowledge of the world, vocabulary, and the information gained from the previously read sentences in a text to formulate their ideas as they read.

Good Readers Use Features Within Text, Story Structure, and Graphic Organizers to Make Meaning

These readers know that graphics can help them organize and relate ideas to each other and can highlight important concepts. Story structure refers to the order of content and events of a narrative or expository text. When students are taught how to read story formats or the structure that fiction plots follow and then the components of nonfiction text in different genre, they significantly increase their appreciation, understanding, and memory for the nonfiction text (which will be described in more depth in Chapter 8).

Good Readers Generate and Answer Questions to Help Them Understand Inferential and Literal Meanings

Research shows that teacher questioning strongly supports and advances students' comprehension, particularly when the questions are those that are described in Figure 7.1 (NICHD, 2000; Omanson, Warren, & Trabasso, 1978). These questions are effective in improving students' comprehension because they

1. Add purpose to students' reading

2. Focus students' attention on what they read

3. Encourage students to monitor their comprehension

4. Help students review content and relate what they have learned to what they already know

5. Require that students understand information to formulate an answer

6. Assist students to ask questions of themselves while reading so that they can better monitor that they truly understand what they are reading

7. Integrate information from different segments of a text

NEW CLASSROOM-PROVEN, RESEARCH-BASED PRACTICES

Teaching Comprehension

Helping students to become more powerful comprehenders is hard work, especially when you differentiate the roles that you play in your comprehension instruction. You can learn how to lead three distinct strands of comprehension lessons, called Comprehension Process Instruction (CPI), and address the six research-based findings, stated previously, so that all your students can become good comprehenders.

Strand 1 Comprehension Lessons

Strand 1 lessons are teacher-directed lessons that provide rich, engaging, expanded explanations and demonstrations of comprehension processes in

COMPREHENSION **99**
INSTRUCTION:
SCIENTIFICALLY
VALIDATED
EFFECTIVE
METHODS

Figure 7.1   Comprehension Challenge Questions

(Comprehension Challenge Questions Are Posted on the Board and Asked Every Day During One Week)

1. Why?

2. Is the most important point _____ or _____?

3. What do you mean by "_____"?

4. If I understand, you mean _____. Is that right?

5. Where will the point you are making not apply? How does _____ relate to _____?

6. If you idea is accepted, what is the greatest change that will occur?

7. Would you say more about _____?

8. What is the difference between _____ and _____?

9. Would this be an example:_____?

10. Is it possible that _____? What else could we do?

11. If _____ happened, what would be the result?

action. Strand 1 lessons implement the four phases of a lesson plan that the National Reading Panel (2000) recommended. The goal of Strand 1 lessons is to preteach students how to make meaning. There are several methods that you can use to reach this goal.

The first is Comprehension Process Motions (CPM). These are hand motions that use kinesthetic and tactical depictions of silent, unobservable mental processes that must be engaged for a student to comprehend and make meaning, as described in greater depth in Block, Rodgers, & Johnson (2004). Posters contained in that publication that can be displayed and used during CPM lessons enable students to see, feel, and initiate the thoughts that expert readers use. Examples of the Comprehension Motion for Inferring and Drawing Conclusions are in Figure 7.2. These are *thinking guides.*

A thinking guide is a graphic depiction of the steps involved in performing a comprehension process. They are available in prepublished commercial formats, such as those that appear in Block & Mangieri (1995a, 1995b, 1996), or they can be teacher-constructed, graphic organizers of the steps and processes expert readers use to set a purpose, infer, draw a conclusion, identify cause and effect, or recognize relevant details, etc.

Figure 7.2   Teach Comprehension Through Thinking Guides and Motions
(Inference Process as an Example of Thinking Guide)

How to Infer

Name: _____

Date: _____

What Is Said or Read +	Interpretations of What = You Know	Inference of What Author Meant

---

A third type of Strand 1 lessons is a think-aloud. A think-aloud is an
instructional method whereby you read a section of text, stop reading, and tell
students the comprehension processes and thoughts you had to understand
that piece of information.

After the introduction and discussion of the processes, read a model aloud,
and tell students what you did to use these one or two comprehension processes
to make meaning as you read. Then have students read silently from a text for
10–20 minutes, depending on grade level. After reading, do not ask literal,
interpretative, or application questions, but those on Figure 7.1 to raise
students' levels of reflection.

COMPREHENSION **101**
INSTRUCTION:
SCIENTIFICALLY
VALIDATED
EFFECTIVE
METHODS

These questions have one characteristic in common. They cannot be answered unless students comprehend the text. Questions such as "What did you like about this book?" can be answered whether or not the student understood the text. Such questions do not improve students' ability to use two comprehension processes to make meaning.

Last, conclude all Strand 1 lessons by saying, "Whenever you come to points in a text like this in the future, remember to think in both these ways, and think about what your mind is doing to help you develop the deepest, fullest meaning."

In summary, Strand 1 lessons begin after you identify the literary processes that students need to comprehend a particular text. Prepare a brief description of one or two of these thinking processes and select a Comprehension Process Motion (CPM), thinking guide (i.e., visual depictions of thinking steps in a comprehension process), or self-stick note that can graphically depict them. When introducing each process, present at least three examples, or think-alouds, so as to teach students *how* and *when* to use the processes.

*Example of a Strand 1 Lesson: Teaching Students How
and When to Use More Than One Comprehension
Process While They Read, and to Recognize
That Many Thoughts Must Occur to Obtain More
Complete Meanings From Text*

This lesson takes several days to complete. It teaches students how to set their own purpose prior to reading, infer, and draw conclusions while they read. The ultimate goal of this lesson is that students will learn how to select and initiate the comprehension processes that are most needed at points in a text when they are needed to make meaning. This lesson contains the following steps.

Step 1: Explain to the students *how* and *at what point* in a text they should set their own purpose (i.e., at about page 3 of a text), how to infer while they read, and how to draw conclusions near the end of a book or chapter. Each of these explanations take place on different days, and students can practice them individually until they can employ them without teacher prompting to do so. You can use the example of an inferring process thinking guide in Figure 7.2 to teach the steps in inferring.

Step 2: When students have learned how to set a purpose (see lesson that teaches that process in Figure 7.3), infer, and draw a conclusion, teach students to use more than one comprehension process when they read a book by using the self-stick note lesson: Make three self-stick notes as shown in Figure 7.3. Then, read two to four pages and do a think-aloud that shows *how* and *where* you set your own purpose for reading. Ask students to state their purposes.

Step 3: Put a self-stick note that asks students to write their purpose for reading on the bottom of pages 2–4 of another text. Ask them to write their purposes on that self-stick note and then to read on.

Figure 7.3   How to Teach Using Self-Stick Notes

Step 1: Read two pages

Step 2: Ask students to set their own purpose for reading

Step 3: Read two additional pages

Step 4: Ask students to infer using inference self-stick notes

Step 5: Ask students to draw inferences until you reach the end of the book using the same process as in Step 4

Step 6: Ask students to draw a conclusion using the draw conclusion self-stick notes

Teach Students How to Think About More Than One Comprehension Process While Reading a Book (Comprehension Process Motions for Inferring and Drawing Conclusions Are Shown by the Arrows on the Following Post-it Notes)

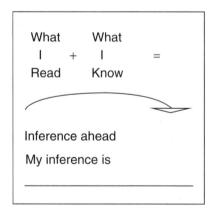

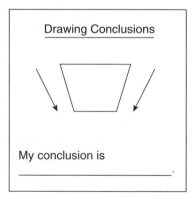

[The *arrows* show the motions students are to make with their hands to create Comprehension Process Motions. These are 2 of 15 that have proven to significantly increase students' comprehension.]

COMPREHENSION **103**
INSTRUCTION:
SCIENTIFICALLY
VALIDATED
EFFECTIVE
METHODS

Step 4: Demonstrate how to infer. Explain that you were able to infer because you recognized clues in the way the author wrote the first three pages. Then, use the Thinking guide in Figure 7.2 to let students create five inferences with you, as they think what will appear on the next page, after you read the page before it. Tell the students what these clues were. Next, place another adhesive note on the edge of page six or seven of a new book. Read pages one to five of this book and write your inference on the adhesive note before you turn the page. Describe how you inferred again. Then, allow students to write their inferences on adhesive notes with a new book.

Step 5: Ask students to make their own inferences and tell you how they did so. They write their inferences on their self-stick notes. They turn the page. If their inference was correct; they put a √ on the back of the self-stick note and write their name or initials. If it is wrong they put an X and write their name or initials.

Step 6: On the next day, students who wrote a √ work in a harder book and repeat the processes as they have learned. Those who wrote an X work with you in a small group to relearn. Follow the steps above again with these students.

Step 7: Teach students how to draw conclusions (the CPM symbol for it appears on the self-stick note in Figure 7.3). Place this self-stick note near the end of the book, at the climax, and before the page in which the author draws the conclusion in that book. Read up to that point and do a think-aloud about how you knew the conclusion. Write it on the self-stick note and then turn the page and describe how your conclusion is like the authors' conclusion and how you knew that was the conclusion that the author was leading you to make. Then, give students another book to practice these comprehension processes alone, while you reteach individually those who have difficulties.

Step 8: Have students place all three self-stick notes shown in Figure 7.3 at appropriate points in a book. As students reach the first self-stick note, they write their purpose, and then place their initials and a √ if their purpose was reached in that book or an X if it was not. Students write their inferences, a √ or an X, and their initials to indicate how correctly they inferred. Last, they write their conclusions, a √ or an X, and their initials on the last self-stick note. When students turn in their self-stick notes you can group them for future reteaching based on which processes individuals mastered and did not master.

Strand 2 Lessons

Strand 2 lessons differ markedly from Strand l lessons. Strand 2 lessons provide more time for students to practice reading texts silently in monitored conditions. Through these lessons, students receive personalized, direct instruction from their teachers in the form of 30-second mini-interventions while they are reading independently and silently. Strand 2 lessons also provide one-on-one instruction through shared readings, paired learning activities, independent silent reading periods, and guided practice sessions.

Strand 2 lessons create time for students to "live within books" while teachers deliver mini-interventions at points of need. The goal of Strand 2 lessons is to provide more time for students to practice engaging the comprehension processes learned in Strand 1 lessons when they read silently, ask for one-on-one mini-interventions from their teachers when they cannot initiate these processes independently, and enjoy books at school. In this strand of comprehension lessons, before students read they are reminded to establish their own purpose, recall the processes taught in previous Strand 1 lessons, and self-initiate these processes.

In subsequent weeks, post a Comprehension Challenge Question on the board each week. This list grows until students ask all the questions on Figure 7.1 automatically and practice them independently while they read silently. While students read, you carry a clipboard with a class roster attached to it. As you move from student to student, ask individuals to describe when they asked themselves the Comprehension Challenge Question, why they asked it, and how they knew the point in a text where they used it was a good one in which to stop and ask that question. Next, mark how well each student did on the class roster you are carrying. You also go to students who raise their hands when they come to a confusing passage. You ask what they tried and why, teach how to overcome that difficulty in the future, and tell them that you will return during the next Strand 2 lesson to see if they can use the processes you taught independently. Last, decide who should join a reteaching group to learn a strategy, address a metacognitive Comprehension Challenge Question, or relearn another comprehension strategy that has not yet become automatic.

*Example of a Strand 2 Lesson: Teaching Students to Ask
Questions of Themselves and Monitor Their Own Comprehension*

To introduce this lesson, you can share with students that a common element exists among highly successful people: they ask questions of themselves and others when they become confused or want to understand completely. This Strand 2 lesson teaches students how to stop and ask for help when confusion arises and to unravel comprehension difficulties for themselves. These lessons differ from traditional silent reading periods because students are told to raise their hands when they come to a point in a text when they are confused. You then conduct a mini-intervention with each student to teach him or her how you knew which process to call upon to unlock a particular unknown meaning. The comprehension process that you used to overcome that confusion is thereby retaught in about 30 seconds.

This mini-intervention is called *PAR*. When students raise their hands when reading silently alone, you ask what a student has tried to overcome the literacy challenge, and you praise the correct aspects of the student's attempt (*P* in PAR is *praise* to build the affective domain). Next, you teach the unknown word or concept (*A* in PAR: *add* cognitive challenge). Finally, you raise the student's level of self-efficacy by holding the student accountable in the future, when similar confusions arise, to use what he or she has been taught (*R* in PAR, to *raise* self-efficacy to increase metacognitive abilities). Using Strand 2 lessons enables students to move to higher levels of understanding more frequently

COMPREHENSION **105**
INSTRUCTION:
SCIENTIFICALLY
VALIDATED
EFFECTIVE
METHODS

because their teachers (and peer leaders) become personal coaches, at their sides when they experience confusion. Through these 30-second mini-interventions, students' silent reading periods are disturbed only momentarily. As a result, they can enter into a more enjoyable flow of living inside an author's message and experience the pleasure of loving to read.

Strand 3 Lessons

Strand 3 lessons are providing a new direction in reading comprehension. The goal of Strand 3 lessons is to teach students how to identify their own comprehension strengths and weaknesses. This strand of comprehension lessons provides time for students to select what they want to learn about comprehension and to choose which processes they want to learn. These lessons are based on the premise that readers usually recognize when comprehension breaks down in their reading and value learning new comprehension processes *after* confusion has been experienced.

Strand 3 lessons occur on a weekly basis so young readers can *select* which comprehension processes they want to learn to increase their understanding and enjoyment. Students are the most aware of the level of effort and drive they are willing to expend to become better comprehenders, and Strand 3 increases that level of effort and drive by fostering (1) students' intentional and deliberate thoughts about their comprehension; (2) a flexible, adaptable understanding; and, (3) an ability to select (and combine) appropriate comprehension processes when needs arise in texts.

Recent studies have demonstrated that although good and poor comprehenders use similar comprehension processes, good comprehenders are willing to persist in using and adapting these processes until they ascertain the meaning (Afflerbach, 2002). Without Strand 3 lessons, poor readers tend to reuse very few processes; they attempt to comprehend every text using the same limited set of comprehension processes, and reading soon becomes a frustrating task to avoid (Block & Pressley, 2002). Their abilities to discover and savor subtle meanings remain untapped, which in turn limits their capacity to kindle the emotions, drive, and desire that emerge from experiencing meaning.

Students need opportunities to discuss new methods they create to make meaning and to identify what they want to learn to comprehend better. In these lessons, students tell their teachers or peers which skills and strategies they use to read text, as well as what kind of help they need to comprehend material more completely. If Strand 3 lessons are not included in a comprehension program, students' ideas about how they can become better readers could be overlooked. In contrast, when students express their metacognitive self-perceptions, they make new discoveries about themselves as readers. Their desires to improve their own comprehension abilities expand (Block, Rodgers, & Johnson, 2004). They seek to read more difficult text and overcome larger comprehension challenges (Block & Rodgers, in press; Block, 2003). Most important, Strand 3 lessons allow students to choose what they want to learn *about the reading process*, not simply to choose a book or discuss a content subject.

Table 7.1   Discovery Discussions: Teaching Students the Process of Asking
Questions and Assessing Their Comprehension

1. Create a chart on which you and students can sign up for discovery discussions. Create a folder in which you can record the information discussed in discovery discussions.

2. Explain to students how to sign up for a discovery discussion. Specify that they can sign up for as many as one every week if they want to discuss new discoveries that they are making about their reading abilities.

3. Hold no more than three discovery discussions a day so you are not depleted of the energy to stay intently focused on each student's story about his or her reading abilities.

4. Allow students to make the first comment to open the discovery discussion. If they do not, begin with a question. Among the best are

   • "What have you discovered about your reading (or writing) abilities?"
   • "What are you learning about comprehension?"
   • "What do you want to learn to comprehend more?"
   • "What is bothering you about your reading abilities?"
   • "What can I do to help you learn to read better?"

5. When students share an insight, paraphrase and ask if you heard them accurately. If you have observed that a student has increased comprehension in a specific way, ask if your observation is accurate. Then the student can agree or explain what they believe has contributed to their growth and can demonstrate the new process.

6. To become a trusted mentor, you cannot rush from one student to another. Rather, provide your undivided attention to single students intently. The most important section of discovery discussions often occurs at the end. It is at this latter point when many students gain the confidence to risk asking a very important question or sharing an insight about their reading weaknesses. Without discovery discussions, many students will not have the courage or opportunity to describe their weaknesses from their perspective. End by asking

   • "What would you like to learn the next time we have reading? and why?"
   • "What is your next goal in reading? When will we revisit this goal to see if it has been reached?"
   • "What do you want to do to help you reach it? How long will it take?"
   • "How can I and others help you the most?"

7. Record the date by which the student wants his or her goal to be reached, develop an action plan to reach it by listing methods and providing time to work on the goal, and return to the written plan on or prior to the day the goal is to be reached.

Example of a Strand 3 Lesson: Discovery Discussions

As described in Table 7.1, Discovery Discussions are one-to-one teacher-student conferences in which you discuss what students have discovered about comprehending text since the last time you met.

A second type of Strand 3 lesson is a "buddy reading," when the pairs discuss *what they are doing to comprehend a book.* It is called *Buddy Beside Me As I Read.* It teaches students how to decode, learn vocabulary, generate and answer

COMPREHENSION **107**
INSTRUCTION:
SCIENTIFICALLY
VALIDATED
EFFECTIVE
METHODS

Figure 7.4   Buddy Beside Me As I Read

Step 1: Student A reads one page

Step 2: Student B summarizes page that was read

Step 3: Student A asks Student B a question about what was read

Step 4: Student A predicts what will happen on the next page

Step 5: The process is repeated with students exchanging places as reader and listener

comprehension questions, infer, become a more fluent reader, and summarize in one lesson (see the Learning Pairs Box in Figure 7.4 for a complete description). This Strand 3 lesson differs from other paired learning activities because when two students read a book together they *do not* discuss the book itself. Instead, students write or discuss what they did *to comprehend* that book. They share what processes they had in common.

In summary, Strand 3 lessons use learning pairs or small groups to provide opportunities to share what they do to comprehend, discuss their strengths and weaknesses, and identify what they want to learn next. You divide students into small teacher-reader groups based on common needs or interests. You work with each group. You allow each student to describe his or her individual skills and weaknesses relative to a particular comprehension process in which everyone in the group is interested (i.e., learning to draw valid conclusions). You and students suggest methods that other group members could try as a means of improving their abilities relative to that process. They list these methods on a chart. Students then report to the class what they learned in their group. Through Strand 3 lessons, readers' abilities to diagnose and overcome their individual comprehension weaknesses improve (Block & Johnson, 2002).

TESTS TO ASSESS COMPREHENSION

The traditional method of measuring students' comprehension has been to ask a series of questions after students read. This assessment method has been followed in classrooms, on standardized tests, and in more recently developed Reading First criterion-referenced state tests. The degree to which these assessments can reliably measure students' ability to draw meaning from text depends on how well they have been taught and learned the comprehension strategies and processes described in this chapter. In many instances, students are given comprehension tests that include questions which measure concepts that students have not been taught in Strand 1, 2, and 3 lessons. You can change this unreliable assessment process.

First, you can ensure that the basic comprehension processes in this chapter have been taught. You can also use other types of comprehension assessments. One of the most effective was described in Table 7.1, Discovery Discussions. When you engage in regularly scheduled Discovery Discussions over the course of the school year, the information you gain documents the rate and depth of individual students' comprehension skill. Similarly, you can administer the Active Reading Chart (Figure 7.5) as a measure of how much students are initiating comprehension processes automatically, and how deep and broad their comprehension abilities are.

Another comprehension test is engaged through the following steps. On your classroom blackboard, write an ongoing list of the comprehension processes that you have taught during a specific grading period. Ask individuals to read to a specific point in a text in which one of the processes on the board should have been engaged to obtain the richest meaning. Ask the student which of the processes listed on the board was initiated at that point in the text. If the student's answer is correct, you have measured that the student knows which comprehension process is needed at that specific point in a text to derive meaning. If the student's answer is incorrect, you have diagnosed a process that needs to be retaught. Another comprehension test also involves the actual measure of comprehension processes as students perform them. The directions for this measure, Comprehension Motions Test, follow.

When you introduce a new comprehension process, teach students to kinesthetically use their hands to mimic the silent mental processes that you intend for them to use while they read. After you have demonstrated this motion, and asked students to practice the Comprehension Process Motion several times, ask students to signal the comprehension process that they are thinking about with the Comprehension Process Motion you taught as you read a book orally. (A complete description and charts to display of the Comprehension Process Motions you can teach appear in the Appendix of Block, Rodgers, & Johnson, 2004.) When students perform a Comprehension Process Motion, stop your reading and ask them to describe the comprehension process they signaled and why that process assisted them to make meaning at that point in the text. Record their comments on a master grid until you have asked every child to describe every Comprehension Process Motion that you have taught.

This comprehension assessment can also occur whenever you ask students to raise their hands when they are reading silently so that you can help them immediately overcome their individual comprehension difficulties. At that point you can re-teach a process that could help them overcome their specific difficulty.

Last, you can keep a classroom monitoring sheet. On it, you list every student's name along the left margin. Every row on the sheet is labeled by a comprehension process that you want to assess. Then, when you ask comprehension questions orally in small or large group discussions, you can place a check in the row and column that indicates that a specific student knew how, and used, a particular comprehension process in answering your question.

There is never a day that goes by that you cannot complete a comprehension assessment and add new information to your classroom checklists and comprehension-monitoring sheets.

ADDRESSING LEARNERS WITH SPECIAL NEEDS

Learners Who Struggle

Struggling readers are less aware of the purposes of reading expository text than their more able reading peers. For this reason, it is important that we

COMPREHENSION **109**
INSTRUCTION:
SCIENTIFICALLY
VALIDATED
EFFECTIVE
METHODS

teach them how to set a purpose more often than regular readers. It is also important to note that struggling readers will lose their comprehension gains whenever they don't make connections of concepts read with their background knowledge (Langer & Close, 2001). For this reason, it is important that students with learning disabilities receive direct instruction individually using the activities in this chapter.

Moreover, Duke and Pearson (2002) remind us that one of the most important findings of NCLB and Reading First research is that comprehension instruction must include both explicit instruction of specific comprehension processes and a great deal of time and opportunity for actual reading, writing, and discussion of text. It is also important, thus, that we teach learning-disabled students when and how to use each of the processes described in this chapter, and we must teach them why a particular process will be successful for them (Hattie, Biggs, & Purdue, 1996).

Moreover, very disabled readers deviated from very good readers in the brain activation patterns whenever reading required them to break up words into their underlying phonologic structure or sound pattern (Barry, 2004). Soon we will have the capability to use brain imaging to diagnose students with reading difficulties, and we will be able to diagnose them earlier and more precisely than we can now. Until this research becomes available, we already have sufficient research data about learning disabilities to tell us that students must be taught using visual, auditory, kinesthetic, and tactile methods, and

1. That words can be broken up into sounds

2. That letters represent these units of language (phonics)

3. That there are sounds of language

Learners Who Are Learning English

English language learners are often placed in small groups in which they receive extra practice in phonics and decoding. Unfortunately, such instruction does not assist them in their ability to find answers in books. Students in higher-level ability groups are often required to give answers in complete sentences, and ELLs are not. This is a second detriment to their ability to comprehend. In addition, students who are placed in the highest-level group are asked to do a second type of comprehension processing that is often not required of English language learners. This is to infer and to apply the text to their lives. Thus, some important qualities we can build into English language learning include (1) requiring ELLs to meet in small groups and practice the comprehension lessons presented in this chapter, (2) requiring them to give answers in complete sentences, and (3) asking them to infer and apply the text to their lives.

Learners Who Excel

Gifted learners profit from active reading charts, which are independent higher-level thinking guides that increase their abilities to ask themselves questions and to monitor their comprehension while they read. Making copies of the

Figure 7.5   Active Reading Chart to Increase Students' Abilities to Ask Themselves
Questions and to Monitor Their Comprehension While They Read

What characters have we met so for?	What seems to be the main conflict or problem as this point?	What questions have I asked myself while I read?	What is my prediction about what will happen next?
Chapter 1:			
Chapter 2:			
(etc.)			

SOURCE: Adapted from the original "Active Reading Chart" created by Carol Santa (1996). In
Project CRISS (p.95). Dubuque, IA: Kendall/Hunt. Used by permission.

chart found in Figure 7.5 can assist gifted students to read by themselves to raise
their comprehension to higher levels while you are working with other groups.

SUMMARY

The purpose of this chapter was to assist literacy coaches and teachers to
increase the number of research-based comprehension practices that are used in
their reading instructional programs. Three strands of lessons have proven to
significantly increase primary students' reading abilities. Literacy coaches can
use this information to build a schoolwide program, assist individual teachers to
increase their students' comprehension abilities, and as a foundation for assessing comprehension instruction when they observe it in action in classrooms.
Teachers can use the information in this chapter to increase their skills in differ-
entiating their comprehension instruction. Students, particularly low-level
students, need the variety described in this chapter before many will develop the
ability to become independent comprehenders. The overarching goal was to
assist each educator to advance the reading abilities for all students. In the
process may the information presented here assist all children to come to love
reading as an instrumental part of their lives and to comprehend more deeply
and broadly, thus increasing the information and pleasure they gain from text.

8

Independent Reading and Shared Reading of Trade Books

With the Practitioner's Voice of Kristen Williams

Ms. William's first graders read trade books every day. They build their decoding, comprehension, vocabulary, fluency, oral language, and writing abilities within the milieu of enjoying high-quality literature. They view reading as a valuable activity that brings meaning and joy, so much so that their attention almost totally rotates around gaining meaning and not on decoding words. Thus, it did not surprise Ms. Williams when she asked her class a question from her phonics program. She queried: What would they get if she took the c off of coat? *Instead of processing this question at the lowest level of thinking about the sounds letters make, the class thought about how useful a coat could be if it were an oat. Almost in unison, the class answered: What they would get if she took the c off of* coat—was A JACKET!! *Ms. Williams credits this meaning-based response to the amount of time that her students spend reading and learning through pleasurable literature. These frequent, independent trade book reading opportunities have changed the way her students think about and process text. The methods she uses to achieve this goal are described in this chapter.*

For many years teachers have seen the advantages of using trade books in their instruction. Research has proven that students receive the following benefits from trade book reading: increased self-esteem; an appreciation for varied literature; and enhanced decoding, vocabulary, fluency, comprehension, and writing abilities (Block & Reed, in press). Prior to 2004, studies conducted to validate independent reading practices produced conflicting results because most were based on observational or correlational data only. The National Reading Panel report (NICHD, 2000) prompted researchers to extend this body of knowledge. Many researchers wanted to examine if sustained silent reading and other types of engagements in book-length reading opportunities affected student achievement. As a result, new scientifically validated practices have been created, and they are described in this chapter.

WHAT TEACHERS NEED TO KNOW ABOUT INDEPENDENT READING PRACTICE

A recent study proved that if today's students are to increase their engagement in and receive pleasure from independent reading, it is important that educators place the very best books in students' hands. This new post-September 11 generation of readers (identified as Generation Y students by the Carnegie Foundation) (Carnegie Foundation, 2001) need to read recently published, high-quality books as the first books they read about a topic if they are to most fully engage in the concepts to be learned. This principle must be followed because students today need to have settings in nonfiction and fiction to which they can readily relate. Today's youth are conditioned to enter new content rapidly, due to their more continuous use of Internet texts, video games, and rapid paced movies and television shows. For this reason, content in trade books must be reported in context that students have experienced or can easily understand.

Thus, for today's teachers to capture students' attention, they must use the very best, most recently published literature relative to concepts that they are introducing (Block & Mangieri, 2003). When you obtain this literature, you will not only have taken the first step toward providing the type of reading instruction that your students want, but you can significantly increase the amount of time which your students spend reading and learning from books at school.

A second major advantage to having students read the best, recently published trade books is that they can more readily engage the learning principle of *fast-mapping* to increase their reading abilities. As previously discussed in Chapter 5, fast-mapping is a term used to denote that students use the same high-level comprehension process at least six times in a row so that they develop the ability to rapidly initiate this high-level metacognitive thinking process as they read independently. Fast-mapping enables students to develop a schema in which they know how it feels to initiate higher-level thinking processes while they read, and they become more sensitized to the need to initiate such comprehension processes at certain points in future texts without having to be prompted by their teacher to do so. This self-initiated, self-prompted cognitive patterning is defined as an *ongoing, self-initiated schema.*

When instruction occurs only through worksheets or teacher-directed reading of short texts, students develop an *externally prompted, stagnant schema*. This type of schema requires external prompts from the teacher before higher-level metacognitive thinking is ignited.

Because prior to enrolling in your class many students may not have ever learned how to develop an ongoing, self-initiated schema, it is important for you to help them develop this schema by providing time for students to read recently published trade books and to couple this with fast-mapping instructional practices. These recently published trade books should be the first books you use to introduce a topic, and the second book you teach can be a classical award-winning text. When you follow this instructional sequence, students can learn to fast-map the use of their own high-level metacognitive processes and self-initiate their own self-prompted schema relative to concepts read.

Another recently published finding is that exemplary teachers use other distinct practices to teach reading through trade books. First, they include twenty minutes of independent reading time accompanied by high-quality teacher monitoring. When their primary-aged students read silently, they continuously move about the room answering students' questions, providing definitions for difficult words the minute students have trouble, and explaining difficult concepts that individuals ask to be clarified. This practice is coupled with the requirement that students read two books on the same topic, back-to-back, to solidify terms and concepts. The first book on a new concept is usually introduced by the teacher, through a shared oral reading, and the second is read independently and silently by students. In addition, these teachers also keep individual student records and ensure that every objective taught is tied to students' demonstrated use of that reading skill in trade book reading.

Exemplary teachers know that this new generation of students values books that show them how to become more self-reliant and that teach ethics and morals. Generation Y readers value worldly characters that are realistic yet exhibit optimism toward the world. They want their books to include the concepts of hope, peace, and caring for others (Block & Mangieri, 2003). This new generation of readers reports that they need books which also intertwine innovative print formats and rapid-paced action in their plots (Block & Mangieri, 2003). They also report that it is important for the content in books to demonstrate how they can become more connected to their peers in positive ways. The students of today are not teacher pleasers; instead they expect their teachers to tell them why they should select and follow certain guidelines as they read and to convince them that it is important to read high-quality books through the valuable, highly effective lessons which the teachers lead.

Providing high-quality books by award-winning authors is also important because these books provide well-crafted English sentences so that students can learn English writing structures and grammatical forms. Such books also follow predictable, well-developed plots so that students can more easily comprehend new words and ideas independently. When such books are used, you can also teach students to comprehend and depend upon the writing structures that characterize fiction and on the specific disciplines described in individual nonfiction selections. When students become aware of authorial writing patterns, this knowledge is known as *tilling the text.* Tilling the text means that students have been taught to skim the textual features of tables of contents and chapter titles and subtitles, as well as the length and depth of individual author's word choices and paragraph structures to predict what will appear in upcoming text. Tilling the text enables students to engage their metacognitive comprehension processes from the moment that they pick up a book to read. This engagement has proven to significantly increase comprehension (Block, 2004a).

As we begin the 21st century, it is important to also note the responsibilities that we hold as educators for building abilities to read a wide variety of genres. The most recent research concerning building comprehension of book-length text focuses on two goals that have been demonstrated to significantly increase students' reading achievement: teaching students *how* to read nonfiction, expository texts, and changing *what* we do when we read books aloud to students (Block, Rodgers, & Johnson, 2004).

The first goal (teaching students *how to read nonfiction*) is important for several reasons. First, the majority of test items on all tests written after 1998 contain nonfiction portions. For students to demonstrate how well they read, they have to know how to comprehend this type of text.

Second, when students learn that they can skim and scan when they read nonfiction, they come to value both fiction and nonfiction texts more (Block, 2004a). When we show them how to "skim and scan until they want to stop and savor," such instruction provides greater affective and cognitive responses not only to nonfiction but to fiction as well (Block & Pressley, 2002; Block & Dellamura, 2001; Block & Mangieri, 2005, 1995a, 1995b, 1996) The reason for this is that if children read everything using the same thought process, they don't learn to use tilling-the-text metacognitive thinking or appreciate the format clues that authors provide when they write nonfiction, poetry, autobiographies, or fiction. When children are taught these formats, the unique clues of each genre, and the special textual characteristics of the writing style within different content domains, students learn to appreciate the wide range of printed materials available to them, which helps increase their knowledge and pleasure from reading.

Third, reading trade books aloud has been cited as the most important activity for building the knowledge students require for vocabulary decoding, comprehension, and later reading success (Anderson, Hiebert, Scott, & Wilkerson, 1985). Research has proven that reading aloud has many benefits, which include inspiring students to write, demonstrating the rhythm and flow of the English language, promoting students' motivation, improving vocabulary, broadening genre appreciation, building comprehension, encouraging visual imagery, and developing concepts of print (Anderson et al., 1985; Loxterman, Beck, & McKeown, 1994; Sticht & James, 1984; Block, 2004b).

Last, it is important to teach children *how* to read nonfiction because our world is becoming more rapidly paced with greater amounts of information being created. Due to this, students may lose a sense of stability and security as to the role that they play in their world and in the world of others. By reading nonfiction they begin to understand that no matter how often events seem chaotic, rapidly paced, or out of control, there are certain rules of nature and laws within disciplines upon which students can depend. This sense of stability and security is becoming very important for Generation Y readers.

RESEARCH THAT TEACHERS CAN USE

Research has just been completed to test the significant effects of trade book reading (Block & Reed, 2004; Block & Reed, in press; Block, 2004b). Results demonstrated that there are 23 statistically significant benefits to students' literacy achievement that arise when the methods described in this chapter are used to build students' independent reading abilities. The most significant effects of book reading occur when trade books are selected by students and teachers to meet the current needs of students. The new-generation readers have distinct reading needs (Block & Mangieri, 2003; Block & Reed, 2004). The reasons behind these needs are that the students of today are faced with a world that is chaotic and coarse, and it must be met head-on without the benefits of adult filters to interpret mass media, trauma, or crises. Without adult filters children experience blunt reality beginning at a very early age. Teachers can no longer anticipate or explain in advance major life-changing events. Past experiences are often irrelevant and invalid sources of information for use in students' future lives. Generation Y students have adult-like thinking patterns at earlier ages and can learn more advanced concepts at earlier ages than students of past generations could.

For example, in a recently completed set of studies, more than 800 preschool through high-school students were interviewed. The objective was to find out what today's students want from their teachers that would improve literacy instruction. "We want teachers to use real books that also teach us how to be kinder and fair" was the most frequently cited response (Block & Mangieri, 2003). When we accomplish this goal for our students, we will have taken another important step in teaching from trade books in ways that statistically significantly increase their literacy achievement on state-based criteria- and norm-referenced tests. New research is presently being conducted to learn more ways that trade books can be incorporated into elementary classrooms to increase students' achievement. Here are some of the questions being researched:

1. Should initial instruction on *most* concepts begin with full-length books that have been published within the last six years?

2. Are newer books necessary for today's students to more rapidly identify with the characters and settings about which they are to read?

3. Is an "instantaneous identity" with content in a nonfiction and fiction book more important for low-achieving students than for their more able-reading peers?

4. How can we measure if students engage a schema and build upon it from page one of a book, and what are the exact effects of this engagement (e.g., will it enable even less able readers to more rapidly decode, learn new vocabulary, and comprehend at higher levels than would be possible through books that do not relate so completely to students' lives)?

NEW CLASSROOM PROVEN, RESEARCH-BASED PRACTICES

Teaching Independent Reading

One of the main goals in helping children become independent readers is to help them transfer comprehension processes independently. Currently there is ongoing research concerned with helping students to become better comprehenders when they read books silently. The following are several research-based methods that are being further explored in present research studies.

Teacher-Reader Groups

The first, scientifically based trade book reading method is called *Teacher-Reader Groups.* In these groups, students re-teach a small group of students a comprehension process the day after or the next few minutes after you have taught that process. A single student becomes the Teacher-Leader of a Teacher-Reader Group. This Teacher-Leader re-teaches what you have taught using either the same book or a different book. This lesson frees the teacher to go around and hear how children are describing the comprehension process. The benefit of Teacher-Reader Groups is that this reading method allows you to understand how much the children have understood from your instructions and what you need to re-teach on the next day. It also helps assist students' internalization of the comprehension process because they have to verbalize the steps in the comprehension process, answer questions, and begin to put the process you just taught in their own words.

In another type of Teacher-Reader Group, a group of students chooses a comprehension process about which they want to learn more. All students who want to become better at using those processes meet together in a Teacher-Reader Group. A specific comprehension process is then re-taught by the Teacher-Leader and discussed by all, using trade books that each student selects to bring to the group. You can begin this type of Teacher-Reader Group by writing scripts for Teacher-Leaders. These scripts will contain three questions or statements that relate to the steps that you taught initially concerning the comprehension process being discussed by the group. For example, if you taught students to infer, using the thinking guide and lesson described in Chapter 7, you could write the following three questions on a sheet of paper to hand to Teacher-Leaders who conduct Teacher-Reader Groups in the future to build inference abilities:

1. What methods have you used to take what you read and add it to what you already know about a topic you are reading?

2. What methods have you used to add together everything that the author has told you in the book already to infer what the author means but does not say?

3. How long does it take you to add all the author clues together to infer, and do you sometimes stop reading to think about the inference the author may want you to make at that point in a book?

During Teacher-Reader Group meetings, students discuss how they accomplish a particular aspect of the reading process. All students bring their favorite books to the group meeting and demonstrate how they make meaning, infer, draw a conclusion, etc. As they demonstrate, they also discuss and ask questions about how they can learn to overcome specific reading problems relative to that domain of comprehension. The suggestions for overcoming these problems are recorded on a Teacher-Reader Group Thinking Chart, which is later shared with the other groups. Students are required to stay with the same group for at least two meetings; however, most remain in the same group for four or more lessons, electing not to change before they feel comfortable that they can perform the comprehension process under discussion independently.

Between each Teacher-Reader Group meeting time, students practice the suggestions they learned. In the next week's meeting, peers teach the new things that they have learned about the aspect of making meaning for which the group has been assembled. The leader of each group records students' findings on the group's Teacher-Reader Group Chart so that the teacher can track each group's progress.

A teacher meets with only one Teacher-Reader Group at a time. At the beginning of the year, other Teacher-Reader Groups either meet at a different time that day (so that the teacher can also be present) or on different days. By midyear, some teachers train students to lead these groups alone so that all students can meet in different groups at the same time. During these lessons, you can move from group to group to note progress being made in each group's understanding of the comprehension process being discussed. Such lessons are conducted most effectively if no more than three Teacher-Reader Groups meet each week so that the students can have three choices of comprehension processes about which they can learn more.

Self-Stick Note Prompts

A second method researched to increase students' independent use of comprehension processes is called *Self-Stick Note Prompts.* This lesson begins by you writing a specific comprehension process that you have taught on a self-stick note and posting it at a point in a book in which that process should be initiated to obtain the richest understanding. Then, students are to write what they did when they used that comprehension process at that particular point in the book. For example, you would write, "Set your own purpose for reading this book" on a self-stick note and post that note after about page three in a book, because it is at this point that this comprehension process should be engaged for the richest understanding of this book to occur. When students are reading the book by themselves and reach that self-stick note, they write the purpose they have set for themselves for reading it on it in the book. In subsequent lessons, you would use self-stick notes to enable students to write their inferences in the middle of a book and the conclusions that they are drawing near the end of the book, before the author writes the conclusion that he or she drew.

After each self-stick note lesson, you can collect every child's book and grade what they wrote on each of these three self-stick notes to determine if they used the one to three comprehension processes you wanted to measure.

Read-Alouds That Build Independent Reading Abilities

Reading trade books aloud to students is one of the best methods of advancing comprehension, higher-level thinking abilities, vocabularies, and an appreciation for literature. It also develops a sense of story—a schema for how stories work. Moreover, reading aloud to preschool and kindergarten children helps them learn the difference between written and spoken language. For example, when students are read to, they see the connection between what they hear and the symbols that make meaning in print (Sticht & James, 1984).

Another reason for the power of this instructional activity is that for one section of each day you become "face-less." As you read, students can befriend an author they have come to love. These authorial friends have closeness to your students that you do not; authorial friends have not corrected students' errors or asked them to take risks. These friends always see students at their very best. Authors can unconditionally transport their student friends to places they've never been, especially when the following books are shared: *Teddy Bear, One Leaf Rides The Wind, The Three Questions, Enemy Pie, Tough Cookie, Paul Revere's Ride,* and *The Clifford Good Deeds* series. Authors also keep students' interest from day to day with cliff-hanging chapter endings (e.g., in *Summer of Fear* and *The View from the Cherry Tree*).

Moreover, when you read to students, slower readers are on equal footing with better, fluent readers. In sharing the beauty and power of the written word, each student experiences the effects that precise, well-chosen words can have on thinking. Through this realization, students often become convinced that the hard work required to create such language is worth it. The steps in an effective reading-aloud experience follow.

Step 1: Select and Practice. Become a good oral reader. Practice reading the book, preferably out loud, before you share it with students. Vary the genres you read to build your students' literary tastes. Vary your voice for each character, and use your voice to create sound effects and build suspense.

Step 2: Decide on a Reading Objective You Want to Teach By Reading this Selection. The objective can be to (1) call attention to an aspect of the author's style that students can use to improve their writing, (2) enjoy and share students' responses to the book at the end of the read-aloud, (3) strengthen a listening or reading comprehension skill, such as asking students to describe what was happening in their thinking as they listened, (4) increase students' speaking ability by having them note a particularly vivid phrase they want to use in their conversations, or (5) build reading vocabulary by writing new words on the board as you read them in the book.

Step 3: Create a Captivating Introduction for Your Reading. This introduction can be an interesting fact about the author of the story (for a list of books that describe author's lives, see Chapter 11, or type the author's name into Google to obtain the Web site they maintain concerning their life experiences and books' histories), an insight that you gained through reading the book, or a description of the first time you read the book and what it meant to you.

Step 4: Decide How Students Will Give a Response to the Reading. Before you read, decide how you will elicit students' responses when the oral reading is finished. After reading, it has proved to be most effective if you allow students to make the first comment. By doing so, you can be sure that students have a chance to tell you what they truly thought was most important about this shared oral reading. When they make the first comments, students are more in charge of the discussion, which has demonstrated to significantly increase their appreciation for read-alouds (Block, 2003). Table 8.1 lists books that children most often request to have read aloud. The list was compiled from contributions made by each of the teachers represented in this textbook and by researchers.

1. Sample questions that you can subsequently ask to solicit other students' responses follow:
   * Was there anything in the story that troubled you?
   * What images, feelings, or memories did the reading stimulate?
   * What was there about the way the book was written or the ideas in the book that influenced you most? Why?
   * Were you disappointed or surprised by something in the book?
   * What questions or comments come to mind? Don't worry about how important a thought or issue may be to others; if it's on your mind, it's important and I want to hear it.

2. Instead of asking students to retell the story to assess their listening and reading comprehension, select a crucial detail and ask students what role that detail played in establishing meaning.

3. To strengthen students' cause-and-effect thinking, ask them to explain why characters behaved as they did. Second- and third-grade students can also discuss whether character actions were prudent or imprudent, appropriate or inappropriate, rational or irrational.

4. To build students' interpretive thinking, ask them to state the theme or moral of the book. Also have them identify generalizations that were not adequately supported.

5. Have younger students re-create the story on flannel boards, as a group or in pairs.

Step 5: If You Are Going to Read a Multichaptered Book, Read From This Book Daily Until It Is Finished So Students Are Not Left Hanging. Each day ask students to share ideas and feelings about events that you read, and then ask, "What is likely to occur in tomorrow's reading?" "How do you know that your inference is likely?" "What comprehension processes did you use or what clues did the author give you?"

Step 6: When You Read, Sit Down. Pull students close. Make sure that everyone is comfortable. Put a sign outside the room asking people to come back to the room at a specified time (when the oral reading time is over). This reduces interruptions between students and their authorial friends.

Table 8.1   Text Sets to Practice Tilling the Text and Award-Winning Chapter Books

Reading Level	Series With Same Book Characters	Author
First Grade	Clifford, The Big Red Dog	Norman Bridewell
	Jullian Jiggs	Phoebe Gilman
	Arthur	Lillian Hoban
	Frog and Toad	Arnold Lobel
	George and Martha	James Marshall
	Little Critters	Mercer Mayer
	Little Bear	Else Minarik
	Amelia Bedilia	Peggy Parish
	Curious George	H. A. Rey
	Henry and Mudge	Cynthia Rylant
	Mr. Putter and Tabby	Cynthia Rylant
	Marvin Redpost	Louis Sachar
	Harry (The Dirty Dog)	Gene Zion
	Nonfiction Books	Eric Carle
Second Grade	Amber Brown	Paula Danzinger
	Pee Wee Scouts	Judy Delton
	Kids of Polk Street School	Patricia Reilly Giff
	Horrible Harry	Suzy Kline
	Kids on Bus 5	Marcia Leonard
	Junie B. Jones	Barbara Park
	Nate the Great	Marjorie Sharmat
	Boxcar Children	Gertrude Warner
	Peter Cottontail	Beatrice Potter
	Magic School Bus	Scholastic
	Encyclopedia Brown	Donald Sobol
	Nonfiction: All About _____	Scholastic
	Ask a Question About Nature	Scholastic
Third Grade	Harry Potter	J. K. Rowling
	Nancy Drew	Carolyn Keene
	The True Confessions of Charlotte Doyle	Avi
	Nothing But the Truth: A Documentary Novel	Avi
	What Do Fish Have to Do With Anything?	Avi
	The Summer of the Swans	B. Byars
	The Pinballs	B. Byars
	Cracker Jackson	B. Byars
	The Wretched Stone	C. Van Allsburg
	Just a Dream	C. Van Allsburg
	Sleeping Ugly	J. Yolen
	Julie of the Wolves	J. C. George
	Sounder	W. H. Armstrong

To reemphasize the importance of reading orally, you should know that Beverly Cleary and Russell Baker state that the turning point in their lives (the point when each decided to become a writer) occurred when a teacher of theirs read something they had written aloud to the class. Both writers say that through this activity, they realized for the first time that others could and did enjoy their writing.

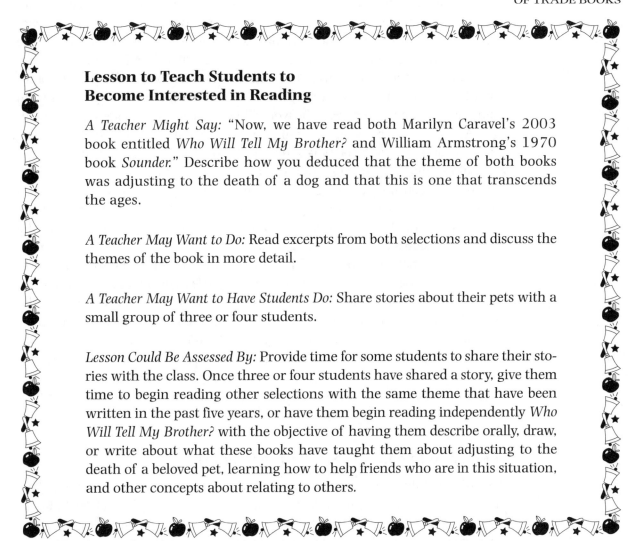

**Lesson to Teach Students to
Become Interested in Reading**

A Teacher Might Say: "Now, we have read both Marilyn Caravel's 2003 book entitled *Who Will Tell My Brother?* and William Armstrong's 1970 book *Sounder.*" Describe how you deduced that the theme of both books was adjusting to the death of a dog and that this is one that transcends the ages.

A Teacher May Want to Do: Read excerpts from both selections and discuss the themes of the book in more detail.

A Teacher May Want to Have Students Do: Share stories about their pets with a small group of three or four students.

Lesson Could Be Assessed By: Provide time for some students to share their stories with the class. Once three or four students have shared a story, give them time to begin reading other selections with the same theme that have been written in the past five years, or have them begin reading independently *Who Will Tell My Brother?* with the objective of having them describe orally, draw, or write about what these books have taught them about adjusting to the death of a beloved pet, learning how to help friends who are in this situation, and other concepts about relating to others.

You can vary the activities you complete in the above steps. For instance, sometimes before you read, you can put a piece of construction paper over the cover of a book and do not show pictures within the book as you read. This lesson is designed to build children's abilities to image. After you finish the book, ask students to describe or draw one or more images that they created as you read. As they describe or show their images, inquire into what they did to image—which details helped them and how they put details together in their minds. Then, ask the class to discuss or draw the photo they deduce that the illustrator would have created to convey the big idea in the book and would have placed on the cover of the book. Ask students to explain the reason for the cover picture chosen by the illustrator and how the picture that they created for the cover was also a valid one to convey the main idea of the book. In subsequent lessons, you can vary the read-aloud experience by introducing facts about the author, connecting students' experiences to the book, discussing the genre, introducing the main characters, or pausing after reading a few pages to help students set their own purposes before reading on.

During reading, you can decide whether students will be allowed to comment while you read or not. If students prefer not to comment during the reading, you can have them raise their hands and ask someone in class to list the names of the students in the order that they raise their hands. When the reading is finished, the students then have the opportunity to contribute in the order that they raised their hands to say something about the book, as you return to the page in the book to re-read the words that triggered each student's comment.

Another valuable instructional variation for read-aloud lessons is to partially cover words in the book if your objective is to build students' independent decoding abilities. In this read-aloud, you place part of a self-stick note over all but the first consonants and first vowels in a word. Then, as you read, when you come to the first self-stick note, perform a think-aloud to demonstrate how you sounded out the first letters of the word and combined those sounds with the comprehension strategies of using semantic and syntactical clues to determine what the partially covered word had to be. Next, as you come to each subsequent self-stick note, ask individual students to describe what they thought as they used the first sounds of the word with context clues to deduce what the word had to be that the author wrote. This lesson enables students to use their phonetic skills, vocabulary knowledge, literal and inferential comprehension processes, structural analysis skills, and context clues in unison to decode the words in the book. This real-world application experience has proven to be more effective, especially for less able readers, than practicing each skill separately (Block & Reed, in press, 2004).

Lesson to Encourage Nonfiction Reading

Allow children to have a friend beside them as they read nonfiction. This is an easy modification to make and will assist children to learn how to fall in love with nonfiction. To engage this lesson, all you do is ensure that anytime that you ask students to independently read a nonfiction selection, two students will be allowed to read it side by side from the same book silently, orally, or through the use of an assisted or repeated reading activity. Allow them to skim and scan a book until they find something of great interest that they want to pause and really learn about. In this way, they do not feel that they have to read every single word in a nonfiction book. They can read nonfiction differently than they read fiction, which increases the pleasure of reading both genres. Nonfiction reading becomes fun because students can pause, reflect more often, and select the sections that they want to savor because these are the parts of the book that are of greatest personal interest. Fiction reading becomes fun because students can be totally transported to a literary character's world and become lost in the experiences that unfold as students read each subsequent word that the author has chosen to transport readers into that character's life.

Two Books at Once Method

The next scientifically validated lesson is entitled *Two Books at Once.* This lesson begins anytime you plan to introduce a new subject, idea, or concept. As you plan this introduction, you select two trade books on that same subject that you share with children. With the first you allow them to skim and scan, as you slowly turn the pages of this book which is shared with the entire class or small group of students. Then, with the second book on the same topic, you ask students what section they want to read as you slowly turn page by page. They will ask you to read the sections that relate to the parts of the first book which captured their attention and interest. This lesson demonstrates and allows students to practice reading nonfiction and shows how such reading experiences are different from fiction reading.

To implement the second phase of the Two Books At Once method, you assemble pairs of nonfiction books on several different topics for which the class has previously expressed interest or your past experiences have proven to be of interest to students of this grade level. Next, allow pairs of children to select two books on the same topic that are of particular interest to them. Then, these pairs read those books as you just demonstrated. When they have finished, they meet with you to describe what they have learned about how to read and learn the most from nonfiction.

In closing, it is important to stop at suspenseful spots when you share fiction or nonfiction. When reading a picture book, be sure the children can see the pictures clearly. If you have a child who needs to keep his or her hands occupied during reading, ask that child to hold the book with you. This diminishes classroom management problems.

TESTS TO ASSESS INDEPENDENT READING

To assess students' independent reading success you can use a *midyear survey.* A midyear survey is conducted after the first half of the year, right before winter break. It is composed of three parts. Each part has questions that each student, Grades 2 and above, responds to in writing. In younger grades, you can ask these questions of students individually and have them respond orally. To get a more valid result for the younger grades, it might be better to have someone else (an adult volunteer or an older student at your school) ask the question. That way students don't give answers they think you want to hear. The three questions that compose a midyear survey are

1. What activity did we do so far this year that has caused you to learn the most about how to become a better reader and why did this lesson help you so much?

2. If we were to use this activity more often in the last half of the year, what do you recommend that we eliminate so that we will have time to do so? Why do you think we could eliminate what you suggested and not hurt others' ability to learn to read better?

3. What have we not done so far this year that you would like us to do? Why would this lesson help you to learn more?

4. What have we done that caused you to learn least, and why did you not learn much with this method?

By conducting a midyear survey right before you leave for winter vacation, you have time over the vacation period to plan the activities that students desire. Some teachers wait until the end of the year to ask students what they most valued in their classes. By changing the timing, through the midyear survey students' needs are addressed and students become partners in planning their own reading lessons.

ADDRESSING LEARNERS WITH SPECIAL NEEDS

Learners Who Struggle

Learners who struggle have proven to profit most from lessons that teach them to till the text. Among the first steps in planning lessons which reemphasize and reteach these tilling-the-text strategies is to identify key features that individual authors use to clue meaning. You then enable learners who struggle to meet with you as you perform think-alouds to demonstrate tilling-the-text strategies that you used to identify the authorial writing pattern and clues to meaning in the book that you are sharing with them. After each think-aloud, ask students to perform it themselves and discuss how that set of thoughts can assist them when they read other books. Define for students that attending to authorial writing style is recognizing the logic that a writer followed when making the book and recognizing how the author divided the parts of the topic into sections and subtopics. In performing this analysis, less able readers can be led to realize that dense concepts and writing styles require more intense use of comprehension and metacognitive processes and that each book they read was built by the author with a specific purpose in mind.

You can also help special learners understand the connections between events in a story by using a story map or story frame and teaching the types of paragraphs that authors use. A *story map* is a graphic in which students write the setting, characters, first event, second event, third event, problem, solution, and theme or moral or lesson of a book as or after they read the text. A *story frame* includes the same information but appears in an outline form. The understanding that these two thinking guides provide increases students' abilities to predict while reading (Loxterman, Beck, & McKeown, 1994). When connections between writing formats are made clear, readers who struggle also begin to think ahead more frequently and gain a greater sense of control over their own reading abilities.

In like fashion, less able readers find it easier to make meaning in reading and writing when they recognize the function that single paragraphs perform in a text. The next section describes the functions of paragraphs and how to teach them. When you provide this information, many learners who struggle come to understand for the first time that sentences are put together in predictable manner. As a result, reading can be viewed "more like a friend" because it begins to possess qualities of dependability and predictability.

The last instructional method is to teach students to recognize authorial writing patterns. Nonfiction writers will usually put their main idea as the first or last sentence of each paragraph. They also will use the remaining sentences in each of their paragraphs to describe details. Usually, an author will write subsequent sentences in a paragraph that describes only how, what, where, when, or why. When learners who struggle learn to pick out which of these five types of details a specific author uses most, they become better able to predict the subject of oncoming sentences in that author's paragraphs. Each of these teaching experiences can build the abilities of learners who struggle with comprehension, decoding, vocabulary, and fluency.

Learners Who Are Learning English

As stated above, both ELLs and learners who struggle profit from explicit instruction about what types of paragraphs authors use. This instruction is a type of tilling-the-text lesson, and it builds students' abilities to use all the clues in a specific author's writing style to fully engage in and comprehend each section that they read. This tilling-the-text lesson is comparable in value to the activities that farmers engage to till the soil, ensuring that all ingredients are present before planting. Through such cultivation, more nutritious fruits (meanings) can be produced. In essence, comprehension advances when students learn how to (1) attend to an author's writing style as they read by scanning the text for subheadings and print features (by using such authorial writing features as the length of paragraphs and the amount of white space left on each page) to determine their own purpose for reading as well as to deduce how much conceptual thought will be required to understand that text; (2) establish their own purposes for reading; (3) use their own background knowledge to expand and not interfere with meaning-making; and (4) initiate metacognitive strategies to make meaning and overcome obstacles while comprehending that specific text. The think-alouds that you can use to teach ELLs to master these comprehension processes are found in Block and Israel (2004).

Learners Who Excel

Many parents and educators request the most recent information concerning gifted learners. The following Web sites can provide this important information. Within these Internet links, you can find information about diagnosing, teaching, and assessing numerous qualities of gifted readers from preschool to Grade 3.

Internet Sites for Parents of Gifted Children

Center for Gifted Education, http://cfge.wm.edu
- Focuses on needs of gifted and talented individuals
- Publishes language arts units for gifted readers
- Offers curriculum resources in reading for gifted and talented children

ERIC Clearinghouse on Disabilities and Gifted Education, http://www.ericec .org
- A resource for parents on a wide variety of topics related to gifted children

The Gifted Child Society, http://www.gifted.org
- Parent forum to address concerns about parenting gifted children

Gifted Children Monthly, http://www.gifted-children.com
- A newsletter for parents of gifted children

National Association for Gifted Children, http://www.nagc.org
- Offers parent resources, booklists, and summer enrichment programs and resources
- Publishes the magazine *Parenting for High Potential*
- Sponsors a Virtual Exhibit hall to search for literacy products and resources

The National Foundation for Gifted and Creative Children, http://www .nfgcc.org
- Provides pamphlets, free resources, recommended reading lists, parent's guide, and information on raising a gifted child.

The National Research Center on the Gifted and Talented, http://www .uconn.edu
- Presents current research on gifted education and talent development
- Offers parent resources for special gifted populations

Smart Kid at Home, http://www.smartkidathome.com
- Site for parents who home school

World Council for Gifted and Talented Children, http://www.worldgifted. org
- International organization for gifted children and support for parents

SUMMARY

This chapter was designed to report recent research-based lessons that increase students' independent reading abilities of books. We now know that independent reading and taking proper steps to share trade books with children significantly increase their reading achievement. In this chapter, we describe the importance of allocating 20 minutes a day to student reading of award-winning trade books with high-quality teacher monitoring. We have discussed how to teach children to read nonfiction different than they read fiction. We have introduced more information about comprehension process motions that can be used to increase students' comprehension of trade books. These motions were initially described in Chapter 7 and are elaborated upon here. We then described three additional methods that can help all children to improve their reading ability: Teacher-Reader Groups, Self-Stick Note Prompts, and reading aloud. To address learners who struggle and English language learners' additional needs, tilling-the-text methods of teaching authorial writing patterns were described. When gifted students' needs are not met, the information provided on the list of Web sites can assist teachers and parents to meet them. When you place students in pairs, teaching them how to read two books back-to-back on the same subject can be especially valuable. Last, to assess students' ability to profit from silent independent reading of trade books, you can administer the midyear survey and monitor their reading continuously.

In closing, all of the information in this chapter was designed to increase the power of the independent reading and shared reading portions of your reading program so that you can increase your students' power of and pleasure from reading.

Figure 9.1   Using a Graphic Organizer to Help Develop Concepts for Writing

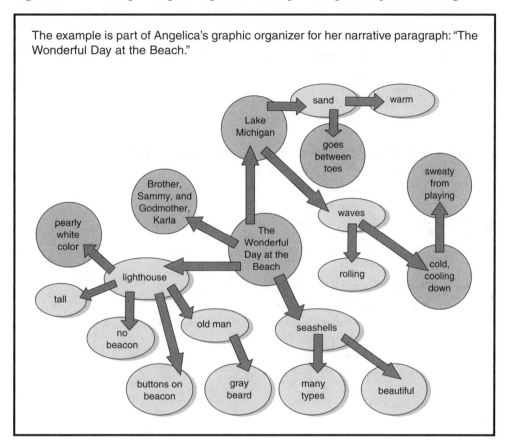

The example is part of Angelica's graphic organizer for her narrative paragraph: "The Wonderful Day at the Beach."

NEW CLASSROOM-PROVEN, RESEARCH-BASED PRACTICES

Teaching Writing

There are a number of practices that classroom teachers can employ to enhance the writing craft in their students. The purpose of this section is to focus on three key practices and provide some concrete sample lessons for each.

Lesson l: Leading Students in Rich Discussions About Writing Using Quality Literature

This is the first lesson and sample activities that help students improve their writing craft. The first two activities in this lesson are related to developing effective reading comprehension as you teach writing. The third activity is intended to apply directly to increasing the quality of student writing.

Activity 1.1: Teaching Students How to
Use Quality Literature as Models of the Writing Craft

One of the best resources to model good writing skills is quality children's literature. Teachers can use literature to illustrate the writer's craft in several ways, (e.g., writing settings, creating memorable characters, showing different points of view, and using lively language effectively). Table 9.1 offers examples

Table 9.1   Books That Illustrate the Writer's Craft

Books That Illustrate How to Write Settings

The Town Mouse and the Country Mouse by Jan Brett
The Teeny-Tiny Woman by Jane O'Connor
Jumanji by Chris Van Allsburg
Charlotte's Web by E. B. White
Bridge to Terabithia by Katherine Paterson

Books That Illustrate How to Write Memorable Characters

The Tale of Peter Rabbit by Beatrix Potter
Frog and Toad are Friends by Arnold Lobel
Charlotte's Web by E. B. White
James and the Giant Peach by Roald Dahl
Hatchet by Gary Paulsen (any Gary Paulsen books)
Roll of Thunder, Hear My Cry by Mildred Taylor

Books That Illustrate Different Points of View

The True Story of the Three Little Pigs by Jon Scieszka
The Three Little Wolves and the Big Bad Pig by Eugene Trivizas
Frog and Toad Together by Arnold Lobel
Doctor De Soto by William Steig
Sarah, Plain and Tall by P. MacLachlan

Lively Language Books

Dr. Seuss Books
Brown Bear, Brown Bear, What Do You See? by Bill Martin Jr.
Koala Lou by Mem Fox
Night Noises by Mem Fox
Chrysanthemum by K. Henkes
Two Bad Ants by Chris Van Allsburg

---

of quality literature that have been used with great success to teach each of these areas. By reading aloud these selections, you can initiate discussions of how each author used a particular writing craft.

Activity 1.2: Read-Alouds With Writing Craft Discussions

After you read a picture book, expository book, poem, or a section or chapter from a longer text, your discussion about the passage should flow naturally. Discussion usually highlights the plot or technical information given in the text. Students are frequently called on to react to the reading in a personal manner. Then, to teach students about the writing craft, you can take the discussion further by focusing on one of the best features of the passage read. For example, in *James and the Giant Peach* by Roald Dahl, characters are well developed. After reading each section, you could lead the children in a fertile discussion about the personality of each character and the words and actions the author used to portray such strong personalities. After such rich discussion, you can also help students extrapolate the learned skill to student writing. For instance, you might ask

MAKING **135**
STUDENTS'
WRITING
COME ALIVE:
STRATEGIES
FOR TEACHING
WRITING

- How could this technique be applied in your writing?
- How could you make your characters have stronger personalities?
- What might they say? What might they do?

Activity 1.3: Teaching Students About the
Writing Craft Through Author or Theme Studies

Author studies have become popular vehicles for promoting reading literacy in classrooms. These studies can also be used to promote writing. Reading and discussing the works of a famous children's author can help children understand the characteristics of the author's work—what the author is famous for including in books. For example, after reading several of Jan Brett's books (*The Mitten, The Gingerbread Baby, The Hat*), Ms. Havera, a second-grade teacher, researched some of Ms. Brett's working techniques. She discovered that Ms. Brett does extensive revisions for her books and that it takes her almost a year to write and illustrate one book. Ms. Havera's students had never realized that a published author of Ms. Brett's stature would ever need to do even one revision. As a result, the students saw the importance of revision in the writing process and were more willing to work at revising their own stories.

Theme studies are another effective way to bring children's writing to life. All of the third-grade teachers in a rural elementary school participated in a Cinderella unit of study. First, teachers shared over 30 different versions of the Cinderella story from around the world. Then students discussed the similarities and differences of each version as they charted and graphed them. After thoroughly analyzing all of the versions, the students embarked on writing and illustrating their own versions. The results were amazing. Reluctant writers who formerly wrote only a sentence or two were writing lengthy versions of their Cinderella stories. Because of their familiarity with the basic format for a Cinderella story as well as their extensive knowledge of all of the possibilities for different versions, students wrote stories that were original and exhilarating to read.

Lesson 2: Teaching Students Practical
Strategies to Enhance Their Writing Craft

This lesson and set of activities enables you to provide real-world activities and exercises that will continually enhance student writing. This lesson includes activities which teach students how to become word enthusiasts, how to develop effective narrative text structures, and how to initiate a specific writing craft through your minilessons.

Activity 2.1: Teaching Students
to Become Word Enthusiasts

> *The difference between the right word and nearly the right word is the same as that between lightning and the lightning bug.*

> —Mark Twain

An excellent author has a way of weaving exact words into beautiful sentences. Authors are articulate in language usage and are able to find just the right word with the precise connotation to share the subtleties of their thoughts. Teachers who are word enthusiasts can create a love for words and their meanings with their students (Sloan, 1996). Teachers can instill pride in their students as they help them learn new words to express their deepest thoughts to their peers, parents, and others in their conversation as well as in their writing. The two goals that teachers should have in helping their students develop their vocabulary are to increase the students' meaning vocabulary and to increase the students' expressive vocabulary.

Activity 2.2: "Word of the Day" (or Week)

There are several versions of this activity that you can initiate to complete the goal of increasing your students' writing vocabulary. Students can keep personal journals or class word walls of interesting words they encounter as they read. Then, you can set aside a few minutes each week to discuss the meaning of new and unusual words after you finish a read-aloud with students.

More important than hearing new words is discussing and learning their meanings. Alphabet books are an excellent source for youngest students to learn new and unusual words. Following are other activities for helping students become wordsmiths.

Activity 2.3: Lively Language Words

The idea for this activity is that the teacher or students select three words from each book they read. The selected words should be those that are considered lively because of their pronunciation and/or their meaning. The selected words should be unusual, not part of everyday language. For example, in *Song and Dance Man* by Karen Ackerman, the Lively Language Words might be: vaudeville, half-moon taps, and grand finale. Think of the kaleidoscope of learning that could develop from the discussion of the selected Lively Language Words within the context of this delightful story of a song and dance man in the good old days.

Activity 2.4: Evolve a Word

Students tend to overuse certain words in their conversations and writings. This activity can help students' vocabulary evolve to higher levels. Mr. Mitchell, a third-grade teacher, found that his students overused the word *awesome,* so he had his students brainstorm a list of alternatives and synonyms. They created a list of over 20 ways to say *awesome* in their writing. Their challenge was to refer to the class list when writing to choose an alternative word for *awesome* or to be even more creative and develop a new synonym. Mr. Mitchell found this technique to be so effective in improving his students' writing vocabulary that throughout the year he and his class developed several more lists to evolve words and grow their vocabularies.

Activity 2.5: Turn a Beautiful Phrase

Developing expressive vocabulary means helping students develop the subtleties and nuances of our language. To begin this activity, you select four or five

MAKING **137**
STUDENTS'
WRITING
COME ALIVE:
STRATEGIES
FOR TEACHING
WRITING

illustrations from an unfamiliar quality children's literature book, such as a Caldecott winner, making sure the author's words are not visible. Provide several copies of each picture and pass them out to the students. Each child is to study his or her picture individually and write ten phrases that could describe the picture. Then the students gather in small groups (one group for each picture) and share the phrases they wrote. As a group, they are to select the three best phrases to share with the class. Students should be able to defend their choices. Then the chosen phrases are compared with the author's words followed by a rich discussion on why the author selected his or her words.

Activity 2.6: Word Mime

This activity can be used to help students understand connotations or shades of meaning. You select a group of action words that are very similar in meaning, such as *ran, trotted, galloped, skittered, sauntered, sprinted, jogged, scampered, scuttled, darted, dashed,* and *scurried.* (Choose a variety of grade-level-appropriate words.) Students are divided into small groups and assigned three or four of the words from the list. They research their words and determine how to act them out so that the subtle shades of meaning are apparent. The rest of the class tries to match the action with the word. This activity has the added benefits of helping students develop and improve their articulation skills when making word choices in their speech.

Activity 2.7: Poetic Expression

Students need to be exposed to poetry so they can learn to love the beautiful language of poetry. You can help children portray their personal reactions to poems through artistic expression. For example, while you orally read some of Shel Silverstein's humorous poems, students could be drawing pictures that come to mind. Other forms of artistic expression could be painting or sculpting with clay. You guide students in rich discussions after the experience. Students' expressions of emotion through their art will be as varied as the students themselves. This activity has the added benefit of helping students to understand that people react differently to the same poetry reading.

Lesson 3: Teaching Students How to Develop Effective Narrative Text Structures

In writing narrative text, student writers need to learn how to make all components of narrative text structures effective in creating the mood and style they desire. This strategy would include such things as creating memorable characters, creating realistic as well as exciting settings, and exploring different points of view. These are all areas of story grammar that can be modeled through quality children's literature. Table 9.1 lists some literature resources for modeling effective narrative text structures.

Memorable characters make a narrative text come alive. How can characters like Charlotte and Wilbur be forgotten? The art of creating memorable characters is a writing craft that can be taught to students. Here are several suggested activities to help students focus on creating memorable characters.

Activity 3.1: Characters We Know

One of the best ways to help students learn about memorable characters is to share memorable characters from quality children's literature. After reading a story or chapter, teachers need to guide students in discussing the main characters, traits of the main characters (supported by actions and words), and personal reactions to the main characters. For example, children in Ms. Huttsell's first-grade classroom love to read stories from the Frog and Toad series by Arnold Lobel. Frog and Toad are very interesting characters who are quite different from each other. Her students created a chart of character traits for Frog and Toad, including examples from the stories to support their choices. A typical entry was similar to this entry for Toad: trait—silly; because—he sings to his seeds.

Activity 3.2: Character Connections

Students can make characters memorable by visualizing their characters and by connecting their characters to themselves or people they already know. Help students visualize their created character by closing their eyes and making a mental picture of their character as they answer basic questions:

- Is my character a boy, girl, animal?
- What does my character look like (size, color, etc.)?
- How does my character move?
- What are my character's facial expressions?

Have students draw their mental image on paper so they can retain it. Then ask students to think about what kind of person their character is and connect their character to a real person or combination of several people they know. Remind them that they must always keep their character connection in mind when they write so that their character says and acts like a real person.

Activity 3.3: Figurative Figures

Authors use figurative language to help readers envision the characters in their stories. For example, in *The Summer of the Swans* by Betsy Byars, Sara speaks of the turmoil in her life by comparing it to a kaleidoscope that has been shaken repeatedly, and the design keeps changing. This metaphor helps the reader understand more about Sara as a character. Teachers need to make sure that students understand the different figures of speech that authors use. They also need to lead children in rich discussions about the meanings of these figures of speech. Bring in a kaleidoscope and let the students experience how it constantly changes.

Creating realistic as well as exciting settings is another important aspect of narrative text structure. The direct representation of the physical world not only adds to the success of the story but also lays the actual "ground" on which the story can proceed. This is accomplished through the use of description that emphasizes the setting. Amateur writers often neglect settings or assume that readers are familiar with their selected settings. The writer needs to create a well-crafted world in which readers willingly allow themselves to believe. Books with excellent examples of setting are included in Table 9.1.

MAKING **139**
STUDENTS'
WRITING
COME ALIVE:
STRATEGIES
FOR TEACHING
WRITING

Activity 3.4: Five-Minute Setting

This is a four-step activity that will help students develop their ability to write creative settings. To help illustrate the activity, there is a sample lesson for conducting the Five-Minute Setting. The teacher is using the setting of a farm from *Charlotte's Web* by E. B. White and a city from *Town Mouse, Country Mouse* by Jan Brett.

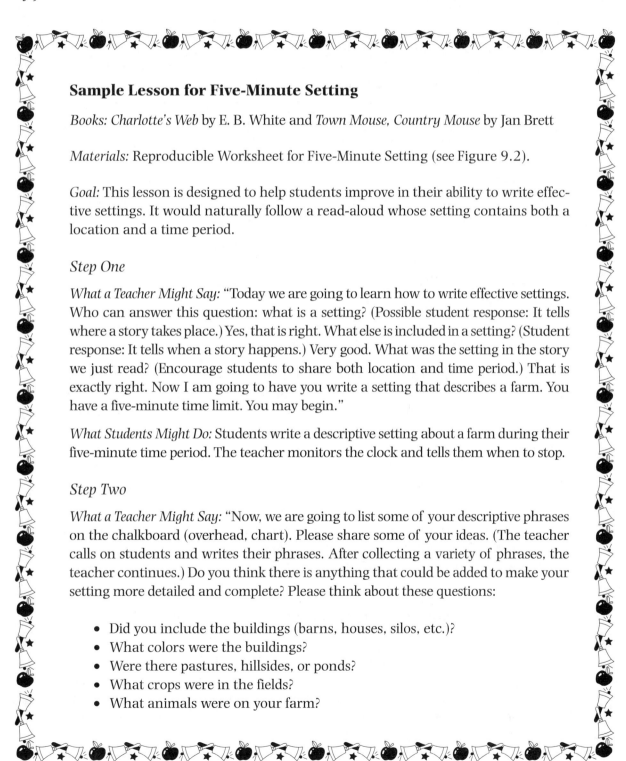

Sample Lesson for Five-Minute Setting

Books: Charlotte's Web by E. B. White and *Town Mouse, Country Mouse* by Jan Brett

Materials: Reproducible Worksheet for Five-Minute Setting (see Figure 9.2).

Goal: This lesson is designed to help students improve in their ability to write effective settings. It would naturally follow a read-aloud whose setting contains both a location and a time period.

Step One

What a Teacher Might Say: "Today we are going to learn how to write effective settings. Who can answer this question: what is a setting? (Possible student response: It tells where a story takes place.) Yes, that is right. What else is included in a setting? (Student response: It tells when a story happens.) Very good. What was the setting in the story we just read? (Encourage students to share both location and time period.) That is exactly right. Now I am going to have you write a setting that describes a farm. You have a five-minute time limit. You may begin."

What Students Might Do: Students write a descriptive setting about a farm during their five-minute time period. The teacher monitors the clock and tells them when to stop.

Step Two

What a Teacher Might Say: "Now, we are going to list some of your descriptive phrases on the chalkboard (overhead, chart). Please share some of your ideas. (The teacher calls on students and writes their phrases. After collecting a variety of phrases, the teacher continues.) Do you think there is anything that could be added to make your setting more detailed and complete? Please think about these questions:

- Did you include the buildings (barns, houses, silos, etc.)?
- What colors were the buildings?
- Were there pastures, hillsides, or ponds?
- What crops were in the fields?
- What animals were on your farm?

(Continued)

(Continued)

- How many animals were there?
- Did you include the time period?

Step Three

What a Teacher Might Say: "I am going to read some descriptive phrases that describe the setting in *Charlotte's Web.* Try to visualize (see a picture in your mind) the setting as I read. On page one, E. B. White says, 'The grass was wet and the earth smelled of springtime. Fern's sneakers were sopping by the time she caught up with her father.' On pages eight to nine, 'It was apple-blossom time, and the days were getting warmer. Mr. Arable fixed a small yard especially for Wilbur under an apple tree, and gave him a large wooden box full of straw, with a doorway cut in it so he could walk in and out as he pleased.' What picture do you see in your mind? What does Wilbur's new home look like? How did the author tell us the time period?" (Guide students in helping recognize the author's craft in writing the setting.)

Step Four

What a Teacher Might Say: "Now, I want you to write a new setting about a town. You have a five-minute time limit."

What Students Might Do: Students will write a new descriptive setting about a town. The teacher will monitor the clock and tell them when to stop.

What a Teacher Might Say: "Okay, class, time is up. Let's share some of the descriptive phrases you wrote about a town." The teacher will repeat Step Two by listing student phrases on the chalkboard, overhead, or chart and Step Three by reading descriptive phrases concerning the new setting from the selected story—*Town Mouse, Country Mouse.*

How This Lesson Might be Assessed

1. Students can count the total number of words used to write the first description (farm) and compare it with the total number of words used to write the second description (town). The second description should have more words because the students will have gotten ideas from the discussion after the first description.

2. Students can circle and then count the number of adjectives in each Five-Minute Setting. The second setting should employ the use of more adjectives.

3. During individual writing conferences, the teacher can help students see the difference in their first and second writings. The teacher should be sure to give each student appropriate praise. Discuss their improvements in writing effective settings and have them share new ideas they have about how to write descriptive settings.

MAKING **141**
STUDENTS'
WRITING
COME ALIVE:
STRATEGIES
FOR TEACHING
WRITING

Figure 9.2   Reproducible for Five-Minute Setting

**Five-Minute
Setting**

Name: _____

Describe a farm setting. _____

_____

_____

_____

_____

_____

_____

_____

Describe a town setting. _____

_____

_____

_____

_____

_____

_____

_____

Answer these questions:	*Farm Setting*	*Town Setting*
How many words did I use to write each setting?		
Circle the adjectives in your settings. How many did you use in each setting?		

Activity 3.5: Guess the Setting

This activity will use unfamiliar settings to hone the skills of creating a realistic environment. First the students will pair up and decide on a particular setting with which neither of them is familiar. They will then do some brief research about that particular setting and come up with a list of descriptive phrases that can best describe the place to someone else who is not familiar with it. The teacher should also encourage the use of a thesaurus as a means of capturing the setting with imagery. The pairs should then report to the class by reading their descriptive phrases. Students should not mention anything about their chosen settings except for the list of descriptive words, and the most successful description can be based on which setting could be guessed with the least amount of prompting phrases.

Exploring different points of view is essential to the writing craft. Teachers need to help students develop an appreciation for point of view through examples from quality children's literature. (See Table 9.1 for a list.) There are three basic points of view that need to be taught to children: *third person omniscient, third person limited,* and *first person.* (*Second person* is seldom used in formal writing.) The *third person omniscient* point of view reveals the most about the author and the direction he or she wishes the characters to take. The author allows his or her voice to be present and crucial to the comprehension and identification of the characters by the reader. This allows the author to evoke human responses to the characters in the story. *Third person limited* point of view allows the author to reveal the action and voice through the eyes of a single character rather than all characters as in the third person omniscient point of view. *First person* point of view is the method by which the author tells the story through the thoughts and actions of one of the main characters using first person language such as *I* and *me.* The author hopes to draw readers to the main character by creating a character with engaging and realistic human qualities. *Second person* employs the use of words such as *you* and *your.* This section offers different ways teachers can explain and illustrate the effects that different points of view have for the reader.

Activity 3.6: Guess the Point of View

Choose descriptive paragraphs from four or five narrative texts. Be careful to select examples that are definitive. Ask students to decide which point of view the passage represents. Follow up any misunderstandings with discussion and ask students to prove the position they have taken. (For younger children, use only first person and third person—not third person limited or omniscient.)

Activity 3.7: Change the Point of View

In this activity, the teacher has students select a short narrative paragraph or poem. Each student must identify the point of view from which the story was initially written. Then, the student changes the author's chosen point of view to something different, such as from third person to first person. Then, the teacher holds a discussion concerning the perceived effects that the changes had for the reader. For learners who excel, this activity can be expanded to

MAKING **143**
STUDENTS'
WRITING
COME ALIVE:
STRATEGIES
FOR TEACHING
WRITING

include all points of view, including third person limited, third person omniscient, and second person.

TESTS TO ASSESS WRITING

Writing is probably the most difficult area of the language arts to assess because of its personal nature. All of us bring our prior knowledge and emotional connections to the reading of a piece of writing, thus creating a subjective reaction to it. Keeping these special assessment issues in mind, the most effective evaluations of a student's writing must be ongoing. By measuring students' progress in relation to each person's areas of need and improvement, the assessment components of the writing program can be individualized to match the needs of each student. When conducted in this manner, such assessments can inform the direction of future instruction. The testing practices that follow adhere to this principle and can assist you to effectively assess your students' writing progress.

Assessment Practice 1: Pocket Pit Stops

This assessment practice is predicated on an additional writing evaluation principle: teachers need to have an effective monitoring system to organize their students' pit stops, or writing challenges that students address, as they journey through the writing process. Using a pocket chart can help organize each student's work steps. The top of the pocket chart should have labels for each stage of the writing process, including the name of writing activities listed above and grammar minilessons that have been taught. Students keep track of their progress by moving their name card to the pocket that describes the objective they have set for themselves for each writing workshop session.

Assessment Practice 2: Maintenance Checklist for Writing

This checklist can be used as a roadmap for the teacher to track each individual student's progress. It can include skills, writing concepts (like writing settings), steps in the writing process, and writing in different genres. Checking for areas of proficiency and deficiency can help teachers plan instructional strategies to meet students' needs. A sample of a Maintenance Checklist for Writing is found in Figure 9.3.

Assessment Practice 3: Focused Feedback

Teachers can give specific assignments that focus on a particular writing skill or concept. These assignments should be very brief and precise. For example, after teaching the Five-Minute Setting minilesson, the teacher could check for mastery of the skill by having the students write a new setting to be used for an assessment. The teacher needs to grade the assignment using the guidelines created in the class discussion and to give students focused feedback on their positive efforts and their areas for improvement.

Figure 9.3   Maintenance Checklist for Writing (Reproducible)

Maintenance Checklist for Writing

Directions: Place a checkmark or date in each column when student has demonstrated mastery.

Names	Writing Process					Narrative Text					Expository Text					
	Brainstorming	Graphic Organizers	Rough Draft	Revision	Editing	Setting	Characters	Point of View	Plot/Action	Problem/ Resolution	Chronological/ Sequential	Compare/ Contrast	Description	Cause/Effect	Problem/Solution	Poetry (label type of poem)

MAKING **145**
STUDENTS'
WRITING
COME ALIVE:
STRATEGIES
FOR TEACHING
WRITING

Assessment Practice 4: Thumbs-Up Critics

Model how to provide constructive criticism when critiquing another writer's work. After numerous examples and minilessons, allow children to critique each other in small groups or with partners. Begin by using this assessment practice with small steps in the writing process. For example, give student critics a focus, such as looking at the quality with which their peers wrote dialogue for their characters or how vivid their settings were. Encourage discussion and positive criticism; hence the idea of "thumbs-up" critics.

Assessment Practice 5: Powerful Portfolios

Portfolios are popular writing assessment measures with good reason. They are an effective tool for collecting student work, which can become the ongoing samples for writing evaluation. One student-selected sample per month is adequate to measure growth. During conferences, teachers can help students notice the progress they have made on their current piece of writing by comparing rough drafts to published pieces and also help students see progress since the beginning of the year. Angelica's teacher was able to use Angelica's two samples of writing ("Tahoe" and "The Wonderful Day at the Beach") to help her see the exceptional growth her writing had when two focused strategies (concept webbing and revising) were stressed. Angelica was amazed at the difference in length and quality. As can be seen in Angelica's examples, portfolios provide a dynamic illustration of student growth throughout the school year.

Assessment Practice 6: Self-Assessment and Self-Reflection

Teachers must play a role in helping students determine and discuss their growth in writing abilities. Students need to learn the art of self-assessment and self-reflection by tapping into their metacognitive processes (Israel, Block, Bauserman, & Kinnucan-Welsch, 2005). Teachers need to guide students in the self-assessment and self-reflection processes with pointed questions that spotlight areas of improvement in their individual writing processes. Through these teacher actions, students can learn to take responsibility for their own writing craft. For this assessment practice to be most effective, individual writing conferences need to be held on a weekly basis. In this manner, students become more expert in reflecting on their writing skills, on concepts that can improve their craft, on steps in the writing processes, and on creation of unique voices in products that they wrote. These writing conferences have proven to be among the most valuable tools to assist students to focus on progress made toward meeting previous goals and on needs for improvement in the following week(s) (Block & Dellamura, 2001/2002).

The steps that produce the most growth in student writing follow. First, get specific feedback from students on their perceptions of individual progress toward previous goals. Then help them focus on future goals. Sample questions you can use to complete both of these steps follow:

- What have you learned about your use of the steps in the writing process this week?
- How have you stretched your writing abilities in specific ways?
- What do you wish you could do better in creating your own writing style?
- What do you want to learn about writing next week? Why?
- What do you want to do to help yourself reach your writing goal?
- How can I best help you reach your next writing goal?

After the writing conferences, help students make plans to improve their writing based on the goals they articulated in their conferences. You can also use the Writing Conference Self-Assessment Worksheet (see Figure 9.4) to chart individual progress toward goals as well as plans for completing future goals. Figure 9.5 is an example of this chart in use, as it contains a partially completed Writing Conference Self-Assessment Worksheet for Lance, a third-grade student.

ADDRESSING LEARNERS WITH SPECIAL NEEDS

The following lessons can be adapted to meet the instructional needs of student writers who struggle, student writers who are learning English, and student writers who excel.

Learners Who Struggle

Writing can be a burdensome task for learners who struggle. Struggling writers need to be exposed to numerous examples of quality children's literature as mentioned previously. Classroom conversations centered on these works should be overstated to emphasize the author's techniques. For example, if the author uses repetition as an effective writing technique, the students can be made aware of this and be encouraged to use a similar technique in their own work.

One of the best ways to provide this extra emphasis and support for struggling students is to have them dictate their stories to the teacher, an instructional aide, or into a tape recorder. Once one of these dictation methods has been employed, struggling writers can compose more than one writing piece per week for publication, which has proven to be necessary to strengthen their writing abilities (Block & Mangieri, 2003). Depending on the level of the struggling student, there are several methods that can be employed to ensure that struggling writers receive the joy and accomplishment of completing two or more published compositions a week. Word processing with a computer may be useful for some students. Alternatively, preschool and kindergarten-level less able students might receive special help while preparing their writings for publication through techniques such as the teacher or an instructional aide translating the dictated story into dotted letters for the student to trace or using the *hand-over-hand* technique (teacher places her hand over the student's hand to guide him or her as each dictated sentence is written). It is very important to

MAKING **147**
STUDENTS'
WRITING
COME ALIVE:
STRATEGIES
FOR TEACHING
WRITING

Figure 9.4   Reproducible Form for Writing Conference Self-Assessment Worksheet

Writing Conference Self-Assessment Worksheet

Name: _____ Month: _____

Date	Writing Conference Goal	Steps to Reach My Goal	Progress

Figure 9.5   Sample of a Completed Writing Conference Self-Assessment Worksheet (Use the Writing Conference Self-Assessment Worksheet to chart individual student progress in self-assessment of and self-reflection on writing)

Writing Conference Self-Assessment Worksheet

Name: Lance   Month: January

Date	Writing Conference Goal	Steps to Reach My Goal	Progress
January 8	I would like to use more exciting words in my writing.	I will learn to use a thesaurus. I will participate in Evolve a Word with a buddy.	I used the word "melancholy" instead of sad. My buddy and I evolved "cool" into "intriguing."
January 15	I want to make my settings more realistic.	My teacher will use Five-Minute Settings to help me improve in writing settings.	
January 22			
January 29			

make connections between the student's spoken word and the idea that what the student said can be written down and later read.

In addition, most of the activities in this chapter can be easily adapted for learners who struggle. One example is to take the Five-Minute Setting and give learners who struggle some supportive help through the use of expository books. When this and other activities in this chapter are adapted for struggling writers, it is recommended that the time limits be removed to prevent students' frustration.

Another effective activity, called *New and Improved Settings,* will also benefit students with limited travel experiences. It expands their understandings of new and diverse settings. Have the struggling student choose a new setting that he or she would like to learn more about; for instance the Rocky Mountains. Choose an expository book about the Rocky Mountains. Then a more capable peer, instructional aide, or the teacher can look through the book with the student and help the student find and list ten descriptive words or phrases that help form a mental picture of the new setting; in this case the mountains. This

MAKING **149**
STUDENTS'
WRITING
COME ALIVE:
STRATEGIES
FOR TEACHING
WRITING

activity could be placed into a game format. The descriptive phrases (not the name of the setting) can be shared with the class for the purpose of guessing the setting being described. The student that conveys his or her setting to the rest of the class with the fewest descriptive phrases has been most successful in describing a "new and improved" setting. See Figure 9.6 for a reproducible worksheet for this activity.

Learners Who Are Learning English

Current research in linguistic diversity supports students' writing in their native language (Nieto, 2000). When ELL students compose in their native language, their volume and creativity increases significantly. These bilingual writing activities promote learning, whereas requiring ELL students to speak in English only is an impediment to academic achievement, especially during the early stages of learning to read and write in a second language (Nieto, 2000). Therefore, ELL students should be encouraged to keep a journal (in their native tongue) of their ideas for writing. Likewise, their compositions (in their native tongue) can be written manually, composed on a word processor, or orally recorded for later use.

As they do with many English-Only students, some teachers of ELL students tend to emphasize form over substance (Jimenez, Smith, & Martinez-Leon, 2003). We recommend that the classroom teacher of ELL students take care not to overemphasize writing form (grammar and punctuation) during the initial stages of creating rough drafts. These areas of mechanics can be attended to when the writing piece is translated for publication. Last, as holds true for struggling writers who are not ELLs, ELLs should be provided with the adaptations described in the prior discussion so that they can also accomplish more than one published composition a week. Above all, teachers of ELL students need to respect their students' native languages, as this is one of the keys for creating a writing environment that promotes ELL's success (Nieto, 2000).

Learners Who Excel

Most classrooms have a few students who are well above average in their academic achievement, although they may not be the most creative or prolific writers in the classroom. Since these students tend to be perfectionists who are accustomed to getting A's, many are afraid of failure or of taking academic risks that might lead to failure (Van Tassel-Baska, 1992). Because of this perfectionist tendency and their tendency to focus on the finished product, it is often hard to challenge gifted writers to rise to their full potential. One thing that classroom teachers can do is to focus these students' attention on improving their abilities in each step of the writing process, especially revision and editing. Learners who excel need to be encouraged to take risks, especially during the revision process. Teachers can encourage this behavior by modeling the effectiveness of using revision to improve a personal piece of writing.

Another way is to find examples of authors who share the ways that they revise a story, as well as how many revisions might be needed before their works are accepted for publication. (Jan Brett is an excellent example, as described

Figure 9.6   Reproducible Form for New and Improved Setting Game

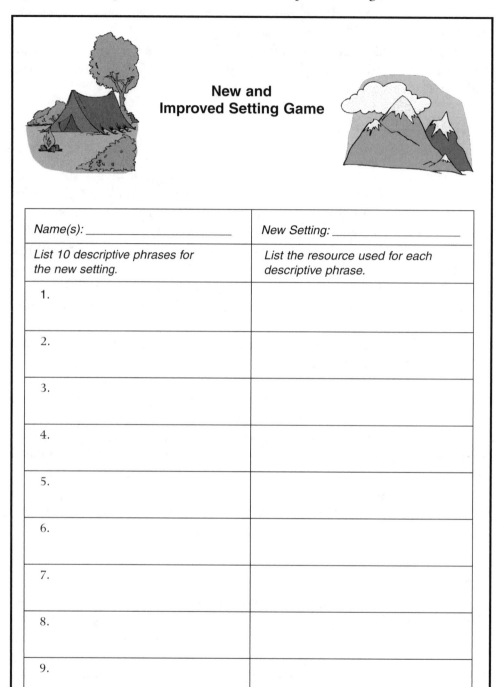

New and Improved Setting Game

Name(s): _____	New Setting: _____
List 10 descriptive phrases for the new setting.	List the resource used for each descriptive phrase.
1.	
2.	
3.	
4.	
5.	
6.	
7.	
8.	
9.	
10.	

Reflection: How many phrases did you have to share before the class guessed your setting?

MAKING **151**
STUDENTS'
WRITING
COME ALIVE:
STRATEGIES
FOR TEACHING
WRITING

previously.) Finally, teachers can praise students for daring to take risks in their writing and help them value the amount of thought and effort they have invested to create finished product.

SUMMARY

Students can become excited about writing and learn how to produce exceptionally well-written and lively works. We discussed five guiding principles for providing instruction that is based on actions that good writers take. Students should be taught to (1) set a purpose for their writing, (2) consider their audience, (3) personally apply the steps in the writing process, (4) utilize all available resources, and (5) use graphic organizers. Then we discussed three lessons that can assist teachers to make students' writing come alive. Teachers need to (1) lead students in rich discussions, (2) foster individual student enthusiasm for writing, and (3) use minilessons to teach students practical strategies that specifically and personally enhance their writing craft. For each of these lesson objectives, many activities were suggested. A sample lesson with step-by-step directions was chosen to model the Five-Minute Setting. Teachers who implement these three lessons, augmented with their genuine personal enthusiasm for writing, can engage students of all levels of entering ability in producing quality pieces of writing. The inevitable result will be student-generated enthusiasm for and increased skill in writing.

10

Metacognition

Monitoring Strategies to Enhance Reading Comprehension

I am not successful when it comes to test taking. My teachers have been asking me to take tests since first grade. Now I am in the sixth grade and I still feel frustrated. In order for me to be more successful when taking a test, I wish I could understand how I think to recall more information. Sometimes my thoughts are confusing and unorganized and I think this makes me not understand what I am reading. My teachers have never asked me what I am thinking. If they did, I would answer by asking them to help me figure out what to do when I get stuck on something I am reading or writing.

—Nicole, a sixth grader who
struggles with test taking and wants
to learn more metacognitive strategies
to monitor her reading and writing

Metacognition is defined as the "awareness and knowledge of one's mental processes such that one can monitor, regulate and direct them to a desired end" (Harris & Hodges, 1995, p. 153). When *Mosaic of Thought* was published in 1997, more teachers became aware of the importance of metacognition (Keene & Zimmerman, l997). When one begins to actually think and understand the mind of a student or reader, one begins to understand that the many thoughts in one's mind are quite similar to a mosaic. The many connected networks in an individual brain are wired differently for each individual, and, as a result, each young reader and writer possesses a different way of thinking and a different way of comprehending. In this chapter, we will describe the research-based instructional and assessment practices that can assist you to advance all students' abilities to think at their highest levels of comprehension and self-directed literacy levels.

WHAT TEACHERS NEED TO KNOW ABOUT METACOGNITION

Good readers use metacognitive strategies to think about and control reading before, during, and after reading the text. Before reading, good readers might clarify their purpose for reading and preview or overview the text. In addition, they might try to activate their prior knowledge of the text being read. During reading, they might monitor their understanding, adjusting their reading speed to fit the difficulty of the text. Throughout reading, highly effective readers also might engage their metacognition whenever they come to difficulties in the text that limit their understanding. At these points, such readers create strategies to help them decode difficult words and comprehend complex ideas. Good readers also utilize their metacognitive monitoring strategies after reading. They check their understanding of what they read. Such readers are very reflective during each phase of the reading process.

Readers who are metacognitively aware recognize when they do not understand a text. By contrast, less metacognitively aware readers often fail to recognize that a reading no longer makes sense to them, or they may not know what to do when they do recognize a comprehension breakdown. We need to teach students to be thoughtful and aware of their own thinking. Awareness of their thinking is necessary for students to be able to monitor their comprehension (Pressley, 2002). In order for most students to reach the high level of metacognitive processing, most teachers must make significant additions to their literacy program (Pressley, 2002; RAND Reading Study Group, 2001; NICHD, 2000).

Reading First legislation supports the use of metacognitive instructional strategies. Chapter 7 introduces the role of metacognition in enhancing comprehension and the value of controlling one's thinking about one's own thinking. This chapter elaborates on the distinct metacognitive processes that can be taught to improve students' literacy. In order for students to comprehend better they need to be taught what strategies to use when a comprehension breakdown occurs. Monitoring is a metacognitive strategy that good readers use when text is confusing or they are no longer gaining meaning from the text.

RESEARCH THAT TEACHERS CAN USE

Flavell's (1979) research delineated many processes within metacognitive thinking and explains the conscious awareness of one's own thoughts. Flavell's

METACOGNITION: **155**
MONITORING
STRATEGIES TO
ENHANCE
READING
COMPREHENSION

model of cognitive monitoring can be categorized into *metacognitive knowledge* and *metacognitive experiences*. *Metacognitive knowledge* consists of knowledge or beliefs about the person (self), the task (reading), and the strategy employed. *Metacognitive experiences* consist of any cognitive or affective experiences that accompany and pertain to any intellectual task such as reading. Flavell highlights the importance of discovering the early competencies that serve as tools for subsequent acquisition of metacognitive strategies, as opposed to cataloguing a child's lack of metacognitive strategies as deficiencies.

Pressley and Afflerbach (1995) compiled and organized a comprehensive list of every conscious process reported in the more than 40 verbal protocols of reading generated through 1995. The studies used in the analysis summarized the conscious processes that are self-regulated and coordinated to produce meaning from text. From this analysis, Pressley and Afflerbach constructed a model known as *Constructively Responsive Reading*. Several major theories contribute to the development of their Constructively Responsive Reading model, including Rosenblatt's (1938) reader response theory which describes the transaction that takes place between a reader, prior knowledge, and a text; and metacognitive theory's (Baker & Brown, 1984) complex model of text processing emanating from cognitive psychology. Schema theory (Anderson & Pearson, 1984) also highlights the importance of background information the reader brings to the reading process. According to Anderson and Pearson, a reader is able to comprehend a message when he is able to bring to mind a schema which gives a good account of the objects and events described in the message.

Pressley and Afflerbach's (1995) model of reading also portrays readers as actively constructing meaning. In this model, good readers monitor comprehension during a reading activity. Exceptionally skilled readers in this model never use only one strategy; rather, they fluidly coordinate a number of strategies to ensure maximum comprehension of the text. Moreover, the National Reading Panel (NICHD, 2000) found that metacognitive strategies to monitor comprehension can be taught at an early age. According to Reading First legislation, students may use several monitoring strategies that can enhance reading comprehension:

- *Identify where a literacy difficulty occurs.* Students should understand where the difficulty occurred and when they were no longer gaining meaning from a text.
- *Identify what the difficulty is.* The difficulty can be related to a particular word or concept in the text.
- *Restate the difficult sentence or passage in their own words.* Students who restate the difficulty that they face will have to work hard at thinking about what it was that did not make sense. A verbal report of the difficulty can help the teacher assess the situation and intervene with more effective instruction. For example, perhaps the reader became confused because he or she had no prior knowledge of the topic and was unable to

apply the topic to information in the text in order to make sense of what was read. When a student verbalizes this difficulty to the teacher, reading instruction can be targeted directly toward strategies that can eliminate this difficulty in the future.

- *Look back through the text.* Looking back should be done with the goal of finding information that is important and will help improve meaning construction and activate comprehension.

- *Look forward in the text for information that might help to resolve the difficulty.* Having students look forward in the text helps them understand how future and present information is going to fit together as a whole. Reading bits and pieces of information is difficult for some readers, and comprehension is limited because the reader is unaware of how the pieces fit together.

When the monitoring strategies listed above are learned and employed frequently and when reading different types of genres or text types, students have been shown to begin to activate monitoring strategies more automatically (Israel, Block, Bauserman, & Kinucan-Welsch, 2005). With continued practice, monitoring strategies become a more natural part of the reading process.

The strategies introduced by the Reading First legislation are also supported by further research in the area of student self-monitoring of comprehension. Braunger and Lewis (1997) included self-monitoring as a strategy critical to reading. Joseph (2005) also emphasizes the importance of teaching self-monitoring. According to Joseph, self-monitoring is defined as attending to an aspect of one's behavior through data-recording procedures. The lack of monitoring strategies prohibits a student from knowing how to change the reading strategies presently engaged when text material becomes increasingly difficult to comprehend. Reading First initiatives should pay close attention to teaching multiple metacognitive monitoring strategies at all grade levels. The following research-based lessons, when applied in the classroom, will provide teachers with specific methods that will significantly increase students' literacy.

NEW CLASSROOM-PROVEN, RESEARCH-BASED PRACTICES

Teaching Metacognition

In the past, it was uncommon to find a teacher providing instructional strategies related to metacognition. However, recent research has identified several ways in which monitoring strategies can be taught. In this chapter, you will learn three of these monitoring strategies.

Metacognitive Monitoring Lesson 1: Metacognitive Reflection Chart

Stemming from a constructively responsive reading framework (Pressley & Afflerbach, 1995), the *Metacognitive Reflection Chart* (Israel, Bauserman, &

METACOGNITION: **157**
MONITORING
STRATEGIES TO
ENHANCE
READING
COMPREHENSION

Block, 2005) can be used to help students monitor their comprehension process. The chart begins with the construction of meaning by the student, then focuses on seeking clarification of this understanding by interacting with a friend or peer to help validate the meaning construction and to extend the student's thinking about the text. When students are asked what they "think" about a text, they are trying to construct meaning by making connections between what they have read or learned and what they already know. When students are asked what they "believe" about a text, they are being asked to monitor their reading based on prior knowledge experiences and on what they have comprehended or understood about the text read to that point.

Alternatively, when students are asked what they "feel" or what they "question" about a text, they are being asked to make an evaluation about what they are reading. This evaluation explains the pattern of thinking used to generate an answer or affect from a reading. Using a metacognitive reflective chart helps organize metacognitive thoughts as they are related to a topic or piece of literature.

Classroom teachers can use this information to increase metacognitive thinking when reading novels or nonfiction or discussing critical issues such as world peace, or to help students monitor their reading comprehension. Table 10.1 is also an important instructional tool because it provides a practical way to help students organize their metacognitive thoughts as well as a pathway to increased monitoring skills. It can be used to identify the valid interpretations at critical points in a text and as an assessment tool.

Metacognitive Monitoring Lesson 2: Look-Backs as Fix-It Strategies

According to Gerald Duffy (2003), *look-backs* are effective metacognitive strategies to help students monitor their reading comprehension. Look-backs can be referred to as strategies in which a reader looks back and forward in a text to remove a meaning blockage. To use look-backs, readers first need to learn how to perform the following metacognitive activities:

- Monitor their acquisition of meaning as they read
- Stop reading momentarily to reflect and initiate new strategies when a problem is encountered

This lesson should be learned using materials that are slightly more difficult than students' independent reading level so that it is likely that problems will be encountered as they read.

According to Duffy, the look-back strategy can be taught by describing it as a revision of thinking similar to that of how a writer thinks when he goes back and re-reads in order to rewrite what he had written. If you tell students that both highly successful readers and writers go about revising their thinking by using this metacognitive strategy, so as to be better readers and better writers,

Table 10.1   Metacognitive Reflection Chart

	Think *I think . . .*	*Believe* *Based on what I know I believe . . .*	*Feel* *This makes me feel . . .*	*Question* *I have questions about . . .*
What I . . . Student Thoughts				
What We . . . Partner Thoughts				
Now I think . . .				

METACOGNITION: **159**
MONITORING
STRATEGIES TO
ENHANCE
READING
COMPREHENSION

students have a more concrete reason and increased motivation for applying the strategy. Once these affective processes are engaged, the five steps in the look-back strategy can be taught as follows:

- *Step 1:* Decide if reading no longer makes sense, and stop. It is important that readers stop when they realize something doesn't make sense. Teachers can encourage readers to stop by modeling, performing a think-aloud of how they engage this metacognitive strategy during a read-aloud, and explaining how to stop reading and begin to regroup and reflect and why.
- *Step 2:* If students are unable to explain what the text is about using a think-aloud, continue to use the look-back strategy, but ask students who understand this metacognitive thought process to verbalize how they would perform it at specific points in a book that you are reading aloud to the class. Helping these students put their thoughts into words not only helps them to focus on where their reading difficulties occur, but enables their peers to hear several different explanations, using varied vernaculars, as to how they can use this metacognition independently in the future.
- *Step 3:* Explain the look-back strategy by telling students they can look back over the text or look forward to gain new information.
- *Step 4:* Explain what a blockage in meaning is and how it can be identified. Tell students that they can ask themselves some questions when a breakdown in comprehension occurs, such as the following: Am I having trouble finding the main idea? Am I unable to visualize the content? Am I having trouble understanding a specific word or sentence? Did I stop understanding because I was not paying attention to what I was reading?
- *Step 5:* Tell students that after they have looked for information to increase acquisition of meaning, they can reread or look ahead to test if the problem related to their comprehension difficulty has been fixed.

When you implement the look-back strategy following this five-step method, students will most likely remember the strategy and employ it when comprehension miscues or breakdowns occur.

An example of Mr. Sullivan's implementation of this lesson follows.

Mr. Sullivan reads a passage from *Gandhi* (Demi, 2001): "Gandhi left his wife at home and went to London to study the law. For a long time he felt completely alone, a foreigner in a strange country."

Mr. Sullivan says: "When I was reading I noticed it said that Gandhi left his wife at home and went to London to study law. Earlier I thought I read that Gandhi was a small boy who was shy and afraid of many things. I guess I am confused about why Gandhi has a wife when he is a small boy. I think I will look back to see what is making me confused about Gandhi."

Mr. Sullivan proceeds looking back in the text and finds the location in the text that caused the difficulty. Mr. Sullivan discovers that Gandhi was thirteen years old when he was married, and this still makes him a small boy according to the author.

Metacognitive Monitoring Lesson 3: The Sentence Verification Technique

Sentence verification technique (Royer, 2001) is an instructional and metacognitive assessment strategy in which students and teacher consider a sentence and change it in three ways. First they paraphrase the sentence— constructing another sentence that has essentially the same meaning. Then they create a meaning-change sentence, in which they change the sentence in a way that changes its meaning. Finally they create a distracter sentence, which is similar in syntactic structure and theme to the original sentence but unrelated in meaning to any sentence in the original passage.

Once students have made the changes, they describe the thoughts they used to do so. Next, students read the original passage, and then on a separate page provide a *yes* or *no* response to the three types of sentences listed above plus the original. Their responses should indicate whether each sentence has the same meaning as the original. Obviously, the original sentence and the paraphrase sentence would have *yes* responses, while the meaning-change sentence and distracter sentence would receive *no* responses. By asking students to tell *why* they chose their responses, the assessment becomes metacognitive. The *why* provides much richer assessment data for understanding student thinking and informing future instruction.

Here is an example of a paraphrase using a sentence from *To Kill a Mockingbird:* "Mockingbirds don't do one thing but make music for us to enjoy."

Paraphrase Sentence: I enjoy listening to mockingbirds because they have such a beautiful sound for all to enjoy.

Asking why the student might select *yes* for the paraphrase sentence helps the teacher understand the thought processes that the student is presently using to aid in comprehension of text. If the responses are not accurate indicators of the message being communicated, the teacher can immediately intervene and teach an effective metacognitive thinking process that can be used in the future to paraphrase meanings in students' own minds to aid in getting their meaning construction back on track.

An example of a sentence verification lesson follows.

METACOGNITION: **161**
MONITORING
STRATEGIES TO
ENHANCE
READING
COMPREHENSION

**Lesson for Primary Teachers to Help
Students Become More Reflective**

A Teacher Might Say: "I love all your new ideas and thoughts you have when I am reading you a story during read-aloud time. Since you have such wonderful thoughts, I am going to see if I can help you use your thoughts to reflect on what I am reading in a different way."

A Teacher May Want to Do: Choose a read-aloud story that is related to a theme or topic students are learning about. For example, when learning about friendships at the beginning of the school year, a teacher may want to read *The Friend* by Sarah Stewart (2004). Choosing stories that relate to classroom themes can initiate reflection and deeper thinking. Begin reading on the first page, "Annabelle Bernadette Clementine Dodd was a good little girl, though decidedly odd. Belle lived every day as if she were grown—she thought she could do *everything* on her own." Stop reading and ask three different questions.

> *Paraphrase:* "What is a different way to say someone lives every day as if she were grown up?
>
> *Meaning-change:* "How can you change the excerpt that I just read to change the meaning of the story?"
>
> *Distracter:* Reread the sentence, "Annabelle Bernadette Clementine Dodd was a good little girl, though decidedly odd." Instead of saying "odd," say "old." Ask the students, "Is there anything strange about what I read that makes you think differently about Belle?"

A Teacher May Want to Have Students Do: Use a two-by-three folded sheet of paper. Have students write a word or draw a picture for each of the different types of questions you have asked and have them explain the meaning of their pictures and how it is related or not related to the original story.

Lesson Could Be Assessed By: When students share their words or pictures, the teacher can assess how students are thinking differently about the story.

TESTS TO ASSESS METACOGNITION

Because statewide tests that assess Reading First objectives do not include a metacognitive evaluation, we wanted to provide two models for your use. Both provide distinct information. You can use one or both repeatedly throughout the year, adapted to match your instructional objectives. Both assist you and students to monitor students' growth toward becoming more automatic, independent metacognitive readers.

Metacognitive Assessment 1:
Metacognitive Monitoring Checklist

Monitoring strategies can easily be analyzed using a metacognitive monitoring checklist (Israel, 2002). To elicit a child's thoughts after reading, the think-aloud strategy can be employed (Block & Israel, 2004). Because think-alouds require readers to stop periodically, reflect on the thinking they do to understand a text, and to relate these thinking processes orally, this metacognitive awareness has shown to significantly increase students' scores on comprehension tests, add to students' self-assessment of their comprehension, and enhance students' abilities to select thinking processes to overcome comprehension challenges while they read (Block, 2004). By using the think-aloud strategy after reading a text, a teacher can measure students' monitoring strategies. This assessment asks students to give a retrospective report of what occurred during their reading process.

Understanding the relation of people's words to their thoughts, Pressley and Afflerbach (1995) offer the opportunity to gather a detailed understanding of readings and reading-related phenomena to better understand the processes of reading. Block and Pressley (2002) focused on reading comprehension and the importance of strategy utilization. Regarding the investigation of monitoring strategies, Pressley states:

> The skilled reader not only monitors but also shifts reading in reaction to what is monitored. Shifting includes the following: attempting to figure out the meaning of a word detected as unknown; deciding whether to interpret text exactly or liberally; deciding whether to attend to or read carefully only certain parts of text that are most likely to be understood or most likely to be helpful; deciding to look up background material before continuing to read the text; attempting to pinpoint the parts of text that are confusing; and deciding to reread material that was not understood initially but that might be understood with more effort. (2002, p. 17)

To obtain knowledge of students' abilities to monitor their comprehension, and to better understand if shifting strategies are being employed, teachers can use the Metacognitive Monitoring Checklist to evaluate the level of metacognitive strategy utilization. After reading a text, the teacher can ask students to perform a retrospective report of the reading of the text. The retrospective report gives them an opportunity to think-aloud their thoughts after reading a specific text. Table 10.2 outlines the directions teachers can use to elicit a retrospective report from a student. Providing detailed directions for students helps guide their thinking and builds their confidence about performing a

METACOGNITION: **163**
MONITORING
STRATEGIES TO
ENHANCE
READING
COMPREHENSION

Table 10.2   Retrospective Report Directions

- Now that you have read the text, I am going to ask you to think about your reading of the text and focus only on your reading comprehension strategies.
- The purpose of the retrospective report is to understand some of the decisions you made to help improve your reading comprehension. You might refer to these has "fix-up strategies." For example, you might want to tell me how you went about determining the meaning of a word that you detected as unknown, or you might want to explain a decision you might have made to better understand the text.
- Everything you say is important.
- Do you have any questions?

retrospective report. Table 10.3 is a checklist that teachers can use to record the retrospective report and check off strategies that are in fact being employed while reading.

Metacognitive Assessment 2: Monitoring Charts

Self-assessments, such as those used in Monitoring Charts, are among the most frequently used and effective metacognitive assessments. To use the Monitoring Chart, ask students to complete it, as described in Table 10.4. This chart helps students record their thoughts related to their metacognitive monitoring thoughts during reading. Teachers in the younger grades can help students monitor their comprehension when reading by pausing at points in a text and asking the group to complete the Monitoring Chart together as a small group of readers. Teachers can also use the Monitoring Chart to record when they note that specific strategies are employed by individuals while they are reading.

ADDRESSING LEARNERS WITH SPECIAL NEEDS

Learners Who Struggle

Struggling readers are less aware of their thinking when they are reading than are their more able reading peers. This is partly why struggling readers have difficulty monitoring their reading. Providing students with knowledge about the monitoring strategies described in this chapter is an important first step to helping these students learn more about the possibilities they have to initiate their metacognitive thinking while they read. Once these students have knowledge of the metacognitive strategies they can use to help them when they have difficulty, they should practice the strategies under teacher direction more frequently than more able readers. Moreover, more capable peers can help struggling readers learn these strategies during the several types of paired reading activities that have been described in this book. Teachers should tell

Table 10.3 Metacognitive Monitoring Checklist

Directions: After students read a text passage, have them give a retrospective report of the reading and use the monitoring checklist to identify which strategies are being employed.

Retrospective Report	(1) Attempted to determine meaning of a word	(2) Decided to interpret text exactly	(3) Decided to interpret text by elaborating on important ideas	(4) Decided to attend to or read carefully only certain parts of text likely to be understood or likely to be helpful	(5) Attempted to pinpoint the parts of text that are confusing	(6) Decided to reread material or look back at the text that was not understand but might be understood with more effort

METACOGNITION: **165**
MONITORING
STRATEGIES TO
ENHANCE
READING
COMPREHENSION

Table 10.4   Monitoring Chart to Increase Students' Abilities to Self-Monitor Their
Comprehension While They Read

Did I identify where the difficulties occurred in the text while reading?	*Can I identify what the difficulty is?*	*Did I try to restate the difficult passage in my own words?*	*Did I look back to locate helpful information?*	*Did I look forward in the text for information that might be helpful?*
Beginning				
Middle				
End				

these more able tutors to stop and think about what they are reading (at the beginning, middle, and end of text) at more difficult sections of a book. As they think, these readers are also taught how to ask their less able reading peer what they would think at these points in a text. If they do not understand, more able reading tutors should re-employ the metacognitive monitoring strategies. Learners who struggle with thinking about their own monitoring strategies can practice these strategies repeatedly then, and by using the lesson that follows.

To begin, combine the following objectives into a single lesson. Tell students that they are going to think about all that they can do to learn the meaning of words they do not know. Next, have them select a predictable book that will be used as a read-aloud book. Call a single child or a small group together. Explain to the students: "Stop reading orally when you come to a word that you don't know. Pay attention to what your mind is doing to try to figure out this word. I am going to pause our reading at times when you stop to think. I'll ask you what you are thinking to learn that word's meaning."

Then begin the read-aloud. You will ask each child who stops to explain his or her thinking. Repeat this lesson on different days until all students have demonstrated that they can independently use the word-learning principles and vocabulary-building strategies. When they have explained their thoughts about understanding the difficult words, ask them to explain what they did to help them monitor their understanding of that word. Finally, students can go back to other metacognitive monitoring strategies they learned previously in this chapter and apply the steps of this lesson to better learn each of them.

Learners Who Are Learning English

A strategy for English language learners, who struggle with reading partly because of their lack of automaticity with English, would be to require them to practice metacognitive strategies using familiar books in their native languages. This modification will help make the transfer of the strategy smoother because they will be more capable in decoding that text and reading with fluency. When English language learners begin to increase their English reading ability, teachers can have them work in small groups to practice metacognitive monitoring of their comprehension. Teachers can also have them verbalize the monitoring strategies they employ while reading so they can hear themselves think aloud about comprehension. In addition, you can help ELL students learn how to ask themselves more questions and to assess their own comprehension by using Discovery Discussion. (See Chapter 7 for more details about Discovery Discussions.) Students can ask questions about how they are overcoming challenges as they read. Asking questions helps them monitor their comprehension. The questions that students generate in the Discovery Discussion can also be used to help ELLs learn new English words.

Learners Who Excel

Most gifted learners already employ a repertoire of metacognitive monitoring strategies without your help. Similarly, most gifted readers can document

METACOGNITION: **167**
MONITORING
STRATEGIES TO
ENHANCE
READING
COMPREHENSION

their monitoring strategies on self-stick notes and place them inside the text with a description of the strategy employed. This will help learners who excel review their thinking and build on their comprehension as they read through the text. Gifted readers should also be encouraged to self-evaluate their own monitoring to detect patterns that occur more frequently. For example, if a gifted reader was having trouble with difficult words in a particular text, that student could ask to spend more time learning the strategies to monitor vocabulary presented in Chapter 5.

SUMMARY

The purpose of this chapter was to help you understand how metacognition can be used to enhance reading comprehension. Monitoring is a metacognitive function that can help students at all levels monitor their understanding of the text. Research-based lessons were provided to help teachers integrate effective metacognitive instruction for less able, ELL, and gifted readers, as well as lessons that can be used throughout their basic instructional programs. Another goal of this chapter was to help teachers use practical lessons and activities to teach monitoring strategies. Three new research-based lessons to teach metacognition were described: monitoring-reflection, look-backs, and the sentence verification strategy. To assess students' understanding of reading comprehension, teachers can use the monitoring checklists and student self-assessment charts to document their utilization and progress related to metacognitive thinking before, during, and after reading. The authors of this book believe that when teachers and literacy coaches instruct students on how to monitor their reading, they will encourage increased levels of self-regulation during the reading task, and fewer learners will struggle with comprehending text.

Including Parents
as True Partners

*My daddy was a traveling salesman and my mommy worked part-time in the
children's book department in the biggest department store in town. On the
nights when my Daddy was in town, he would read stories to my brother and
me at bedtime. Other times he would read outside on the porch and neighbor
kids would always join us because they all knew that with every story my
daddy made up or read, he would make the experience special for them. He
always made us laugh.*

—Sally Hahn, a personal narrative of
her experiences growing up and learning

WHAT TEACHERS NEED TO KNOW ABOUT
INCLUDING PARENTS AS SERIOUS PARTNERS

Reading First legislation has emphasized that parents are an integral part of
their children's education and has mandated that schools and teachers include
parents as meaningful partners in their children's literacy development. Reading First supports the notion that success in school starts with reading. It is
important that teachers and parents together help children become readers
and literacy lovers. We need to give full recognition and respect to the fact
that parents are the first to hold aspirations for their children's success and that
they dedicate themselves to working toward it. They trust us as teachers, and
we must return this respect by offering them ideas and suggesting experiences
with which they can support their children's learning through activities with
children at home. The purpose of this chapter is to provide teachers, and literacy coaches with strategies and ideas for including parents and families as true

partners with the goal of developing positive partnerships that can help bridge the achievement gap and support all young learners.

As the International Reading Association's position statement, entitled *Family-School Partnerships: Essential Elements of Literacy Instruction in the United States,* states:

> Family involvement is a potentially powerful element of effective literacy instruction. The International Reading Association believes parents, family and community members, teachers, school administrators, researchers, and policymakers must be aware of its importance and must receive information and training that allow them to effectively execute their respective roles in establishing family involvement in literacy learning. (2002)

Research on family literacy supports the notion that when families get involved with their child's literacy development, students' early literacy skills are developed (Jordan, Snow, & Porche, 2000). Likewise, when literacy engaged environments are created, students have increased access to print-rich materials (Neuman & Celano, 2001). When families like Sally's demonstrate a value of literacy, parents can model effective literacy behaviors (Nistler & Maiers, 2000). Literacy-oriented engagements help promote literacy development. These approaches to family literacy suggest the important value of reading and talking together as a family.

A growing body of research indicates that the way in which a parent speaks with a child about reading may have as much or more to do with later reading achievement of the child than actual time spent reading to the child. *A Parent's Guide to No Child Left Behind* (2003) stresses the importance of reading to children at home, especially at an early age in a child's literacy development.

Children who enter school with language skills (e.g., understanding that print reads from left to right and top to bottom) and prereading skills are more likely to learn to read well in the early grades and succeed in later years. It is never too early to start building language skills by talking with and reading to children.

Teachers can model successful parent involvement programs that establish a belief that parents are a positive resource in the education process. Nistler and Maiers (2000) have designed an effective parent involvement program that is based on the belief that parents are a powerful, underused source of knowledge. They believe parents are an untapped resource in today's classrooms. Several elements of success should be incorporated into parental involvement programs, according to Nistler and Maiers. The elements of success are as follows

- Maintain a positive relationship between teacher and parents
- Recruit new parent volunteers on an ongoing basis
- Value parent input
- Engage participants in a variety of literacy activities
- Empathize with family challenges

NEW CLASSROOM-PROVEN, RESEARCH-BASED PRACTICES

Including Parents as Partners

In this chapter, we are going to provide you with specific examples of how parents can assist with each of the major components of Reading First and the other critical elements discussed throughout this book. This section begins with a self-assessment form that teachers can use to evaluate their own values and attitudes related to parent partnerships. Following this are examples that teachers can share with parents to give them a clearer sense of how literacy processes interact and to invite their conscious participation in development of oral language, phonemes and phonemic awareness, phonics, vocabulary, fluency, comprehension, independent reading, writing, and metacognition. Each of the five Reading First components and four additional identified components that were discussed in greater detail in this book will be presented.

First, a brief overview of the key points related to the component will be highlighted. Following will be family experiences that can pleasurably be done with their child at home. The ideas here have been implemented by many teachers. Jennifer Medved, a first-grade teacher in a midwestern school district, suggests placing the ideas in a parent letter or parent newspaper so children can take the ideas home and share them with their families. The chapter closes with a summary of parent resources that can assist families with further literacy engagements at home. These can also be added to the parent newsletter or sent in an e-mail message. A teacher or school might even consider scheduling a series of family literacy nights, with individual nights like "Vocabulary Night" or "Metacognition Night" in order to introduce families more fully to the component ideas and opportunities for family reading, perhaps with benefit of a translating family member, letting children show parents the work in the classroom and presenting children's fiction and nonfiction books that families can borrow from the school resource center or public library.

PARENTS AS SERIOUS PARTNERS SELF-ASSESSMENT

According to the International Reading Association, an outcomes-based approach to preparing educators to include parents as serious partners should include attention to the interconnected roles of the school, family, and community in children's learning and development (IRA, 2002). Educators partnering with parents should take into account the values and attitudes of parents. The goals of an outcomes-based approach are to encourage programs that interconnect family and school. One of the first steps teachers can take is to reflect on their own values and attitudes about building family partnerships. The *Parents as Serious Partners Self-Assessment (PSPS)* in Table 11.1 is provided for teachers to reflect on their own values and attitudes related to parent partnerships. All teachers and school personnel can use it to begin the conversation about their beliefs and understanding of the elements of effective parent partnerships.

Table 11.1   Parents as Serious Partners Belief Self-Assessment for Educators

Use the assessment to reflect on the areas of strengths and areas that need further refinement.

1 = Strongly Disagree   5 = Strongly Agree

1. I am aware of the importance of family-school connections, and I am committed to the concept of partnerships with the families of all children.   1   2   3   4   5

2. I am able to think systematically about family-involvement attitudes and practices and learn from my experiences.   1   2   3   4   5

3. I understand the benefits of different types of family involvement, as well as the barriers to their implementation.   1   2   3   4   5

4. I am aware of the way cultural assumptions and life experiences influence interpretations of events, and respect the beliefs, values, opinions, lifestyles, and childrearing practices of families.   1   2   3   4   5

5. I am willing to build on family diversity in the classroom, at the school site, and in the home.   1   2   3   4   5

6. I am willing to work collaboratively with other professionals and with families and students to develop a common vision of partnerships.   1   2   3   4   5

7. I am willing to assume responsibility for initiating, supporting, rewarding, and monitoring various types of partnership activities, ensuring access for all parents, and respecting all types and levels of participation.   1   2   3   4   5

PARENT-FRIENDLY EXAMPLES THAT PARENTS CAN USE TO ASSIST WITH THE MAJOR COMPONENTS OF READING FIRST

Oral Language

Parents can help develop oral language at home by encouraging children to express themselves verbally. At home parents can read aloud, engage in meaningful conversations, recite certain pages in a book or from a favorite poem, and encourage children to speak with relatives on the phone.

Home Study Buddies

Home Study Buddies can be determined at school by the teacher. At school students begin homework assignments and also exchange phone numbers so they can consult each other at home. Each is responsible for being sure the Study Buddy receives and completes all the work for days he or she is absent. In schools that do not assign homework, struggling readers and writers benefit from Study Buddies by being allowed to pair with a person who has the same hobby or reading interests. They can meet to share work on their hobbies at home. They can also keep each other informed of upcoming television and community events relative to the hobby area. Parents can support the children by giving them time to discuss assignments and activities for a brief period of time at home. Home Study Buddies serves multiple purposes. Most important, they encourage children to develop oral language speaking skills with peers. This builds confidence and increases students' willingness to develop oral language in school situations.

Family Opportunities to Help Oral Language Development

A Parent Might Say: "We are going to visit our grandparents today and you could ask them about their favorite childhood stories and memories."

A Parent May Want to: Help children think in advance about questions that they would like to ask. This can be done in the car or on the bus to the grandparents' house.

A Parent May Want to Suggest: Retell to other members of the family the stories that their grandparents told.

Phonemes and Phonemic Awareness

Parents can assist their child with early reading strategies by understanding the concept of phonemic awareness. Phonemic awareness is the ability to hear, identify, and manipulate the individual sounds in spoken words. One way parents can help is to practice rhyming words and segment the word into sounds.

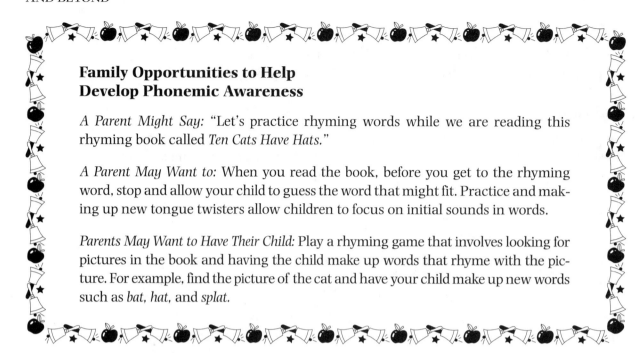

**Family Opportunities to Help
Develop Phonemic Awareness**

A Parent Might Say: "Let's practice rhyming words while we are reading this rhyming book called *Ten Cats Have Hats.*"

A Parent May Want to: When you read the book, before you get to the rhyming word, stop and allow your child to guess the word that might fit. Practice and making up new tongue twisters allow children to focus on initial sounds in words.

Parents May Want to Have Their Child: Play a rhyming game that involves looking for pictures in the book and having the child make up words that rhyme with the picture. For example, find the picture of the cat and have your child make up new words such as *bat, hat,* and *splat.*

Phonics

Research has determined that students need systematic phonics that teaches sounds, letters, and spelling patterns in the context of literature. Parents can assist their child with reading by doing the following:

- Review words learned in school.
- Begin with high-frequency letters and move to less-frequent letters. For example, begin practicing with *a, b,* and *c,* and vowels, *a* and *i.* Words that begin with *v, w,* and *x* can be practiced once the high-frequency words have been practiced.
- Parents can practice word families at home and spelling patterns of frequently used words in the house.

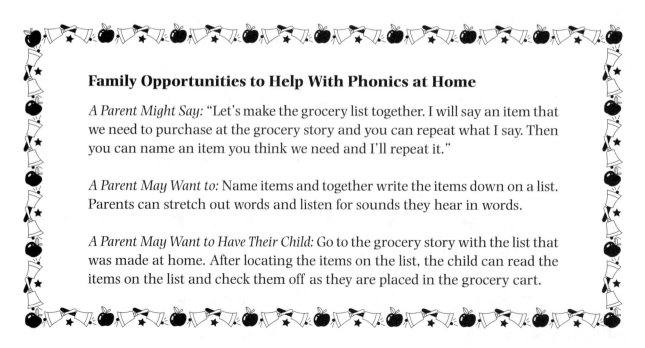

Family Opportunities to Help With Phonics at Home

A Parent Might Say: "Let's make the grocery list together. I will say an item that we need to purchase at the grocery story and you can repeat what I say. Then you can name an item you think we need and I'll repeat it."

A Parent May Want to: Name items and together write the items down on a list. Parents can stretch out words and listen for sounds they hear in words.

A Parent May Want to Have Their Child: Go to the grocery story with the list that was made at home. After locating the items on the list, the child can read the items on the list and check them off as they are placed in the grocery cart.

Vocabulary

Teachers can help parents promote vocabulary growth and language development in meaningful ways by communicating to them effective ways to define words during a read-aloud experience at home (Dickinson & Smith, 1994). Teachers can communicate that daily attention to and seeking meaning of exact words also builds literacy (Dickinson & Tabors, 2001). In Chapter 5, ten research findings were presented to guide teachers to help students increase their own vocabularies. Following are five research findings that parents can easily implement in home experiences to increase and enhance vocabulary development with their child. The five research-based findings can guide parents to a more complete understanding of methods to promote vocabulary development. Five easy-to-implement methods were selected to build confidence and an appreciation for support in strengthening vocabulary at home.

Parent Tip 1: High-Frequency Words Are Important

Parents can help children develop vocabulary by learning high-frequency words. High-frequency words that parents can practice with their child can be provided by the teacher at the beginning of the year or periodically during the school year. Words that are provided should be grade and developmentally appropriate. The more thoroughly children can learn high-frequency vocabulary, the better able they will be at comprehending text that contains these or similar words.

Parent Tip 2: Teach Important Words That Transfer

Since the many high-frequency words encountered in reading are characteristic of a core of word families, the learning of one word creates a key to unlocking the meaning of several dozen other new words. Parents can begin with picturable nouns and concrete-referent words. For example, parents can choose books with nouns that can easily be represented by a picture or mental image. A book on cars, trucks, houses, and toys is a great place to begin developing vocabulary.

Parent Tip 3: Provide Rich, Effective
Experiences When Learning Word Meaning

Parents can help their child learn the meaning of words by providing varied, tactile, dramatic, kinesthetic, oral, and written exposure to a word's meaning.

Parent Tip 4: Provide Multiple Exposures to Words and Meanings

Repeated exposures increase the size of the visual unit that children recognize, so that they can eventually know many words with the same letter or meaning-based patterns automatically (Samuels, 2003). You can provide such exposure by giving your child a range of effective vocabulary-building learning experiences for each word (and the family of words it represents). This repeated, successive use of a word is called *fast-mapping* (Block, 2004). Fast-mapping gives at least six consecutive opportunities to independently apply the word and meaning just learned so that its use becomes automatic.

Parent Tip 5: Link Vocabulary to Common Themes

As we discussed in Chapter 5, word consciousness develops even more deeply when vocabulary words are tied to a common theme. Parents can relate to high-interest themes and topics with words that students experience daily. For example, when reading a fiction book, parents can help their child look for common themes related to child-selected vocabulary words. A child might begin to notice words related to building friendships or words related to traveling.

Fluency

Fluency is reading with speed, accuracy, and proper expression without conscious attention. Parents can help their child build fluency by reading poetry together. Rereading familiar books also helps children build fluency, especially if the child is able to read along with the parent. Helping children to make puppets and perform short skits using the puppets from the books they are reading is another method parents can use to help their child increase fluency.

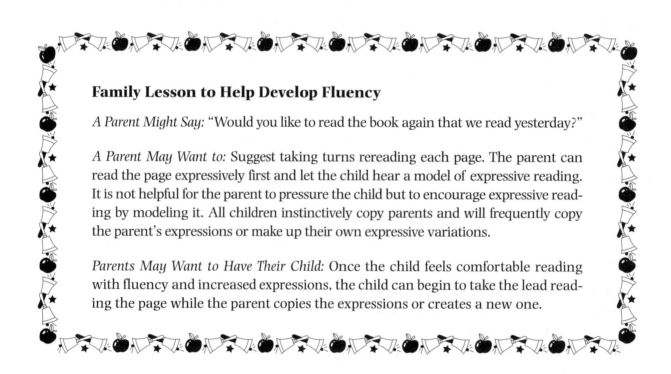

Family Lesson to Help Develop Fluency

A Parent Might Say: "Would you like to read the book again that we read yesterday?"

A Parent May Want to: Suggest taking turns rereading each page. The parent can read the page expressively first and let the child hear a model of expressive reading. It is not helpful for the parent to pressure the child but to encourage expressive reading by modeling it. All children instinctively copy parents and will frequently copy the parent's expressions or make up their own expressive variations.

Parents May Want to Have Their Child: Once the child feels comfortable reading with fluency and increased expressions, the child can begin to take the lead reading the page while the parent copies the expressions or creates a new one.

Comprehension

Reading comprehension is the construction of meaning from text. Parents can assist their child by helping them think more deeply about what they are reading. One way to do this is to use the think-aloud strategy. This strategy serves multiple purposes, such as vocabulary development, fluency, and more metacognitive, or conscious, ways of thinking. Four think-aloud strategies that can be demonstrated by parents while reading any text are revising prior knowledge, recognizing the author's writing style, determining word meaning, and asking questions (Block and Israel, 2004).

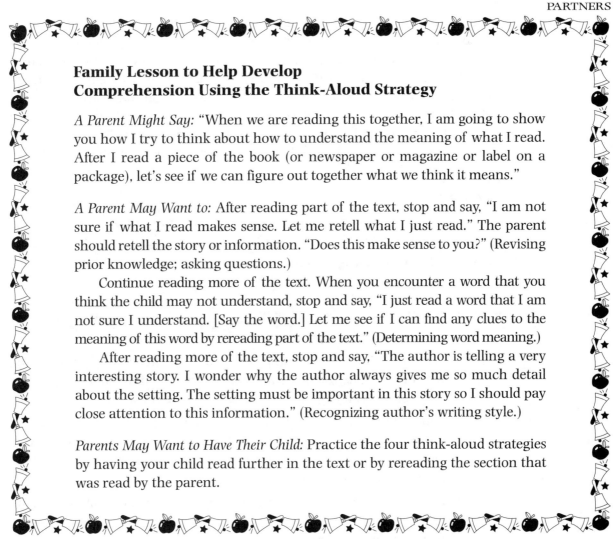

**Family Lesson to Help Develop
Comprehension Using the Think-Aloud Strategy**

A Parent Might Say: "When we are reading this together, I am going to show you how I try to think about how to understand the meaning of what I read. After I read a piece of the book (or newspaper or magazine or label on a package), let's see if we can figure out together what we think it means."

A Parent May Want to: After reading part of the text, stop and say, "I am not sure if what I read makes sense. Let me retell what I just read." The parent should retell the story or information. "Does this make sense to you?" (Revising prior knowledge; asking questions.)

Continue reading more of the text. When you encounter a word that you think the child may not understand, stop and say, "I just read a word that I am not sure I understand. [Say the word.] Let me see if I can find any clues to the meaning of this word by rereading part of the text." (Determining word meaning.)

After reading more of the text, stop and say, "The author is telling a very interesting story. I wonder why the author always gives me so much detail about the setting. The setting must be important in this story so I should pay close attention to this information." (Recognizing author's writing style.)

Parents May Want to Have Their Child: Practice the four think-aloud strategies by having your child read further in the text or by rereading the section that was read by the parent.

Independent Reading

There are many ways for parents to encourage their child to read independently at home. Parents can model reading independently for extended periods of time. Choosing varied reading materials, such as newspapers, magazines, and books, also models good reading habits for children. This will provide a model and help children understand that spending time reading independently is an enjoyable experience. Parents can provide assistance by making sure quiet time and quiet places are provided in the evening and on weekends. Time can be set aside when the entire family is engaged in independent reading tasks. Going to the library also provides quiet space where independent reading is modeled. If children find books they like to read, encourage them to become familiar with other books written by the same author.

Sustained Silent Evenings

To help parents with increasing independent reading at home, parents can begin having occasional Sustained Silent Evenings (SSE). In school, students benefit from sustained silent reading activities. SSE has been created to provide opportunities for children to watch their parents read silently and read silently themselves. A modification of SSE that can provide increased writing time can be time to have Sustained Silent Reading or Writing time (SSRW). Parents should read or write in the same room as their children. They should share what they read about that is of value to them. Likewise, a discussion about writing can also take place. Children and adolescents who are involved in these types of activities build a stronger foundation than those who do not have this experience (Block, 1990).

Writing

Writing is a wonderful way of expressing thoughts and ideas. Parents can encourage their child to write more at home by providing them with opportunities to write. Below is a list of ten ways parents can encourage writing at home.

1. Show your children that you think that *writing is IMPORTANT.* Show them how you *use writing* all through your day. For example, show them the grocery list you prepare.

2. *Write with your child.* Use the stories you read together as vehicles for writing prompts. You and your child can write a different ending to the story, or you can help them to write a letter to the author.

3. Show your child *how much you like to write* by showing them a story or poem you have written. You can even share with them something you wrote in school or at the office; for example, a newsletter you have prepared or even a memo.

4. *If you don't like to write* ask someone else to help your child with writing. Grandparents or friends who enjoy writing might enjoy sharing their writing experiences.

5. *Buy writing supplies as gifts.* Children love to have a new pad of blank paper and a cool pen to write with. Writing supplies can also include new writing storybook software.

6. *Take your child to a newspaper office.* The people working there will give your child new ideas as they observe people who love their writing processes. Local bookstores usually invite authors to sign books. This is a wonderful time to take your child to the bookstore and meet an author.

7. *Keep a journal when taking a family trip.* Journals encourage children to reflect on their experiences. It also helps them document favorite activities. The journal can also be used as a record of the trip. Promote reading by having your children read excerpts from their journals.

8. If your child speaks a language in addition to English, *help your child write in your home language.*

9. *Teach your children how to revise their writing.* Have children write a rough draft of a letter they are writing to another family member before they write the final draft.

10. When your children find stories or books or poems that they like a lot, *have them copy the poem and change certain words to make a new story.*

Copying a story or poem also helps children better understand how words are used to develop stories. Changing the words is a creative way to model good writing.

Metacognition

When students involve metacognition, or "a consciousness of one's own thinking processes before, during, and after reading, writing, speaking, listening, and viewing," they experience full comprehension that is emotional, cognitive, and efferent (Block, 2004, p. 292). Metacognition aids students in "the development of insightful comprehension and creative composition, learning how to learn, and enhancing their motivation as well as their positive attitudes toward reading" (Block, 2004, p. 396).

Parents can help their child become more metacognitive by asking them four simple questions during any reading experience. After each question, asking *why* provides much more insight for understanding your child's thinking.

Family Opportunity to Help Develop Metacognition

A Parent Might Say: "I would like to know what you are thinking about what you are reading," or "Would you like to tell me about what you are thinking?"

A Parent May Want to: Ask your child the following four questions. After each question ask one more question by saying, "And why."
- What do you think you believe about what you just read?
- What do you know about what you just read?
- What do you feel about what you just read?
- What do you question about what you just read?

Parents May Want to Have Their Child: Have their child practice asking the same questions back to the parent.

RESOURCES FOR PARTNERING PARENTS

Teachers can help parents by providing them with resources that will assist them in promoting literacy experiences at home. Following are lists of easy-to-obtain resources and informative Web sites.

Free Resources From the Department of Education

The following list of resources can be obtained free from the Department of Education by calling 1-800-228-8813 or visiting the Web site at www.edpubs .org.

- *Put Reading First: Helping Your Child Learn to Read, A Parent Guide Preschool Through Grade 3*
- *No Child Left Behind: A Parent's Guide*
- *Helping Your Child Become a Reader*
- *Helping Your Child Succeed in School*
- *Helping Your Child With Homework*

Web Sites

- http://www.ed.gov/print/nclb/methods/reading/readingfirst.html. This site provides a brief summary of the facts about Reading First from the Department of Education. The Web site provides helpful information about how Reading First will improve reading instruction. The Web site also gives an introduction to the application process for states that wish to seek Reading First grants.
- http://www.ed.gov/programs/readingfirst/index.html. Summary of the Reading First legislation and the purpose of Reading First.
- http://www.nifl.gov. The National Institute for Literacy, an independent federal organization, supports the development of high-quality state, regional, and national literacy services. *Partnerships for Reading* is a program promoting child literacy administered by the National Institute for Literacy.
- http://www.reading.org. The International Reading Association promotes parents as partners by published several parent booklets in the areas of reading and literacy. The booklets may be obtained from this Web site.

SUMMARY

The purpose of this chapter was to assist teachers with ways to develop positive and effective relationships with parents. Educators can use this information to reflect upon, evaluate, and change their active role in efforts related to building parent and family partnerships. Including parents as serious partners takes time. It is important to begin thinking about the roles in which parents are being utilized to interconnect literacy in school and at home. May the information presented in this chapter provide a framework to give parents the information and assistance they need to support their child's literacy development.

References and Suggested Readings

CHAPTER 1

Block, C. C. (2004). *Teaching comprehension: The comprehension process approach.* Needham Heights, MA: Allyn & Bacon.

Block, C. C., & Dellamura, R. (2000/2001). Better book buddies. *The Reading Teacher, 54*(4), 364–370.

Block, C. C., Oakar, M, & Hirt, N. (2002). The exemplary literacy teachers continuum: Preschool to grade 5. *Reading Research Quarterly, 50,* 173–191.

Cullinan, B. (Ed.). (1992). *Invitation to read: More children's literature in the reading program.* Newark, DE: International Reading Association.

Dehaene, S., Naccache, L., Cohen, L., Le Bihan, D., Mangin, J., Poline, J., et al. (2001). Cerebral mechanisms of word masking and unconscious repetition priming. *Nature neuroscience, 4,* 752–758.

Demb, J., Boynton, G., & Heeger, D. (1988). Functional magnetic resonance imaging of early visual pathways in dyslexia. *Journal of Neuroscience, 18,* 6939–6951.

Demonet, J., Price, C., Wise, R., & Frackowiak, R. (1994). A PET study of cognitive strategies in normal subjects during language tasks: Influence of phonetic ambiguity and sequence processing on phoneme monitoring. *Brain, 117,* 671–682.

Dyson, A. H. (2000, April). *The persistence of contrary pedagogical order.* Paper presented at the annual meeting of the American Educational Research Association, New Orleans.

Eden, G. F., VanMeter, J. W., Rumsey, J. M., Maisog, J. M., Woods, R. P., & Zeffiro, T. A. (1996). Abnormal processing of visual motion in dyslexia revealed by functional brain imaging. *Nature, 382,* 66–69.

Frequently asked questions about No Child Left Behind. (n.d.). Retrieved April 1, 2004 from www.ed.gov.

Jensen, E. (2000). Moving with the brain in mind. *Educational Leadership, 58,* 34–37.

Learning disabilities and early intervention strategies: Hearing before the Subcommittee on Education Reform, of the Committee on Education and the Workforce, House of Representatives, 107th Cong., (2002) (testimony of G. Reid Lyon).

Lyon, G. R. (2002). Reading development, reading difficulties, and reading instruction: Educational and public health issues. *Journal of School Psychology, 40,* 3–6.

National Center for Educational Statistics (2003). *Nation's report card.* Washington, DC: U.S. Department of Education.

National Institute of Child Health and Human Development, NIH, DHHS. (2000a). *Report of the National Reading Panel: Teaching Children to Read* (00–4769). Washington, DC: U.S. Government Printing Office.

National Institute of Child Health and Human Development, NIH, DHHS. (2000b). *Report of the National Reading Panel: Teaching Children to Read: Reports of the Subgroups* (00–4754). Washington, DC: U.S. Government Printing Office.

No Child Left Behind: A Toolkit for Teachers. (n.d.). Retrieved Sept. 24, 2004, from www.ed.gov/teachers.

Presseisen, B. (1987). Teaching thinking and at-risk students. *Educational Research and Improvement, 7*(1), 77. Reading First, www.ed.gov.

Shaywitz, S. (1999). Brain imaging. *Educational Leadership, 56,* 21–28.

Simos, P., Breier, J., Flether, J., Bergman, E., & Papanicolaou, A. (2000). Cerebral mechanisms involved in word reading in dyslexic children: A magnetic source imaging approach. *Cerebral Cortex, 10,* 809–816.

Simos, P. G., Fletcher, J. M., Bergman, E., Breier, J. I., Foorman, B. R., Castillo, E. M., et al. (2002). Dyslexia-specific brain activation profile becomes normal following successful remedial training. *Neurology, 58*(8), 1203–1213.

Snow, C., Burns, S., & Griffin, P. (Eds.). (1998). *Preventing reading difficulties in young children.* Washington, DC: National Academy Press.

State assessments (n.d.). Retrieved Oct. 3, 2004, from www.ed.gov/teachers.

CHAPTER 2

Anderson, V., & Roit, M. (1996). Linking reading comprehension instruction to language development for language-minority students. *The Elementary School Journal, 96,* 295–309.

Au, T. K., Depretto, M., & Song, Y-K. (1994). Input vs. constraints: Early word acquisition in Korean and English. *Journal of Memory and Language, 33,* 567–582.

Beals, D. E. (2001). Eating and reading: Links between family conversations with preschoolers and later language literacy. In D. K. Dickinson & P. O. Tabors, (Eds.), *Beginning literacy with language: Young children learning at home and school* (pp. 433–456). Baltimore, MD: Paul H. Brookes.

Block, C. C., Rodgers, L., & Johnson, R. (2004). *Teaching comprehension in kindergarten through grade 3: Building success for all students.* New York: Guilford.

Bloom, L. (1990). Development in express: Affect and speech. In N. Stein & T. Trabasso (Eds.), *Psychological and biological approaches to emotion* (pp. 215–245). Hillsdale, NJ: Erlbaum.

Bohannan, J. N., III. (1993). Theoretical approaches to language acquisition. In J. B. Gleason (Ed.), *The Development of language* (3rd ed.) (pp. 239–297). New York: Macmillan.

Cazden, C. B. (1992). Revealing and telling: The socialization of attention in learning to read and write. *Educational psychology: An international journal of experimental educational psychology, 12,* 305–313.

Choi, D. H., & Kim, J. (2003). Practicing social skills training for young children with low peer acceptance: A cognitive-social learning model. *Early Childhood Education Journal, 31,* 41–46.

Chomsky, C. (1965). *Aspects of a theory of syntax.* Cambridge, MA: MIT Press.

Clark, E. V. (1997). Conceptual perspective and lexical choice in language acquisition. *Cognition, 64,* 309–343.

Coger, L. I., & White, M. R. (1982). *Readers theatre handbook: A dramatic approach to literature* (3rd ed.). Glenview, IL: Scott, Foresman.

Collier, M. (1987, December). *Amount of time needed to read oral proficiency: Research study concerning English Language Learners' ability to catch up.* Paper presented at the annual meeting of the National Reading Conference, San Diego, CA.

Conrad, N. K., Gong, Y., Sipp, L., & Wright, L. (2004). Using Text Talk as a gateway to culturally responsive teaching. *Early Childhood Education Journal, 31,* 187–192.

Corson, D. (2001). *Language diversity and education.* Mahwah, NJ: Lawrence Erlbaum Associates.

Cutler, A., & Clifton, C. (1999). Comprehending spoken language: A blueprint of the listener. In C. M. Brown, & P. Hagoort (Eds.), *The neurocognition of language* (pp. 123–166). New York: Oxford University Press.

Delpit, L. (1995). *Other people's children.* New York: New Press.

Dickinson, D. K., & Tabors, P. O. (2000). *Early literacy at home and school: The critical role of language development in the preschool years.* Baltimore, MD: Paul H. Brookes.

Gleason, J. B. (2001). The development of language: An overview and a preview. In J. B. (Ed.). *The Development of Language* (pp. 1–39). Needham Heights, MA: Allyn & Bacon.

Graves, M. F., Juel, C., & Graves, B. B. (2004). Reading Instruction for English-Language Learners. In A. M. Ramos & M. Kriener (Eds.), *Teaching reading in the 21st century,* (pp. 496–541). Boston, MA: Allyn and Bacon.

Halliday, M. A. K. (1975) Learning how to mean: Exploration in the development of language. London: Edward Arnold.

Halliday, M. A. K. (1987). Spoken and written modes of meaning. In R. Horowitz & S. J. Samuels (Eds.), *Comprehending oral and written language* (pp. 55–82). San Diego, CA: Academic Press.

Harris, T. L., & Hodges, R. E. (1995). *The Literacy Dictionary.* Newark, DE: International Reading Association.

Jaggar, A. (1985). Allowing for language differences. In G.S. Pinnell (Ed.), *Discovering language with children* (pp. 111–122). Urbana, IL: National Council of Teachers of English.

Jewell, M., & Zintz, M. (1986). *Learning to read naturally.* Dubuque, IA: Kendall/Hunt.

Johnson, D. W., Johnson, R. T., & Holubec, E. J. (1994). *The new circles of learning: Cooperation in the classroom and school.* Alexandria, VA: Association for Supervision and Curriculum Development.

Johnson, J. S., & Newport, E. L. (1989). Critical period effect in second language learning: The influence of maturational state on the acquisition of English as a second language. *Cognitive Psychology, 21,* 60–99.

LaBerge, D., & Samuels, S. J. (1974). Toward a theory of automatic information processing in reading. *Cognitive Psychology, 6,* 292–323.

Ladson-Billings, G. (1994). *The Dreamkeepers.* San Francisco: Jossey-Bass.

Lapp, D., Block, C. C., Cooper, E. J., Flood, J., Roser, N., & Tinajero, V. (2004). *Teaching All the Children: Strategies for Developing Literacy in an Urban Setting.* New York: Guilford.

Levelt, W. J. M. (1999). Producing spoken language: A blueprint of the speaker. In C. M. Brown & P. Hagoort (Eds.), *The neurocognition of language* (pp. 84–122). New York: Oxford University Press.

Menn, L., & Stoel-Gammon, C. (2001). Phonological development: Learning sounds and sound patterns. In J. B. Gleason (Ed.), *The development of language* (pp. 70–124). Needham Heights, MA: Allyn & Bacon.

Moerk, E. L. (1992). *A first language taught and learned.* Baltimore, MD: Paul H. Brookes.

Morrow, L. M. (2001). *Literacy development in the early years: Helping children read and write* (4th ed.). Needham Heights, MA: Allyn & Bacon.

Pelligrini, A. D., Galda, L., Bartini, M, & Charak, D. (1998). Oral language and literacy learning in content: The role of social relationships. *Merrill-Palmer Quarterly, 44,* 38–54.

Perfetti, C. A. (1999). Comprehending written language: A blueprint of the reader. In C. M. Brown and P. Hagoort (Eds.) *The neurocognition of language* (pp. 167–197). New York: Oxford University Press.

Piaget, J., & Inhelder, B. (1969). *The psychology of the child.* New York: Basic Books.

Pinker, S. (1994). *The language instinct.* New York: Harper Collins.

Sachs, J. (2001). Communication development in infancy. In J. B. Gleason (Ed.), *The development of language* (pp. 40–69). Needham Heights, MA: Allyn & Bacon.

Samuels, J. (2002). The development of fluency. In J. Samuels & A. Farstrup (Eds.). *What research has to say about reading instruction* (pp. 237–249). Newark, DE: International Reading Association.

Samuels, S. J. (2002). Reading fluency: What is it? How can I teach it? How can I measure it? *Instructional Leader, 15*(6), 1–2, 11–12.

Skinner, B. F. (1957). *Verbal behavior.* Boston: Appleton-Century-Crofts.

St. Amour, M. J. (2003). Connecting children's stories to children's literature: Meeting diversity needs. *Early Childhood Education Journal, 31,* 47–51.

Sulzby, E. (1986). Kindergarteners as writers and readers. In M. Farr (Ed.), *Advances in writing research, Vol. 1: Children's early writing* (pp. 33–54). Norwood, NJ: Ablex.

Vygotsky, L. S. (1978). *Mind in society: The development of psychological processes.* Cambridge, MA: Harvard University Press.

Whitehurst, G. J., Arnold, D. S., Epstein, J. N., Angell, A. L., Smith, M., & Fischel, J. E. (1994). A picture book reading intervention in day care and home for children from low-income families. *Developmental Psychology, 30,* 697–689.

Wigfield, A., & Eccles, C. (l996). Social and motivating influences on reading. In P. D. Pearson, R. Barr, M. Kamil, & P. Mosenthal (Eds.). *Handbook of reading research* (pp. 423–452). New York: Longman.

CHAPTER 3

Adams, M. J. (1990). *Beginning to read; Thinking and learning about print.* Cambridge, MA: MIT Press.

Adams, M. J. (1995). *Advances in learning and behavioral disabilities.* Greenwich, CT: JAI Press.

Beck, I., & McKeown, M. (1991). Conditions of vocabulary acquisition. In R. Barr, M. Kamil, P. Mosenthal, & P. D. Pearson (Eds.), *Handbook of reading research, Vol. 2* (pp. 789–814). New York: Longman.

Beck, I., McKeown, M. G., & Kucan, L. (2002). *Bringing words to life: Robust vocabulary development.* New York: Guilford.

Beck, I. L., Perfetti, C.A., & McKeown, M.G. (1982). Effects of long-term vocabulary instruction on lexical access and reading comprehension. *Journal of Educational Psychology, 74,* 506–521.

Block, C. C. (2004). *Teaching comprehension: The comprehension process.* New York: Guilford.

Block, C. C., & Mangieri, J. N. (2003). *Exemplary literacy teachers: Literacy success in grades K-5.* New York: Guilford.

Block, C. C., Rodgers, L., & Johnson, R. (2004). *Teaching comprehension in kindergarten through grade 3: Building success for all students.* New York: Guilford.

Bus, A. G., van Ijzendoorn, M. H., & Pellegrini, A. D. (1995). Joint book reading makes for success in learning to read: A meta-analysis on intergenerational transmission of literacy. *Review of Educational Research, 65,* 1–21.

Carroll, J. M., Snowling, M. J., Hulme, C., & Stevenson, J. (2003). The development of phonological awareness in preschool children. *Developmental Psychology, 39*(5), 913–923.

Dickinson, D., & Smith, M. (1994). Long-term effects of preschool teachers' book readings on low-income children's vocabulary and story comprehension. *Reading Research Quarterly, 29,* 104–122.

Dickinson, D. K., & McCabe, A. (2003). The comprehensive language approach to early literacy: The interrelationships among vocabulary, phonological sensitivity, and print knowledge among preschool-aged children. *Journal of Educational Psychology, 95*(3), 465–481.

Dickinson, D. K., & Tabors, P. O. (Eds.). (2001). *Building literacy with language.* Baltimore: Paul H. Brookes.

Dodds, D. (1991). Dialing for members. *Currents, 17*(3), 38–40.

Durkin, D. (1993). *Teaching them to read* (6th ed.). Boston: Allyn & Bacon.

Ericson, L., & Juliebo, M. F. (1998). *The phonological awareness handbook for kindergarten and primary teachers.* Newark, DE: International Reading Association.

Gans, K. D. (1994). *Learning through listening* (2nd ed.). Dubuque, IA: Kendall Hunt.

International Reading Association (2004). *Language and Literacy in American Preschools.* Position statement. Newark, DE: author.

Mastropieri, M. A., & Scruggs, T. E. (1991). Reading comprehension: A synthesis of research in learning disabilities. In T. E. Scruggs & M. A. Mastropieri (Eds.), *Comprehension Research and Practice* (pp. 345–367). Mahwah, NJ: Erlbaum.

McKeown, M. G., Beck, I. L., Omanson, R. C., & Pople, M. T. (1985). Some effects of the nature and frequency of vocabulary instruction on the knowledge and use of words. *Reading Research Quarterly, 20,* 522–535.

Miller, W. H. (1993). *Complete reading disabilities handbook: Ready-to-use techniques for teaching reading disabled students.* West Nyack, NH: Center for Applied Research in Education.

Morrow, L. M., Tracey, D. H., Woo, D. G., & Pressley, M. (1999). Characteristics of exemplary first-grade literacy instruction. *The Reading Teacher, 52*(5), 462–476.

Mwalimu & Kennaway, A. (1989). *Awful aardvark.* Boston: Little, Brown.

National Institute of Child Health and Human Development, NIH, DHHS. (2000). *Report of the National Reading Panel: Teaching Children to Read* (00-4769). Washington, DC: U.S. Government Printing Office.

National Institute of Child Health and Human Development, NIH, DHHS. (2004). Child Development and Behavior Branch (CDBB), NICHD, Report to the NACHHD Council, September 2004. Washington, DC: U.S. Government Printing Office.

Rosenshine, B., & Stevens, S. (1984). Reciprocal protocols: A review of nineteen experimental studies. *Review of Educational Research, 64,* 470–530.

Shaywitz, S. (1999). Brain imaging. *Educational leadership, 56,* 21–28.

Shaywitz, B. A., Shaywitz, S. E., Blachman, B. A., Pugh, K. R., Fulbright, R. K., Skudlarski, P. et al. (2004). Development of left occipitotemporal systems for skilled reading in children after a phonologically based intervention. *Biological Psychiatry, 55*(9), 926–933.

Snow, C. E., Burns, M. S., & Griffin, P. (1998). *Preventing reading difficulties in young children.* Washington, DC: National Academy Press.

Stanovich, K. E., & Cunningham, A. E. (l993). Where does knowledge come from? Specific associations between print exposure and information acquisition. *Journal of Educational Psychology, 85,* 211–229.

Stewart, M. T. (2002). *"Best Practice"? Insights on literacy instruction from an elementary classroom.* Newark, DE: International Reading Association.

Stewart, M. T. (2004). Early literacy instruction in the climate of No Child Left Behind. *The Reading Teacher, 57*(8), 732–743.

Wells, D. (1986). Leading grand conversations. In N. Roser & M. Martinez (Eds.) *Book talk and beyond* (pp. 263–271). Newark, DE: International Reading Association.

CHAPTER 4

Adams, M. J. (1990). *Beginning to read: Thinking and learning about print.* Cambridge, MA: MIT Press.

Baumann, J. F., Hoffman, J. V., Moon, J., & Duffy-Hester, A. M. (1998). Where are teachers' voices in the phonics/whole language debate? Results from a survey of U.S. elementary classroom teachers. *The Reading Teacher, 51*(8), 636–650.

Berent, I., & Perretti, C. A. (l995). A rose is a REEZ: The two-cycles model of phonology assembly in reading English. *Psychological Review, 102,* 146–184.

Block, C. C., & Dellamura, R. (2000/2001). Better book buddies. *The Reading Teacher, 54*(4), 364–370.

Block, C. C., & Mangieri, J. N. (2003). *Exemplary literacy teachers: Literacy success in grades K–5.* New York: Guilford.

Cassidy J., Roettger, R., & Wixson, K. (1987). Linguistic readers revisited. *Elementary Reading Instruction,* Research Report 3, San Diego, CA: Macmillan.

Clymer, T. (1963, reprinted 1996). The utility of phonic generalizations in the primary grades. *The Reading Teacher, 50*(3), 182–187.

Duffy, G. G., & Hoffman, J. V. (1999). In pursuit of an illusion: The flawed search for a perfect method. *The Reading Teacher, 50*(1), 10–17.

Gaskins, R. W., Gaskins, J. C., & Gaskins, I. W. (1991). A decoding program for poor readers—and the rest of the class too! *Language Arts, 68*(3), 213–225.

Goswami, U. (2000). Phonological and lexical processes. In M. L. Kamil, P. B. Mosenthal, P. D. Pearson, & R. Barr (Eds.). *Handbook of reading research, Vol. 3* (pp. 251–267). Mahwah, NJ: Erlbaum.

Harris, T. L., & Hodges, R. E. (1995). *The literacy dictionary.* Newark, DE: International Reading Association.

International Reading Association (1997). *Phonics Instruction.* Position statement. Newark, DE: author.

Jensen, E. (2000). Moving with the brain in mind. *Educational Leadership, 58,* 34–37.

Michael, P. A. (1994). *The child's view of reading.* Boston: Allyn & Bacon.

National Institute of Child Health and Human Development, NIH, DHHS. (2000a). *Report of the National Reading Panel: Teaching Children to Read* (00–4769). Washington, DC: U.S. Government Printing Office.

National Institute of Child Health and Human Development, NIH, DHHS. (2000b). *Report of the National Reading Panel: Teaching Children to Read: Reports of the Subgroups* (00–4754). Washington, DC: U.S. Government Printing Office.

Olson, D. R. (1977). From utterance to text: The bias of language in speech and writing. *Harvard Educational Review, 47,* 257–281.

Rubin, H. (1988). Morphological knowledge and early writing ability. *Language and Speech, 31,* 337–355.

Shaywitz, S. (1999). Brain Imaging. *Educational Leadership, 56,* 21–28.

Stahl, S. A., Duffy-Hester, A. M., & Stahl, K. A. (1998). Everything you wanted to know about phonics (but were afraid to ask). *Reading Research Quarterly, 33*, 338–355.

Stanovich, K. E., & Cunningham, A. E. (1993). Where does knowledge come from? Specific associations between print exposure and information acquisition. *Journal of Educational Psychology, 85*, 211–229.

Tannen, D. (1985). Relative focus on involvement in oral and written discourse. In D. R. Olson, N. Torrance, & A. Hildyard (Eds.), *Literacy, language and learning: The nature and consequences of reading and writing* (pp. 124–147). Cambridge: Cambridge University Press.

Venezky, R. L. (1997). The literary text: Its future in the classroom. In J. Flood, S. B. Heth, & D. Lapp (Eds.). *Handbook of research on teaching literacy through the communicative and visual arts* (pp. 528–535). New York: Macmillan.

CHAPTER 5

Beck, I., & McKeown, M. (1991). Conditions of vocabulary acquisition. In R. Barr, M. Kamil, P. Mosenthal, & P. D. Pearson (Eds.), *The handbook of reading research Vol. 2* (pp. 789–814). New York: Longman.

Beck, I., & McKeown, M. (2002). *Bringing words to life: Robust vocabulary development.* New York: Guilford.

Beck, I. L., Perfetti, C.A., & McKeown, M.G. (1982). Effects of long-term vocabulary instruction on lexical access and reading comprehension. *Journal of Educational Psychology, 74*, 506–521.

Biemiller, A. (2001). Teaching reading and language to the disadvantaged: What we have learned from field research. *Harvard Educational Review, 47*, 518–543.

Biemiller, A., & Slonim, M. (2001). Estimating root word vocabulary growth in normative and advantaged populations: Evidence for a common sequence of vocabulary acquisition. *Journal of Educational Psychology, 93*, 498–520.

Block, C. C. (2004). Effects of trade book reading on literacy achievement. *Illinois Reading Journal 32*(4), 3–8.

Block, C. C. & Graham, M. (2000). *Elementary students as co-teachers and co-researchers.* Paper presented at the annual meeting of the National Reading Conference, Charleston, SC.

Block, C. C., & Mangieri, J. N. (2003). *Exemplary literacy teachers: Literacy success in grades K-5.* New York: Guilford.

Block, C. C., & Mangieri, J. N. (2005). *Powerful vocabulary for reading success.* New York: Scholastic.

Block, C. C., Rodgers, L., & Johnson, R. (2004). *Teaching comprehension in kindergarten through grade 3: Building success for all students.* New York: Guilford.

Block, C. C., Stanley, C., & McDonough (in press). Effects of audio-tape supported instruction on students' vocabulary and comprehension instruction. *Journal of Literacy Behavior.*

Brabham, E. G., & Lynch-Brown, C. (2002). Effects of teachers' reading aloud styles on vocabulary acquisition & comprehension of students in the early elementary grades. *Journal of Educational Psychology, 94*, 465–473.

Dickinson, D., & Smith, M. (1994). Long-term effects of pre-school teachers' book readings on low-income children's vocabulary and story comprehension. *Reading Research Quarterly, 29*, 104–122.

Dickinson, D. K., & Tabors, P. O. (Eds.). (2001). *Building literacy with language.* Baltimore: Paul H. Brookes.

Durkin, D. (1993). *Teaching them to read* (6th ed.). Boston: Allyn & Bacon.

Fry, E. B. (2004). *The vocabulary teacher's book of lists.* Indianapolis, IN: Jossey-Bass.

Gorman, M. (1993). Footprints on the classroom wall. *The Reading Teacher, 47*(2), 98.

Gough, P. B., Alford, J. A., & Holly-Wilcox, P. (1981). Words and contexts. In O. L. Tzeng & H. Signer (Eds.), *Perception of print: Reading research in experimental psychology* (pp. 66–78). Hillsdale, NJ: Erlbaum.

Harris, T. L., & Hodges, R. E. (1995). *The literacy dictionary.* Newark, DE: International Reading Association.

Hart, B., & Risley, T. R. (1995). *Meaningful differences in the everyday experiences of young American children.* Baltimore: Paul H. Brookes.

Hirsch, E. G., Jr. (2001). *Overcoming the language gap: Make better use of the literacy time block.* The Core Curriculum. Washington, DC: American Federation of Teachers.

Leu, D. J., & Kincer, C. K. (1995). *Effective literacy instruction* (4th ed.). Upper Saddle River, NJ: Simon & Schuster.

Levin, J., Levin, K., Glassman, G., & Norduall, D. (l992, April). Vocabulary instruction: *How much is enough; how much is too much.* Paper presented at the annual conference of the American Educational Research Association, Chicago, IL.

Mangieri, J. N. (1972). *Difficulty of learning basic sight words.* Unpublished dissertation, University of Pittsburgh.

Manzo, A.V. (1981). Using proverbs to teach reading and thinking; or come faceva mia nonna (The way my grandmother did it). *The Reading Teacher, 24*(2), 411–416.

Moll, L. (1997, December). *Bilingual schools, literacy, and the cultural mediation of thinking.* Paper presented at the National Reading Conference, Scottsdale, AZ.

National Institute of Child Health and Human Development, NIH, DHHS. (2000a). *Report of the National Reading Panel: Teaching Children to Read* (00–4769). Washington, DC: U.S. Government Printing Office.

National Institute of Child Health and Human Development, NIH, DHHS. (2000b). *Report of the National Reading Panel: Teaching Children to Read: Reports of the Subgroups* (00–4754). Washington, DC: U.S. Government Printing Office.

National Institute of Child Health and Human Development, NIH, DHHS. (2004). Child Development and Behavior Branch (CDBB), NICHD, Report to the NACHHD Council, September 2004. Washington, DC: U.S. Government Printing Office.

Nichelson, L. (1998). *Quick activities to build a very voluminous vocabulary.* New York: Scholastic.

Pressley, M., & Afflerbach, P. (1995). *Verbal protocols of reading: The nature of constructively responsive reading.* Hillsdale, NJ: Erlbaum.

RAND Reading Study Group (2001). *Reading for understanding: Toward an R & D program in reading comprehension.* Technical report for the Office of Educational Research and Improvement. Washington, DC: OERI.

Samuels, S. J. (2002). Reading fluency: What is it? How can I teach it? How can I measure it? *Instructional Leader, 15*(6), 1–2, 11–12.

Snow, C. (2003). Assessment of reading comprehension: Researchers and practitioners helping themselves and each other. In A. Sweet & C. Snow (Eds.), *Rethinking reading comprehension* (pp. 254–269). New York: Guilford.

Snow, C. E., Burns, M. S., & Griffin, P. (1998). *Preventing reading difficulties in young children.* Washington, DC: National Academy Press.

Stewart, M. T. (2002a). *"Best Practice"? Insights on literacy instruction from an elementary classroom.* Newark, DE: International Reading Association, and Chicago: National Reading Conference.

Stewart, M. T. (2002b). *WRITING: "It's in the bag." Ways to inspire your students to write.* Peterborough, NH: Crystal Springs Books.

Stewart, M. T. (2004). Early literacy instruction in the climate of No Child Left Behind. *The Reading Teacher, 57*(8), 732–743.

Taka, M. L. (1997). *Word game bingo and adult literacy students: Sight word acquisition and reading comprehension.* Unpublished master's thesis, University of Auckland, Auckland, New Zealand.

Tan, A., & Nicholson, T. (1997). Flashcards revisited. Training poor readers to read words faster improves their comprehension of text. *Journal of Educational Psychology, 89,* 276–288.

Yopp, R. H., & Yopp, H. K. (2003). Ten important words: Identifying the big ideas in informational text. *Journal of Content Area Reading, 2*(1), 7–13.

CHAPTER 6

Chomsky, C. (1978). When you still can't read in third grade: After decoding, what? In S. J. Samuels (Ed.), *What research has to say about reading instruction.* Newark, DE: International Reading Association.

Deno, S. L. (1985). Curriculum-based measurement: The emerging alternative. *Exceptional Children, 52,* 219–232.

Dowhower, S. L. (1987). Effects of repeated reading on second-grade transitional readers' fluency and comprehension. *Reading Research Quarterly, 22,* 389–406.

Huey, E. B. (1908). *The psychology and pedagogy of reading.* Cambridge, MA: MIT Press.

Kuhn, M. R., & Stahl, S. (2000). *Fluency: A review of developmental and remedial strategies: Report No. 2–008.* Ann Arbor, MI: Center for the Improvement of Early Reading Achievement (CIERA).

LaBerge, D., & Samuels, S.J. (1974). Toward a theory of automatic information processing in reading. *Cognitive Psychology, 6,* 292–323.

Logan, G. D. (1997). Automaticity and reading: Perspectives from the instance theory of automatization. *Reading and Writing Quarterly, 13,* 123–246.

National Institute of Child Health and Human Development, NIH, DHHS. (2000). *Report of the National Reading Panel: Teaching Children to Read* (00–4769). Washington, DC: U.S. Government Printing Office.

O'Shea, L. J., Sindelar, P. T., & O'Shea, D. J. (1985). The effects of repeated readings and attentional cues on reading fluency and comprehension. *Journal of Reading Behavior, 17,* 129–142.

O'Shea, L. J., Sindelar, P. T., & O'Shea, D. J. (1987). The effects of repeated readings and attentional cues on reading fluency and comprehension on learning disabled readers. *Learning Disabilities Research, 2*(2), 103–109.

Pinnell, G. S., Pikulski, J. J., Wixson, K. K., Campbell, J. R., Gough, P. B., & Beatty, A. S. (1995). *Listening to children read aloud.* Washington, DC: Office of Educational Research and Improvement, U. S. Department of Education.

Rasinski, T. (2003). *The Fluent Reader.* New York: Scholastic.

Samuels, J. (2003). The development of fluency. In J. Samuels & A. Farstrup (Eds.), *What research has to say about reading instruction* (pp. 237–249). Newark, DE: International Reading Association.

Samuels, S. J. (1976). Automatic decoding and reading comprehension. *Language Arts, 53,* 323–325.

Samuels, S. J. (1979). The method of repeated readings. *The Reading Teacher, 32,* 403–408.

Shaywitz, B. A., Shaywitz, S. E., Blachman, B. A., Pugh, K. R., Fulbright, R. K., Skudlarski P., et al. (2004). Development of left occipitotemporal systems for skilled reading in children after a phonologically based intervention. *Biological Psychiatry, 55*(9), 926–933.

Snow, C. E., Burns, M. S., & Griffin, P. (1998). *Preventing reading difficulties in young children.* Washington, DC: National Academy Press.

Thurlow, R., & van den Broek, P. (1997). Automaticity and inference generation. *Reading and Writing Quarterly, 13,* 165–184.

Torgesen, J. K. (1986). Computers and cognition in reading: A focus on decoding fluency. *Exceptional Children, 53*(2), 157–162.

Vygotsky, L. S. (1978). *Mind in society: The development of higher psychological process.* Cambridge, MA: MIT Press.

CHAPTER 7

Afflerbach, P. (2002). Teaching reading self-assessment strategies. In C.C. Block & M. Pressley (Eds.), *Comprehension instruction: Research-based best practices* (pp. 96–111). New York: Guilford.

Atwell, N. (1998). *In the middle. New understanding about writing, reading, and learning.* Portsmouth, NH: Boynton/Cook.

Baker, L. (2002). Metacognition in comprehension instruction. In C. C. Block & M. Pressley (Eds.), *Comprehension instruction: Research-based best practices* (pp. 77–95). New York: Guilford.

Barry, P. (2004, November). *Brain activation pattern differences between good and poor achievers.* Presentation to the City of Philadelphia Consortium for the Health of Children. Philadelphia, PA: City of Philadelphia Schools.

Block, C. C. (1998, November). *New millennium reading.* Presentation to the Nobel Learning Communities' Biannual Board Meeting, Philadelphia, PA.

Block, C. C. (1999). The case for exemplary teaching especially for students who begin first grade without the precursors for literacy success. *National Reading Conference Yearbook, 49,* 71–85.

Block, C. C. (2000c). *How can we teach all students to comprehend well?* Research paper No. 4. New York: Scholastic.

Block, C. C. (2003). *Literacy Difficulties* (2nd ed.). Boston: Allyn & Bacon.

Block, C. C. (2004). *Teaching comprehension: The comprehension process approach.* Needham Heights, MA: Allyn & Bacon.

Block, C. C., & Johnson, R. (2002). The thinking process approach to comprehension development: Preparing students for their future comprehension challenges. In C. C. Block, L. B. Gambrell, & M. Pressley (Eds.), *Improving comprehension instruction: Rethinking research, theory, and classroom practice* (pp. 54–80). San Francisco: Jossey-Bass.

Block, C. C., & Mangieri, J. (1995a and b, 1996). *Reason to read: Thinking strategies for life through literature, Vols. 1–3.* Menlo Park, CA: Addison.

Block, C. C., & Mangieri, J. N. (2003). *Exemplary literacy teachers.* New York: Guilford.

Block, C.C., Oakar, M., & Hirt, N. (2002). The exemplary literacy teachers continuum: Preschool to grade 5. *Reading Research Quarterly, 50,* 173–191.

Block, C. C., & Pressley, M. (Eds.). (2002). *Comprehension instruction: Research-based best practices.* New York: Guilford.

Block, C. C., & Rodgers, L. (in press). Developing K–3 students' comprehension abilities: Using comprehension motions. *The Reading Teacher.*

Block, C. C., Rodgers, L., & Johnson, R. (2004). *Comprehension process instruction.* New York: Guilford.

Cain-Thoreson, C., Lippman, M. Z., & McClendon-Magnuson, C. (1997). Windows on comprehension: Reading comprehension processes as revealed by two think-aloud procedures. *Journal of Educational Psychology, 89*(4), 579–590.

Chall, J. (1998). *Teaching children to read.* Cambridge, MA: Brookline.

Chall, J. S. (1983, 1993). *Stages of reading development.* New York: McGraw-Hill.

Collins, C. (1991). Reading instruction that increases thinking abilities. *Journal of Reading, 34,* 510–516.

Duke, N. K., & Pearson, P. D. (2002). Effective practices for developing reading comprehension. In A. E. Farstrup & S. J. Samuels (Eds.), *What research has to say about reading instruction,* (3rd ed.) (pp 203–242). Newark, DE: International Reading Association.

Durkin, D. (1978). What classroom observations reveal about reading comprehension. *Reading Research Quarterly, 14*(4), 481–533.

Hattie, J., Biggs, J., & Purdue, N. (1996). Effects of learning skills intervention on student learning: A meta-analysis. *Review of Educational Research, 66,* 99–136.

Keene, E. O., & Zimmerman, S. (1997). *Mosaic of thought: Teaching comprehension in a reader's workshop.* Portsmouth, NH: Heinemann.

Kintsch, W. (1999, April). *Comprehension transfer model.* Paper presented at the annual meeting of the American Educational Research Association, New Orleans, LA.

Langer, J., & Close, E. (2001). *Improving literacy understanding through classroom conversation.* Albany, NY: Center for English Learning & Achievement.

Moll, L. (1997, December). *Bilingual schools, literacy, and the cultural mediation of thinking.* Paper presented at the National Reading Conference, Scottsdale, AZ.

National Institute of Child Health and Human Development (1999). *Progress report to the National Institute on Child Health and Human Development.* Washington, DC: U.S. Government Printing Office.

National Institute of Child Health and Human Development, NIH, DHHS. (2000). *Report of the National Reading Panel: Teaching Children to Read: Reports of the Subgroups* (00–4754). Washington, DC: U.S. Government Printing Office.

National Institute of Child Health and Human Development, NIH, DHHS. (2004).Child Development and Behavior Branch (CDBB), NICHD, Report to the NACHHD Council, September 2004. Washington, DC: U.S. Government Printing Office.

Omanson, R., Warren, R., & Trabasso, T. (1978, April). *Comprehending text through strategies.* Paper presented at the annual meeting of the American Educational Research Association, New Orleans, LA.

Paris, S. G., Wasik, B. A., & Turner, J. (1991). Portfolio assessment for young readers. *The Reading Teacher, 44*(8), 680–682.

Pearson, P. D., & Fielding, L. (1991). Comprehension instruction. In P. D. Pearson, E. Barr, P. Mosenthal, & M. Kamil (Eds.), *Handbook of reading research, Vol. 2,* (pp. 815–860). Mahwah, NJ: Erlbaum.

Pressley, M., & Afflerbach, P. (1995). *Verbal protocols of reading: The nature of constructively responsive reading.* Hillsdale, NJ: Erlbaum.

Shaywitz, S. (1999). Brain Imaging. *Educational Leadership, 56,* 21–28.

CHAPTER 8

Anderson, R., Hiebert, E., Scott, R., & Wilkerson, R. (1985). *Becoming a nation of readers: The report of the commission on reading.* Washington, DC: U.S. Government Printing Office.

Block, C. C. (2003). *Literacy Difficulties* (2nd ed.). Boston: Allyn & Bacon.

Block, C. C. (2004a). Effects of trade book reading on literacy achievement. *Illinois Reading Journal, 32*(4) 3–8.

Block, C. C. (2004b, December). *Metacognitive assessments: Effects of metacognitive intervention on students' comprehension and vocabulary success.* Paper presented at the annual meeting of the National Reading Conference, San Antonio, TX.

Block, C. C., & Dellamura, R. (2000/2001). Better book buddies. *The Reading Teacher,* *54(4),* 364–370.

Block, C. C., & Israel, S. (2004). The ABCs of performing highly-effective think-alouds. *The Reading Teacher, 58(2),* 154–167.

Block, C. C., & Mangieri, J. N. (1995a and b,1996). *Reason to read: Thinking strategies for life through literature, Vols. 1–3.* Menlo Park, CA: Addison.

Block, C. C., & Mangieri, J. N. (2003). *Exemplary literacy teachers: Promoting success for all children in grades K–5.* New York: Guilford.

Block, C. C., & Mangieri, J. N. (2005). *Powerful vocabulary for reading success.* New York: Scholastic.

Block, C. C., & Pressley, M. (2002). *Comprehension instruction: Research-based best practices.* New York: Guilford.

Block, C. C., & Reed, K. M. (2004). *Effects of trade book reading on students' comprehension, vocabulary, fluency and attitudes.* Research Report No. 11002004. Charlotte, NC: Institute for Literacy Enhancement.

Block, C. C., & Reed, K. M. (under review). *Adding twenty minutes of instruction to the reading program: Effects on vocabulary, comprehension, fluency, and attitudes.*

Block, C. C., Rodgers, L., & Johnson, R. (2004). *Comprehension process instruction.* New York: Guilford.

Carnegie Foundation (2001). *Generation Y: Research report on the changing dynamics that comprise the new younger generation.* New York: Carnegie Foundation Press.

Loxterman, J. A., Beck, I. L., & McKeown, M. G. (1994). The effects of thinking aloud during reading on students' comprehension of more or less coherent text. *Reading Research Quarterly, 29(4),* 353–366.

National Institute of Child Health and Human Development, NIH, DHHS. (2004). Child Development and Behavior Branch (CDBB), NICHD, Report to the NACHHD Council, September 2004. Washington, DC: U.S. Government Printing Office.

National Institute of Child Health and Human Development, NIH, DHHS. (2000). Report of the National Reading Panel: Teaching Children to Read (00–4769). Washington,DC: U.S. Government Printing Office.

Sticht, T., & James, J. (1984). Listening and reading. In P. D. Pearson (Ed.), *Handbook of reading research* (pp. 888–920). White Plains, NY: Longman.

CHAPTER 9

Blachowicz, C., & Fisher, P. (2001). *Teaching vocabulary in all classrooms* (2nd ed.) Upper Saddle River, NJ: Merrill Prentice Hall.

Block, C. C., & Dellamura, R. (2000/2001). Better book buddies. *The Reading Teacher,* *54(4),* 364–370.

Block, C. C., & Mangieri, J. N. (2003). *Exemplary literacy teachers: Promoting success for all children in grades K–5.* New York: Guilford.

Brett, A., Rothlein, L., & Hurley, M. (1996). Vocabulary acquisition from listening to stories and explanations of target words. *Elementary School Journal, 96,* 415–422.

Britton, J., Burgess, T., Martin, N., McLeod, A., & Rosen, H. (1975). *The development of writing abilities (11–18).* London: Macmillan.

Butler, A., & Turbill, J. (1984). *Towards a reading-writing classroom.* Portsmouth, NH: Heinemann.

Calkins, L. M. (1994). *The art of teaching writing.* Portsmouth, NH: Heinemann.

Cole, M. (1990). Cultural psychology: A once and future discipline. In J. Berman (Ed.), *Nebraska's symposium on motivation: Cross cultural perspectives, 37.* Lincoln: University of Nebraska Press.

Dixon-Krauss, L. (2002). Using literature as a context for teaching vocabulary. *Journal of Adolescent & Adult Literacy, 45*(4), 310–318.

Dole, J. A., Sloan, C., & Trathen, W. (1995). Teaching vocabulary within the context of literature. *Journal of Reading, 38,* 452–460.

Emig, J. (1971). *The composing processes of twelfth graders.* Champaign, IL: National Council of Teachers of English.

Fitzgerald, J. (1989). Enhancing two related thought processes: Revision in writing and critical thinking. *The Reading Teacher, 43*(1), 42–48.

Graves, D. H. (1975). An examination of the writing processes of seven-year-old children. *Research in the Teaching of English, 9,* 227–241.

Graves, D. H. (1983). *Writing: Teachers and children at work.* Portsmouth, NH: Heinemann.

Graves, D. H., & Hansen, J. (1983). The author's chair. *Language Arts, 60,* 176–183.

Harmon, J. M. (2002). Teaching independent word learning strategies to struggling readers. *Journal of Adolescent & Adult Literacy, 45*(7), 606–615.

Hennings, D. G. (2000). Contextually relevant word study: Adolescent vocabulary development across the curriculum. *Journal of Adolescent & Adult Literacy, 44,* 268–279.

Israel, S., Block, C. C., Bauserman, K., & Kinucan-Welsch, K. (2005). *Metacognition in literacy learning: Theory, assessment, instruction, and professional development.* Mahwah, NJ: Erlbaum.

Jimenez, R. T., Smith, P. H., & Martinez-Leon, N. (2003). Freedom and form: The language and literacy practices of two Mexican schools. *Reading Research Quarterly, 36*(4), 488–508.

Lipson, M. Y., & Wixson, K. K. (2003). *Assessment and literacy instruction of reading and writing difficulty: An interactive approach* (3rd ed.). Boston, MA: Allyn & Bacon.

Murray, D. H. (1982). *Learning by teaching.* Montclair, NJ: Boynton/Cook.

National Institute of Child Health and Human Development, NIH, DHHS. (2000). Report of the National Reading Panel: Teaching Children to Read: Reports of the Subgroups (00–4754). Washington, DC: U.S. Government Printing Office.

Nieto, S. (2000). *Affirming diversity: The sociopolitical context of multicultural education* (3rd ed.). New York: Longman.

No Child Left Behind Act, P.L. 107–110. (2002).

Oldfather, P. (1995). Commentary: What's needed to maintain and extend motivation for literacy in the middle grades. *Journal of Reading, 38,* 420–422.

Perl, S. (1994). The composing processes of unskilled college writers. In S. Perl (Ed.), *Landmark essays on the writing process* (pp. 39–62). Davis, CA: Hermagoras.

Peterson, R., & Eeds, M. (1990). *Grand conversations: Literature groups in action.* New York: Scholastic.

Rosenblatt, L. (1978). *The reader, the text, the poem: The transactional theory of the literary work.* Carbondale: Southern Illinois University Press.

Ruddell, R. B. (1995). Those influential literacy teachers: Meaning negotiators and motivation builders. *The Reading Teacher, 48*(7), 454–463.

Sloan, M. S. (1996). Encouraging young students to use interesting words in their writing. *The Reading Teacher, 50*(5), 268–269.

Tierney, R. J. (1983). Writer-reader transactions: Defining the dimensions of negotiation. In P.L. Stock (Ed.), *Forum: Essays on theory and practice in the teaching of writing* (pp. 147–151). Upper Montclair, NJ: Boynton/Cook.

Tompkins, G. E. (2000). *Teaching writing: Balancing process and product* (3rd ed.). Upper Saddle River, NJ: Merrill Prentice Hall.

Tompkins, G. E. (2003). *Literacy for the 21st century* (3rd ed.) Upper Saddle River, NJ: Merrill Prentice Hall.

Turner, J., & Paris, S. G. (1995). How literacy tasks influence children's motivation for literacy. *The Reading Teacher, 48*(8), 662–673.

Van Tassel-Baska, J. (1992). *Planning effective curriculum for gifted learners.* Denver, CO: Love.

Vygotsky, L. S. (1978). *Mind in society: The development of higher psychological process.* Cambridge, MA: MIT Press.

Vygotsky, L. S. (1986). *Thought and language.* Cambridge, MA: MIT Press.

Walker, B. J. (2000). *Diagnostic teaching of reading: Techniques for instruction and assessment* (4th ed.). Upper Saddle River, NJ: Merrill.

Yager, S., Johnson, D. W., & Johnson, R. T. (1985). Oral discussion, group-to-individual transfer, and achievement in cooperative learning groups. *Journal of Educational Psychology, 77*(1), 60–66.

Yager, S., Johnson, R. T., Johnson, D. W., & Snider, B. (1986). The impact of group processing on achievement in cooperative learning groups. *The Journal of Social Psychology, 126*(3), 389–397.

Reference List of Children's Literature

Charlotte's Web by E. B. White

Frog and Toad Series by Arnold Lobel

If You Were a Writer by Joan Lowery Nixon

James and the Giant Peach by Roald Dahl

The Mitten, The Gingerbread Baby, The Hat by Jan Brett

Song and Dance Man by Karen Ackerman

The Summer of the Swans by Betsy Byars

Town Mouse, Country Mouse by Jan Brett

There's a Light in the Attic, Where the Sidewalk Ends by Shel Silverstein

What Do Authors Do? by Eileen Christelow

CHAPTER 10

Anderson, R., & Pearson, D. (1984). A schema-theoretic view of basic processes in reading. In D. Pearson, R. Barr, M. Kamil, & P. Mosenthal (Eds.), *Handbook of reading research* (pp. 289–331). New York: Longman.

Armbruster, B. B., Lehr, F., & Osborn, J. *Put Reading First: The Research Building Blocks for Teaching Children to Read.* Retrieved Jan. 10, 2005, from http://www.nifl.gov/partnershipforreading/publications/reading_first1.html

Baker, L., & Brown, A. L. (1984). Metacognitive skills and reading. In P. D. Pearson, R. Barr, M. Kamil, & P. Mosenthal (Eds.), *Handbook of reading research* (pp. 353–394). New York: Longman.

Block, C. C. (1990). *SSE and adolescents, 45 minutes of silent reading.* Fort Worth, TX: Texas Christian University.

Block, C. C. (2004). Effects of trade book reading on literacy achievement. *Illinois Reading Journal, 32*(4), 3–8.

Block, C. C., & Israel, S. (2004). The ABCs of performing highly-effective think-alouds. *The Reading Teacher, 58*(2),154–167.

Block, C. C. & Pressley, M. (Eds.). (2002). *Comprehension instruction: Research-based best practices.* New York: Guilford.

Braunger, J., & Lewis, J. P. (1997). *Building a knowledge base in reading.* Newark, DE: International Reading Association.

Cooter, R. (2003). Teacher "capacity-building" helps urban children succeed in reading. *The Reading Teacher, 57*(2),198–204.

Demi. (2001). *Gandhi.* New York: Henry Holt.

Dickinson, D., & Smith, M. (1994). Long-term effects of pre-school teachers' book readings on low-income children's vocabulary and story comprehension. *Reading Research Quarterly, 29,* 104–122.

Dickinson, D. K., & Tabors, P. O. (Eds.). (2001). *Building literacy with language.* Baltimore: Paul H. Brookes.

Duffy, G. G. (2003). *Explaining reading: A resource for teaching concepts, skills, and strategies.* New York: Guilford.

Flavell, J. H. (1979). Metacognition and cognitive monitoring: A new area of cognitive developmental inquiry. *American Psychologist, 34*(10), 906–911.

Harris, T. L., & Hodges, R. E. (1995). *The literacy dictionary.* Newark, DE: International Reading Association.

Israel, S. (2002). *Understanding strategy utilization during reading comprehension: Relations between text type and reading levels using verbal protocols.* Unpublished doctoral dissertation. Teachers College, Ball State University, Muncie, IN.

Israel, S. E., Bauserman, K., & Block, C. C. (2005). *Unlocking thinking processes through metacognitive assessment strategies.* Newark, DE: Thinking Classroom/Peremena.

Israel, S., Bauserman, K., & Block, C. C. (in press). *Metacognitive assessment strategies.* Newark, DE: Thinking Classroom/Peremena.

Israel, S., Block, C. C., Bauserman, K., & Kinucan-Welsch, K. (2005). *Metacognition in literacy learning: Theory, assessment, instruction, and professional development.* Mahwah, NJ: Erlbaum.

Jordan, G., Snow, C., & Porche, M. (2000). Parents engaged in language development activities Project EASE: The effort of a family literacy project on kindergarten student's early literacy skills. *Reading Research Quarterly, 3*(4), 524–546.

Joseph, L. (2005). The role of self-monitoring in literacy learning. In S. Israel, C.C. Block, K. Bauserman K. & Kinucan-Welsch, (Eds). (2005). *Metacognition in literacy learning.* Mahwah, NJ: Erlbaum.

Keene, E., & Zimmerman, S. (1997). *Mosaic of thought: Teaching comprehension in a reader's workshop.* Portsmouth, NH: Heinemann.

National Institute of Child Health and Human Development (2000). *Report of the National Reading Panel: Teaching children to read: An evidence based assessment of the scientific research literature on reading and its implications for reading instruction.* (NIH Publication No. 00–4769), Washington, DC: U.S. Government Printing Office.

Neuman, S., & Celano, D. (2001). Access to print in low-income and middle-income communities: An ecological study of four neighborhoods. *Reading Research Quarterly, 36*(1), 8–26.

Nistler, R., & Maiers, A. (2000). Stopping the silence: Hearing parents' voices in an urban first-grade family literacy program. *The Reading Teacher, 53*(8), 670–679.

Pressley, M. (2002). Metacognition and self-regulated comprehension. In A. Farstrup & S. J. Samuels, (Eds.), *What research has to say about reading instruction* (3rd ed.) (pp. 291–309). Newark, DE: International Reading Association.

Pressley, M., & Afflerbach, P. (1995). *Verbal protocols of reading: The nature of constructively responsive reading.* Hillsdale, NJ: Erlbaum.

RAND Reading Study Group (2001). *Reading for understanding: Toward an R & D program in reading comprehension.* Technical report for the Office of Educational Research and Improvement. Washington, DC: OERI.

Rosenblatt, L. (1938). *Literature as exploration.* New York: Modern Language Association.

Royer, L. (2001, December). *Effects of the sentence verification technique in increasing students' metacognitions during reading.* Paper presented at the annual meeting of the National Reading Conference, Scottsdale, AZ.

Samuels, J. (2003). The development of fluency. In J. Samuels & A. Farstrup (Eds.). *What research has to say about reading instruction* (pp. 237–249). Newark, DE: International Reading Association.

Snow, C. (2003). Assessment of Reading Comprehension: Researchers and practitioners helping themselves and each other. In A. Sweet & C. Snow (Eds.), *Rethinking reading comprehension* (pp. 254–269). New York: Guilford.

CHAPTER 11

Block, C. C. (1990). *SSE and adolescents, 45 minutes of silent reading.* Fort Worth, TX, Texas Christian University.

Block, C. C. (2004). Effects of trade book reading on literacy achievement. *Illinois Reading Journal. 32*(4), 3–8.

Block, C.C., & Israel, S. (2004). The ABCs of performing highly-effective think-alouds. *The Reading Teacher, 58*(2), 154–167.

Cooter, R. (2003). Teacher "capacity-building" helps urban children succeed in reading. *The Reading Teacher, 57*(2), 198–204.

Dickinson, D., & Smith, M. (1994). Long-term effects of pre-school teachers' book readings on low-income children's vocabulary and story comprehension. *Reading Research Quarterly, 29,* 104–122.

Dickinson, D. K., & Tabors, P. O. (Eds.). (2001). *Building literacy with language.* Baltimore: Paul H. Brookes.

International Reading Association. (2002). *Family-School Partnerships: Essential Elements of Literacy Instruction in the United States.* Position statement. Newark, DE: author.

Israel, S., Bauserman, K., & Block, C. C. (2005). *Metacognitive assessment strategies.* Newark, DE: Thinking Classroom/Peremena.

Jordan, G., Snow, C., & Porche, M. (2000). Parents engaged in language development activities Project EASE: The effort of a family literacy project on kindergarten student's early literacy skills. *Reading Research Quarterly, 3*(4), 524–546.

Neuman, S., & Celano, D. (2001). Access to print in low-income and middle-income communities: An ecological study of four neighborhoods. *Reading Research Quarterly, 36*(1), 8–26.

Nistler, R., & Maiers, A. (2000). Stopping the silence: Hearing parents' voices in an urban first-grade family literacy program. *The Reading Teacher, 53*(8), 670–680.

Samuels, J. (2003). The development of fluency. In J. Samuels & A. Farstrup (Eds.), *What research has to say about reading instruction* (pp. 237–249). Newark, DE: International Reading Association.

U.S. Department of Education (2003). *A parent's guide to no child left behind* (EAT0060P). Washington, DC: U.S. Government Printing Office.

Index

**CORWIN
PRESS**

The Corwin Press logo—a raven striding across an open book—represents the union of courage and learning. Corwin Press is committed to improving education for all learners by publishing books and other professional development resources for those serving the field of K–12 education. By providing practical, hands-on materials, Corwin Press continues to carry out the promise of its motto: **"Helping Educators Do Their Work Better."**